for
Business
Students

Dorothy Farmiloe

Communication for Business Students

EDITORIAL CONSULTANTS
Philip Walsh, *Algonquin College*
Mary Finlay, *Seneca College*

Holt, Rinehart and Winston of Canada Limited
TORONTO

Communication for Business Students was published in the original edition under the title *Creative Communication for Career Students* and in the second edition under the title *Creative Communication for Business Students*. Copyright © 1974, 1977 by Holt, Rinehart and Winston of Canada, Limited.

Canadian Cataloguing in Publication Data

Farmiloe, Dorothy, 1920-
   Communication for business students

Includes index

ISBN 0-03-920277-1

1. Communication in management.   2. Commercial correspondence.   3. Business report writing.

HF5718.F37   651.7   C81-094012-4

Acquisitions Editor: *Joe McKeon*
Editor: *Richard Tallman*

Printed in Canada
   2   3   4   5   85   84   83   82

Contents

Foreword

You are holding in your hands the new edition of Dorothy Farmiloe's *Communication for Business Students*, a textbook many of your fellow students and teachers in Canadian community colleges have found eminently useful during the last ten years. You may be interested in knowing why so many others have found this book profitable, and why we think this is the best book of its kind on the market.

As you know, community college students are different from high school or university students. Today's typical business college student is dedicated to the idea of a career in the world of commerce and has chosen the community college as the quickest and most efficient means of attaining this goal. This student requires a practical, action-oriented textbook in communication: *Communication for Business Students* fulfils this need.

If you glance through it, you'll see that this book is above all a practical one. It tackles the actual kinds of communication problems you are most likely to encounter in your business career, and it does so in a modern way, recognizing that the contemporary business person must be adaptable to ever-changing situations, aware of the personal factors that may arise in any business situation, and alert to respond promptly and decisively both in solving problems and in seizing opportunities. *Communication for Business Students* aims at helping the student to develop these qualities.

The fact that this book is Canadian, not just in its language and local references but in its overall outlook, also sets it apart from the other books aimed at the community college business student, most of which are American. Obviously, as a Canadian you'll feel more at home with the Canadian place names used here; but more than that, the Canadian business contexts cited throughout our book will help you to develop self-confidence, an important quality in successful communication in the world of business.

This new edition differs from the original in several significant ways.

The text itself has been streamlined and reorganized and references and research materials have been broadened and brought up to date. The sections on "The Job Application Package" and "Research Methods" have been expanded considerably, and the book has sprouted an appendix containing a mini-handbook of grammar and style for easy consultation. Teachers will be glad to know that the new Instructor's Manual contains many suggestions for class assignments and activities and that there are many new chapter exercises in the text.

This new edition of *Communication for Business Students* does not change any of the things that made the book the popular success it has been, but it makes a good product even better.

Philip Walsh
Algonquin College
Ottawa

Introduction

Business, Communication, and Your Future

In the fast-moving world in which you will spend your business career, over the next twenty, thirty, forty, or more years, you can expect to see a lot of change. The way you work, the facts that are important to you, the goods or services you produce, the people you work with, the amount of time you spend at the office — all these will likely change, and change drastically, during your working career.

The facts you learned in school will soon be forgotten. The procedures learned while working at your first job may soon become old-fashioned. The business environment will certainly change from day to day. What will remain through time is what you take from your education and develop over the years — your ability to communicate.

You are planning a career in business. Do you intend to become a clerk in a small town car rental agency? The president of a multinational conglomerate? A bookkeeper? A secretary? A purchasing agent? A manager? A sales representative? Whatever role you assume, your best asset will always be your ability to communicate. It may well be that in the future people in business will understand that every member in the company, from janitor to president, is essential to the entire operation. Values may shift, and people may come to feel a greater sense of self-esteem, realizing that everyone contributes something very special to the overall effort. But whether or not the present sense of anxious competition among employees changes, the need for efficiency will not. In fact, many business people believe that in the future we will have to become more and more efficient. The key to efficiency in business is the quality of communication.

Make no mistake about it: the business person who will get a job, be successful, be promoted, develop a satisfying role, be able to change roles from time to time, be respected by fellow workers, have a sense of self-worth, and be best equipped to change with the times will be the one who can communicate well.

In business, people often use "scenarios" to plan for the future. A scenario is a fantasy — a description of what might happen, and how your business might be affected by changing times. An automobile manufacturer, for example, might want to work with scenarios involving more government regulation, more demanding consumers, rising oil prices, greater competition from Japanese imports, the development of much more efficient batteries, or the appearance of hydrogen as a new fuel for cars. By considering different responses to some or all of these possibilities, a car maker could develop strategies for continuing to operate a profitable business.

Let's consider a scenario for the future of business in general. Microprocessors and various types of electronic communications equipment are almost everywhere. Telephone connections wire the whole Earth together. Word-processing equipment makes it possible to edit and re-edit text copy, then print, store, or transmit it instantly. There is little cash in use, and all banking transactions take place in "real time," that is, at the speed of light. Computers can communicate with each other over telephone lines. Virtually everyone has an automatic telephone answering device, so that calls are never missed. There is much less manufacturing being done. More and more people process, package, and sell information. Many, if not most, work at home much of the time. Most business people are able to operate small computers. The data banks of news agencies, government institutions, and libraries are available to all through telephone lines and video screens. Everyone has access to the computing power of the largest and fastest computers. The largest computers are about the size of a basketball. Personal files of correspondence, facts, and figures can be called up instantly on the video screen. Alphanumeric keyboards have largely replaced pen and paper. People separated by vast distances can work together as if their offices were next door.

What has changed? Well, it now takes much less raw energy to get things done. The products of business are different. But the key to success is still effective communication.

In fact, the basics of business communication, particularly written communication, will probably become much more important during your business career. Why should writing become more important in an electronic world where telephone use is rising and computers can "talk" to each other across continents? Simply because we are surrounded by more and more data, so it becomes more and more necessary for human beings to make sense out of it. Writing makes sense because it objectifies information, giving you a record which is the same for different people in different times and places. The more data available, the more valuable becomes any writing that collects, analyses, and synthesizes information so it can be quickly and easily understood.

Today it is very common for a company to be floundering in a sea of numbers: sales figures, budget figures, interest rates, exchange rates, inflation factors, growth projections, past and future costs, industry-wide data, tax rates, government statistics. The person who can make sense out of this stuff, and rearrange it into information that can be read and understood, is a valuable person indeed.

As we learn to do more business by telephone, it becomes essential to have objective records of what has been transacted. You need a written record to refer to, after you have forgotten the details. If you can distill a half-hour business call into two concise and accurate paragraphs, or simply a list of fifteen or twenty points, you have a record of your transaction that can be stored, recalled, or transmitted at will. It makes little difference whether your record exists on paper or in some electronic form. The important questions are: Is it accurate? Does it make sense? Can it be easily understood?

The greatest enemy of communication is too many words. Whatever you have to say, say it simply. And write it simply, too. It was clearly the experience of business people through the sixties and seventies that as electronic media flourished, people became less and less willing or able to read large masses of writing. Just as clearly, in this electronic environment the person who stands out from the crowd, gets jobs, gains promotions, and succeeds while others fail is the person who can listen and read carefully, speak well, and, above all, write clearly, accurately, and concisely.

If you take your business communication seriously, the world of business will take *you* seriously. It's that simple.

Part One
Background for Writing

Theory and Practice

Spelling and Punctuation

Chapter One

Theory and Practice

Some people never get beyond the apprenticeship mentality and are content to follow routine without ever going into the principles behind what they are doing. If you want to advance out of that class and become an expert in your particular field, you will want to master theory as well as technique. This is as true of verbal communication as it is of any craft. The craft of writing requires an awareness of audience and a style suitable to that audience. The principles of effective business communication can be summed up under the heading the Five C's.

The Five C's

1. **Clear.** This is the most important component of verbal communication. If your message isn't clearly expressed in the first place, the content, however important, gets lost in an impenetrable fog. Clarity, of course, also requires that writing be logical and organized.
2. **Concise.** Keep your material brief and to the point. Most business persons haven't the time to read three-page letters or twenty-page reports. Use point form and graphic devices wherever and whenever they will contribute to easier understanding. Remember, though, that concision is relative and must be balanced by the need for completeness.
3. **Complete.** When you have all the information in your letter or report, it will have a sense of wholeness and completeness. Knowing how to get the information you need and knowing when you have gotten it are important for your writing to be complete.
4. **Correct.** Your work must be written in good, correct English. Train yourself to check your own spelling, grammar, form, facts.

3

5. **Considered.** Your material should be audience-directed, that is, adapted to your reader or listener. If you comprehend the position of the other person you will *consider* his abilities and feelings as well as your own. This will affect the tone of your communication. *Consideration* stems from *courtesy*; both are attributes of a civilized person.

Clear, concise, complete, correct, considered. Memorize these five words and apply them as a check list against your own writing until their application becomes automatic.

Practice

It makes sense to study the principles behind any skill if you want to master what goes into the finished form. It makes sense to watch Wayne Gretzky in action if you want to make it in big league hockey. But you'll never get there if you restrict your interest to watching and reading. You have to get out on the ice yourself and practise if you want to develop your potential. Once you understand the principles you have to apply them.

A tremendous flood of information is funnelled into periodicals and journals today. The sheer weight of words appearing in print is staggering. The latest developments in technical fields, new laws and projected laws, current twists and trends of the economy — all this along with comment and viewpoint can be confusing to say the least. Some articles cover changes that haven't had time to appear in books and even these developments may be superseded by further changes often before the article appears in print. Question: Can modern career persons cope with this information overload? Answer: Yes. They have to if they are going to keep up in their fields. One practical suggestion on *how* is to take a course in rapid reading. Being able to speed read is a valuable asset in any profession.

How to Skim Read

Obviously, you can't read everything that appears in print in your interest area. If your college has a reading lab you are fortunate, for you can double or triple your reading speed through daily practice there. Barring this kind of help, you can skim read. Like this:

• Before you devour any of the reading material in a periodical, run through the table of contents for an article that appeals to you. After you have located it, take note of the subheading underneath the title. This is usually a brief summary of the article itself and will clue you in to the focus of the piece.

4

- Read the first and last paragraphs (in a longer piece, the introduction and conclusion). Then go back and glance through the rest of it rapidly, noting headings or key words and phrases.
- Now you may want to read the whole piece with care in order to absorb the detail in it.
- Next, think about what you have read.
- Finally, analyse and condense the author's ideas.

Practise these steps yourself: read, think, analyse, condense. Before you go any further into this textbook, take an hour to skim read the rest of it — if you haven't done so already — following the procedure outlined for you here. Do this for the textbooks for all your courses at the beginning of the term before your workload gets too heavy. It helps to know what your destination is before you beetle off down the highway.

Précis Writing

A précis is a condensed version or summary of a piece of writing. Weekly practice in précis writing, with emphasis on the 5 C's, is the best possible apprenticeship in the art of business communication. As a preliminary step to the précis exercises at the end of this chapter, browse through the periodicals in your college library until you find one that is especially pertinent to your major field of study and your career choice. If you can, buy a subscription on the recommendation of your instructor(s). Until your copies start coming in, pick up an issue from a newsstand or have your bookstore order a copy for you. You will need your own copy because you will be marking up the pages. If buying a subscription isn't feasible, then photocopy articles from periodicals you have found useful. (Libraries don't appreciate mutilated magazines on their shelves so don't mark theirs.) Here is a list of guidelines for précis writing:

- Find an article that interests you.
- Read the article as many times as necessary to understand it. To test your understanding, turn the magazine over and see if you can repeat back in a general way the ideas it contains.
- Decide on the most important point the author is trying to put across. Decide which sentence above all others states this point.
- Underline this topic sentence. Do not underline more than two sentences.
- Put a checkmark in the margin beside statements that support the topic sentence. Half a dozen checkmarks should be enough.
- Write a brief paragraph condensing these ideas in your own words.

Don't add comment of your own for straight précis writing.
- Omit fillers and figures. Fillers are interesting anecdotes that illustrate the author's topic. Your précis can do without them and without most of the statistics.
- Now rewrite. Change the order of the sentences if necessary. Then condense still further, striving to get a clear, concise, and complete précis in as few words as possible.

The Clipping File

There is another benefit to be gained from browsing through periodicals in the library in your search for précis material. Straight précis writing is a more-or-less mechanical exercise but the information in the articles may give you something to think about. Save some of the articles, especially those that bear on your career. One way to improve your communicative ability is to *have something to write and talk about*. This seems like simplistic advice until you think about it. It isn't easy to master a fund of knowledge and to become so familiar with it that you can comfortably carry on a conversation in the area if the subject comes up. A thorough background knowledge of a topic and an up-to-date file of recent developments in that topic area will give you confidence, whether you are talking to a prospective employer or preparing a report for the Chamber of Commerce. Begin now to build that knowledge and that confidence by starting a clipping file. Be sure to write a complete bibliographic reference at the top of each journal, magazine, or newspaper article you include in your file. (Bibliographic style is discussed in Chapter 8, Library Research.)

Most professionals have a file of this nature. Some firms have an executive assistant whose main duty is to clip short articles and prepare summaries of longer ones for busy executives. Large organizations have a librarian who does this. You don't have that kind of help yet, but don't wait to begin your file until you do. Begin looking for material now. Save anything that relates in a general way to your future career. Be on the lookout for articles about related fields. You might start, for example, with the general topic of successful career persons, filing under separate subheadings. You may decide that some topic mentioned in one of the articles interests you more than the person — and this will be the subject for you to concentrate on.

Make yourself an expert on some aspect of your future career. You may not be attracted to successful career persons as such, but find something to make your own. And continue to clip and file everything you come across that relates to it.

Where to Find Material

The *Financial Post*, the *Financial Times of Canada*, the business section of any big city newspaper, the pages of the business periodicals — all these are good sources of articles for your files. Provided you don't contravene copyright regulations, you can photocopy material from the library. If you find an article of interest in your own periodical, make a précis of it and include this in your file. Beware of cutting up a periodical, even one of your own. Remember that when you cut out one article, you may also be hacking up another on the other side of the page. You can also use notecards on which you jot down the name of the periodical and the date of publication, the title of the article, the author, the page number. List the points of interest in the article on the back of the card. When you want to refer to the original again you will have the information there for ready reference.

Radio talks, newscasts, and television documentaries are further sources of information. Again you can take notes or if it is extremely valuable you might record the whole thing on a tape recorder for later analysis. Once your interest is aroused you will find any number of sources as well as the ones mentioned here.

How to File Your Information

Start simply with two or three major headings. Later, as you collect more material, you will find subheadings necessary. File your clippings and notes in a manila folder, arranging the material alphabetically under the subject headings. The information won't do you or anyone else much good if it is all jumbled together in a desk drawer. You'll waste time searching through it when you want a specific piece. Successful career people haven't time to be messy. Your college bookstore probably sells inexpensive cardboard filing boxes that will do for your clippings for the time being.

Prepare your file as the professional you hope to be. Practice may not make perfect but it does form habits that, if they are the right ones, will save you endless time and frustration later. Part of this textbook is devoted to theory, the other to the exercises that test the theories and help you put them into practice. One is wasted without the other. Practise doing each assignment as conscientiously as a work order from your employer.

Terminology

The words *periodical, magazine,* and *journal* often are used interchangeably, but there are useful distinctions between the three. *Pe-*

riodical is an inclusive term referring to all publications that appear periodically — whether daily, weekly, monthly, bi-monthly, quarterly, or semi-annually. A *magazine* is directed toward a broad, general, popular audience; its pagination begins anew with each issue; it most often is published six times or more a year. A *journal*, on the other hand, is directed toward a professional, special interest audience; its pagination is consecutive throughout each volume (or year); it tends to be published quarterly (although some journals appear monthly). Magazines tend to include a lot of advertising; journals don't. The real difference, of course, is that the popular treatment in magazine articles simplifies often complex issues and topics, whereas the professional treatment in journals can be so esoteric that only an audience of specialists and peers can understand the true complexity of the topic or problem. In establishing your clipping file and writing précis you should not limit your coverage to what magazines have to offer. In most instances you will only be skimming the surface of a subject.

Précis Writing in Business

The clipping file, started now, will be used later in conjunction with written and oral reports for this course. The précis exercises prepare you for more complex forms of written communication. Starting with the simple précis, you can progress to critical writing in which you compare two articles with differing viewpoints and add comment of your own.

The purpose of the précis assignments is three-fold: the preliminary browsing in the library introduces you to the wide variety of periodicals in your field; it stimulates you with new ideas and develops your critical reading and thinking ability; and it gives you practice in summarizing and writing. This triple nature of précis writing cannot be overemphasized because it puts into practice almost everything we have said so far about communication.

In the contemporary business world the ability to reduce material to essentials is an extremely valuable skill. You will be using it all the time for interpreting memos, letters, and reports; for your own writing; for filling in forms; and for taking notes.

While searching for material for your précis assignments, note how current periodicals make use of summaries to conserve the reader's time. The column entitled "News Summary" on the first page of the *Globe and Mail's* Report on Business section and the condensed news items from *Time* and *Newsweek* are examples of précis.

Business Periodicals

The following list of periodicals is by no means complete. Your college library probably has a variety of others that will be just as helpful for your assignments.

Administrative Digest
Advertising Age
Business Automation
Business Week
CA
CGA
Canadian Business
Canadian Journal of Economics
Canadian Marketeer
Changing Times
Cost and Management
Data Management
Data Processing Magazine
Economist
Executive

Financial Post
Financial Times of Canada
Fortune
The Globe and Mail
Journal of Accounting
Journal of Marketing
Journal of Retailing
The Magazine of Wall Street
Marketing
Modern Office Procedure
Monetary Times
Sales Management
U.S. News and World Report
Wall Street Journal

Toward More Expressive Prose

Think Ahead

One of the necessities for good writing of any kind is the ability to think clearly. But like a great many words in the English language, we use *think* very loosely at times. We use it to mean anything from interpreting what we see ("I think that's John driving up.") to expressing opinion ("I think so too.") In its truest sense, though, thinking is the mental process that enables us to see logical relationships. Logic allows us to relate past experiences to the present and the future. Thinking enables us to plan ahead.

Good writing requires disciplined planning and thinking. Weak thinking that tries to hold splintered thoughts together always results in weak and splintered writing. The principal characteristic of good writing is clarity. Spell out in your own mind what you want to say before you start writing. In any planned communication there is usually ample opportunity to think the message through before you write it down, and then to revise its written form.

A written message has a tremendous edge over an oral one in that you can rewrite what you have written, whereas once spoken words have left your mouth they are apt to go echoing down the corridors of the listener's mind for a long time — there is nothing on earth you can do to call them back. Take advantage of whatever time you have to plan before you write, and to revise after you have written.

What to Think About

Before you can adequately plan what you are going to say, you have to decide why you want to say it. Formulate clearly in your own mind the *purpose* of your letter or report. If, for example, you are the recipient of a series of bills from the Snugger Auto Accessories Company for seatcovers you did not order or receive, how do you handle the situation? You could fill your letter with angry phrases like *burned up, you've got your nerve, mad enough to, damn seatcovers, stupid company.* You're going to tell them a thing or two, all right.

But is your purpose here to be as insulting as you can, or to straighten out the mistake and stop the bills from coming? You can't argue with a computer but you can with the head of the company. It's a good idea in letters of complaint to go right to the top. Tear up that first letter and write — calmly — to the top person in the company. He or she will see that your letter is channelled to the right department. Think the matter through and decide what you want to achieve.

```
Dear Sir:

I know your computers can't read because they
don't answer my letters.  They keep right on
billing me for seatcovers I neither ordered nor
received.

Perhaps someone in your billing department fed
the computer the wrong information.  Perhaps
```

you have a customer whose name is similar to mine.
At any rate, I'm not your person and I don't owe
you the $39.50 shown on the enclosed statement.

I'll be grateful for your assistance in
straightening this out.

Sincerely yours,

Diction

Diction is your selection of words for the expression of your ideas. You don't need a vocabulary stuffed like a dictionary. In many cases the use of large words does not help at all. They may alienate your reader if it seems you are trying to write over the reader's head. Or the reader may misunderstand you if he or she doesn't know the meaning of the words. Everyday diction will generally achieve your purpose.

There may be a special occasion, however, when you will need an exceptional word. The greater the variety of ammunition you have in your arsenal, the greater the chance of hitting your target without blasting everything in sight. You can call people liars or you can suggest that they are manipulating the truth to their own advantage. Build up your vocabulary to give yourself a greater command of the language and, therefore, a greater command of the situation.

Tone

When the diction is consistent it sets the tone for the writing. Tone is the writer's attitude toward the reader or listener, and there is no mistaking the tone in the words of that intended first letter to the Snugger Company. Those fire-breathing phrases fairly scorch the paper. Emotion has a great deal to do with tone. If you are angry, worried, or deliriously happy, avoid expressing these extremes in business writing. A skilled writer is not only aware of the tone of the communication but also controls it. Tone, then, is the emotional quality of writing. Business writing should not be full of ranting and raving, weeping, and laughing; neither should it be a dry, absolutely objective monotone.

Decide ahead of time on the tone you want to establish and choose only words that support it. Ideally, good diction is a family of words all of which are related and working harmoniously together. One ill-chosen word can ruin the whole tenor of a sentence or paragraph.

In the following sentence, if the word *liar* were used, it would disrupt the tone:

With all due respect for your integrity, I suggest you are mistaken in your facts.

Connotations

Many words have different associative meanings to different people, for the simple reason that each of us has had unique yet culturally restricted experience in our reading, writing, and speaking, and, especially, in our living. Hence, the same word can *connote* different things to different people. A clear example of this was given to Canadians in September, 1980, when Prime Minister Pierre Trudeau refuted a provincial insistence during the Constitutional Conference that Canada be a "free association of provinces." Trudeau explained that "free association" meant something rather different to the various provinces: to Quebec, freedom to separate from the federation; to Newfoundland and Nova Scotia, freedom to limit the mobility and job opportunities of Canadians from outside those provinces; to Alberta, freedom to get all it can from its oil wealth without consideration of the needs of all Canadians; to other provinces, freedom to restrict free trade, land ownership, and so on. The "free association," in other words, could have whatever meaning any provincial government chose to give it; the choice of words, in this case, was so imprecise that the meaning was clouded, and for each provincial premier the meaning had at least as much to do with his personal provincial experience as it did with a dictionary definition of the words.

If you are unsure of how the connotations of words can affect communication, consider the word *business* and the many usages it has.

- Let's get down to business.
- No more monkey business, please!
- I'm taking business in college.
- The stage business was poorly directed in *Death of a Salesman*.
- He really gave me the business.
- She means business.
- We would be glad to do business with you.
- It's none of your business.
- The business office was seething with busyness.
- She's in business for herself.

Obviously, *business* can be used in various ways, and it can be received

12

in various ways, too. If you were to ask a random selection of friends and acquaintances what *business* and *business person* mean, you could arrive at a reasonable definition of what people think of business. But your survey might tell you more about local and regional and contemporary attitudes toward business (i.e., connotations) than about what the *denotation* or dictionary definition of the word actually is. And if you were to conduct your survey in Tokyo, Tel Aviv, and Timmins, you might get quite different responses.

No matter how careful you are in your choice of words, no matter how careful to control your tone, there are times when you will run into this sort of trouble because of your reader's attitude. Some word of yours may trigger a different reaction from the one you expect. The background experiences that make each of us unique make it impossible for any two persons to translate words into exactly the same meaning. Words pick up emotional connotations that stick like burrs and cause all kinds of prickly problems. To Winston in Orwell's *1984*, rats mean the worst horror possible. To the medical scientist using rats in his research, rats mean help toward a cancer cure. In many situations connotative words can become barriers preventing the message from reaching its goal the way it was meant to.

Remember that words imply different things to different people. Successful transmission of a message means it has been understood as clearly as was intended. As sender of the message, you bear the major portion of responsibility: the choice of words is yours.

Precision in Language

Language continues to grow to keep pace with advances, particularly those in science and technology. *Splashdown* grew out of the need for a word to describe the return of a space capsule, and *capsule* itself has acquired additional meaning. Unfortunately, words have a tendency to spread in the wrong direction at times. There is no excuse for a perfectly good verb like *use* to swell into *utilize*, for example. If you keep in mind the second of the five C's (concise) you will be able to resist this urge toward fat English.

Except for special occasions when professional language is needed, use everyday English to express your thoughts. If a lawyer is speaking to another lawyer or drawing up a contract, he or she is justified in using the specialized terminology of the profession, but these same terms can be very confusing to the poor clients who may think the lawyer is showing off or trying to confuse them for ulterior motives.

This works the other way as well. A doctor who is aware of audience, for example, will explain the diagnosis and proposed treatment of Johnny's stomach ache in simple terms to a parent with little education

13

but will give the same diagnosis in more specific, professional language to a parent with more education and comprehension. The professional — doctor, lawyer, Indian chief, or business person — who always hides behind the mysterious language of the profession, or who never uses it for fear of being misunderstood, needs a greater awareness of audience. This, of course, relates to *purpose*. If you have a clear purpose in mind for your writing, you are aware of the audience it is intended for.

Style

When we apply the word style to prose, what do we mean? First of all, style has much to do with quality. Writers usually think of it as the set of characteristics that identify another writer, as when we speak of Hemingway's style or Leacock's style. We also use the word to place a work in a certain period of time, as "in the style of eighteenth century" or "the style of the thirties." And the word as used in the *CP Style Book* or the *MLA Style Sheet* describes format and technical detail.

Your writing — if it has style — will reflect your personality to some extent. Unfortunately, many of us are unaware of the composition of our own personalities. I have heard student conversations in college corridors that reveal flashes of real wit and vitality, yet these same students, asked to write a business letter, freeze up and fill it with such stilted language as "this will acknowledge receipt of" or "beg to remain."

Write the way you talk and don't go out of your way to reach for unaccustomed phrases. You wouldn't dream of saying you "wound slowly o'er the lea" on your way home — you'd say you "cut across the field." In the same way, as far as possible, be yourself in your writing.

Expressive Verbs

The use of strong verbs is one way to put more punch in your writing. Since verbs are the words that move the sentence forward, let them bear the weight of your meaning. You can strengthen your sentences considerably just by getting rid of weak little phrases like "there is" and "there are" and "it is" and bringing the action verbs up front where they can do their work more readily.

Not this: There is too much time being wasted by office gossiping.
This: Office gossiping wastes too much time.

Not this: It is his attention to detail that earned him the promotion.
This: His attention to detail earned him the promotion.

In the first example above we are replacing a weak verb with a strong one by using the active voice instead of the passive. A verb is in the active voice when its subject performs the action, and is in the passive voice when the subject is acted upon.

Active: He hit the ball.
Passive: The ball was hit by him.

Use the active voice wherever possible for direct statement.

Sports announcers know that direct action demands direct statement. Imagine the unnecessary suspense if the hitter's name is fumbled out only at the end of the sentence. (The ball was just slammed into centre field by — guess who — Carter.) Business writing, like sports coverage, calls for fast delivery; the punch should not be left for the end as in a mystery story.

The use of expressive verbs can put more color and more muscle into any kind of writing. Under the pen of a sportswriter, a boxer doesn't just hit — he jabs, punches, pounds, slashes, lands a swift uppercut. Skill in the imaginative use of verbs will go a long way toward enabling you to write a better-than-average letter. This introductory paragraph from a letter of application derives much of its potency from its verbs:

Gentlemen:

Your ad in today's Financial Post interests me for several reasons. Evidently, securing management potential for your North Bay office presents a real problem for your firm. Understandably, you are seeking the best person available to head up this important branch....

Constructing the Paragraph

The paragraph is the basic building block of most writing. If you can put together a well-written and interesting paragraph, you can turn out a longer piece of work just as well. The principles are the same. For anything longer than one paragraph you develop your paragraphs singly and then fit them together following a preconceived plan or blueprint. There are two basic methods of paragraph planning — both are discussed below — and you can follow either.

Where do you start? Decide first of all what the *key point* of your communication is. After you determine this, you have to decide where in the paragraph you are going to put this important statement. It can go in the first sentence, in which case you will be leading out from it, or it can come at the end after you have worked up to it.

From the Specific to the General

The main point of your communication, especially if you are writing a report, often will be your recommendation. The preferred place for this is right at the beginning. This method starts with the most important statement followed by supporting detail and ends with a general conclusion as in this example:

I am recommending a trial period of staggered work hours for our department. Experiments along this line among Ontario government employees have been successful. Follow-up surveys of those who opted for starting times other than 8:30 show that they are now enjoying a considerable reduction in travelling time and are suffering less from chronic commuteritis. If a work schedule tailored to individual needs means happier and more productive employees, it is certainly worth considering.

From the General to the Specific

This method starts with a broad general statement followed by specific detail and works up to the main point. Business writers who wish to soften a hard blow (an unfavorable recommendation or the dismissal of a worker, for example) usually use this method. It is effective, also, where a writer wants to clinch an argument or suggestion. In the following example of going from the general to the specific, note the images that liven the writing:

As readers of the company's Business Bulletin, we are normally fed a strict diet of unappetizingly dry articles on management techniques and policies. In the current issue, however, we are served a surprising change of fare: "How to Drive Your Employees Crazy." This tongue-in-cheek article details the ins and outs of employer-employee relations. I recommend the article to you, both for the meat of its message and for its stimulating style.

Transitions

Each sentence in a paragraph must be connected in some way to the sentence ahead. This can be done by repeating a noun or referring to it or to a preceding idea in some way. In addition, you can connect sentences and add smoothness to your writing by the use of transitional devices such as *although, however, for example, therefore, meanwhile,* and/ or related expressions. These should be used unobtrusively. Note how skilfully the writer of the paragraph above uses transitional devices to connect his sentences.

Creating smooth transitions between sentences and paragraphs, however, should not be a contrived, self-conscious part of the act of writing. As you write (and read) more, this will become as natural as it is for all good writers. Polishing transitions to improve the flow and sense of your writing can only occur after you have written something, not while you are writing. And, if there is an organized logic in what you have to say, each sentence and paragraph inevitably will point the way to the next.

A Word about Reading

In spite of other methods of communication, the printed word is here to stay. The best way to improve your own writing is to read, and to read with awareness. Build up a vocabulary so you will be able to choose the best words for what you want to say. Reading develops an ear for language just as listening to records develops an ear for music.

Education is a continuous process. Start your own personal reading list now. Reading the book review sections in business magazines and newspapers will alert you to other books you want to read. Don't forget that problems of pollution, energy shortages, poverty, and over-population all interact with problems in business. Never has the need been greater for the business person to be well-informed on a broad variety of topics, so don't limit your reading too narrowly to your own field.

Exercises

1. Using your college library, compile a list of periodicals that will be helpful to you in your chosen career. Discuss the strengths and weaknesses of these periodicals with your instructor and fellow students.
2. Begin your clipping file of articles relating to your chosen career.
3. Bring in for class discussion an article relating in some way to one of the following topics:
   a. the changing work ethic
   b. the energy crisis
   c. inner city problems
   d. the state of the economy
   e. the GNP and the limits of growth
   f. multinational corporations
4. Prepare a bibliography of books and government reports on the topic chosen above. Note that the article you selected only touches on the topic.

5. Following the guidelines for précis writing on pages 5-6, prepare a précis of a one-page article from a current business periodical.
6. Prepare a précis of the following news item:

Philip Kives changes success saga
by Roger Newman

Perhaps current business textbooks should be expanded to include a chapter on Philip Kives who has been rewriting all the standard rules for success during the past 12 years.

Mr. Kives is a former country fair gadget demonstrator who now heads a world-wide marketing company with annual sales of $87.8 million. His company—K-tel International Inc. of Winnipeg and Minneapolis—had a $3.2 million profit last year from sales of record albums and gadgets in 40 000 stores in 14 countries.

K-tel, in fact, has made money in 12 of the 13 years since it was founded in 1962. Basically, Mr. Kives has done this by adapting the skills of his old profession to the larger arena of international commerce.

He is, undoubtedly, one of Canada's most prominent exponents of hard-sell advertising. When K-tel embarks on a promotion campaign, it buys large blocks of television time in specific target cities and then floods these markets with endlessly repeated commercials for the product that is being offered.

Mr. Kives also shuns the modern trend to low-key advertising that concentrates on the sophisticated and the amusing. To him, the only object is to sell. As a result, K-tel commercials almost always feature a brassy high-pitched announcer who breathlessly exhorts viewers to run to their nearest store to buy a particular record or gadget.

The K-tel president's philosophy is that you have to bang people on the head to get their attention. And he says that the hard-sell saturation approach has worked extremely well for his company.*

7. Discuss the pros and cons of Philip Kives' method of selling. Compare his method with a more sophisticated television commercial.
8. List five names that you would choose for a child and analyse the reasons for each choice. (Emotional connotations? Pleasant sound? Name of someone you admire? Or what?)
9. List five names you would NOT choose for a child. Analyse your reasons.
10. Suggest three different names for a new boutique catering to the college crowd and featuring casual clothes. Analyse your choices.

*From *The Globe and Mail*, January 29, 1976. Reprinted by permission of Roger Newman.

11. Put the following sentences into more expressive prose by replacing the italicized verbs with stronger ones.
    a. The meeting *began* at 2:00 with a strong address by the president.
    b. We *hope* you will like doing business with us.
    c. For the past three years, federal planners *have been working on* the problem.
    d. As an innovative, forward-looking person, you *want* more active involvement in administrative affairs.
    e. These qualities will *put* you up the ladder to general management.
12. Construct a brief paragraph describing a problem you encountered the first week of school. Recommend a solution to the problem. Go from the specific to the general by putting your recommendation in the first sentence.
13. Construct a brief paragraph describing a film or television program you saw recently. Go from the general to the specific. (*Note*: For exercises 12 and 13, put into practice the points covered in this chapter concerning diction, precision of language, tone, and style. Before handing in your assignment, use the Five C's as a checklist to ensure that your communication is clear, concise, complete, correct, and considered.
14. Revise the following to improve tone and/or diction:
    a. Although it is against our policy, because you have been a profitable customer we are repairing your cooler free of charge.
    b. Would it be asking too much to ask you to take time to come in and let us give you an estimate on resurfacing your driveway. You will have to come in from 9:00 to 4:00 Monday thru Friday.
    c. The odor of this cat food is not offensive.
    d. Our Snowgal snowboot must be treated with a silicone spray to prevent salt damage, otherwise it's the pits.
15. Revise the following sentences to make them more concise and direct:
    a. The question you asked is not a question that can be easily answered; your question raises another question.
    b. We deliver goods to our customers on a C.O.D. basis.
    c. In terms of price this model is rather expensive.
    d. It is obvious that one of us who are now in this room is the one who is responsible for the commission of this error.

Chapter Two
Spelling and Punctuation

The two most apparent weaknesses in writing are spelling and punctuation. Even the best ideas in business will get no further than the wastebasket if poor spelling and punctuation mar them. No person who depends in part on written communication can afford not to be accurate.

Spelling

Why don't you teach them how to spell?" Business and industry have been voicing this complaint to educators ever since the products of the elementary school "look-see" (word recognition) reading method of twenty-five years ago came on the market. Through the "look-see" method, children were taught to read by recognizing a whole word instead of sounding it out syllable by syllable as taught under the old phonetic system. When phonics were temporarily abandoned, children began to confuse *elephant* with *telephone* (some mistake!) or to leave syllables out altogether (*elphant, telphone*). These reading habits continue to contribute to the spelling peculiarities of recent graduates of universities and community colleges to the extent that poor spelling causes more office headaches than persistent unwanted salespeople do.

Fortunately, you can improve your spelling with the help of a dictionary. Once you land that first job, your boss won't care whether you can spell a word off the top of your head or whether you have to look it up as long as the correct word appears in your written work. So this is a good time to get into the habit of checking your own spelling. Carry a pocket dictionary to class with you now, and keep it on your desk at work later.

20

Eventually you may have a secretary who will do your spelling for you, or you may be a secretary yourself. Some secretaries could profit from a pep talk on spelling. The amount of correspondence they send out with spelling and typing errors can be appalling — and sometimes funny. Consider the mistake made by one secretary who typed out a report from the *broad* of directors instead of from the *board* of directors. Even if you have a secretary you will have to sign the letters you dictate and you will have to know whether the secretary has made any mistakes or not. (*Never* sign *anything* you haven't read.) Anyway, you can't carry a secretary around in your pocket all the time. A dictionary is a handy source of reference, too.

Uses of the Dictionary

The commonest reason we reach for a dictionary, other than to check for spelling, is for the meaning of a word. But dictionaries contain much more than definitions. From brief biographical sketches to lists of synonyms, a wealth of information is condensed in a good dictionary. The guide near the front of the dictionary tells what it contains and how to use the information. Once you know how to unlock the resources inside, a dictionary is an education in itself.

Sometimes perhaps too much so. One college student, at the end of his first semester, arrived a few minutes late for his English exam — with the dictionary he was required to bring. The examination room was full so he was put in a small classroom nearby, which had no clock on the wall. Halfway into his first paragraph he stopped to check the spelling of a word. Two hours later, while he was still fascinated by reading the dictionary without the pressure of others around him taking the exam, he noticed that students were leaving the examination room down the hall. Too late, he returned to the work. He failed the exam but learned a great deal about the dictionary.

The following entry* for *native* illustrates just how much content can be found for one quite ordinary word in a dictionary. The best way to "read" a dictionary and to become familiar with it, as the failed scholar mentioned in the preceding paragraph did, is to look up the synonyms and read their entries after reading the entry you began with.

*From the *Dictionary of Canadian English: The Senior Dictionary*. Published by W. J. Gage Limited, Toronto, 1967. Reprinted by permission of Gage Educational Publishing Limited.

na·tive (nā′tiv) *n.* **1** a person born in a certain place or country: *He is a native of Montreal.* **2** one of the original inhabitants of a place, as contrasted with conquerors, settlers, visitors, etc.; especially, a member of a less civilized race: *The natives were quite suspicious of strangers.* **3** *Derogatory.* a member of a less civilized race, usually not white. **4** an animal or plant living in the place where it originated. [< Med.L *nativus* a native < L *nativus.* See NATIVE, adj.]
—*adj.* **1** born in a certain place or country: *He is a native son of Winnipeg.* **2** belonging to one because of his birth: *one's native land.* **3** belonging to one because of his country or the nation to which he belongs: *one's native language.* **4** born in a person; natural: *native ability, native courtesy.* **5** of or having to do with the original inhabitants: *native customs, native huts.* **6** originating, grown, or produced in a certain place: *The Manitoba maple is native to Canada.* **7** found pure in nature: *native copper.* **8** found in nature; not produced: *Native salt is refined for use.* **9** go **native,** live as the less civilized natives do. [< L *nativus* innate, ult. < *nasci* be born. Doublet of NAÏVE.] —**na′tive·ly,** *adv.* —**na′tive·ness,** *n.*
Syn. *adj.* **4 Native, natural** = belonging to someone or something by birth or nature. **Native** emphasizes the idea of being born in a person, as contrasted with being acquired: *He has native artistic talent.* **Natural** emphasizes being part of the nature of a person, animal, or thing, belonging by birth or because of essential character: *Sugar has natural sweetness.* **5** aboriginal. **6** indigenous.

In checking the spelling of a word, you may find an alternate form listed. The preferred form is usually given first and the variant spelling follows, as in **program, programme**. Where two spellings exist and are listed in separate entries, the one containing the complete information is the preferred spelling.

Dictionaries also list plurals if they are irregular. (Is it indexes or indices?) If a noun has a troublesome or irregular plural it appears after the singular form (**knife**, n. [pl. knives]). Dictionaries sometimes give sample sentences; for example, for a word used only in the plural (*knickers* are back in), or for plurals used in a singular sense (office *politics* is a dangerous game). On page 25 there is a review of the rules for forming plurals.

Further, dictionaries tell you whether a word should be capitalized or not (*Southern Hemisphere* is, *southern* isn't). They also indicate when to use a hyphen (*re-educate, window-shopping*). Bear in mind, however, that not all dictionaries follow the same style. Some dictionaries are better than others, and some do not include all of the parts of an entry as discussed here. Some don't indicate hyphenation at all; others do so only occasionally. Some include more usages for each word than others. And, most significant, not all dictionaries spell words the same. A British dictionary, for example, will spell *honour*, an American dictionary *honor*, and Canadian dictionaries can be found that spell the word each way. The most important thing is to select a good dictionary and stick with it.

Pronunciation

The key to the pronunciation symbols is usually given at the beginning of the dictionary and repeated on every page or every other page throughout. In the sample above, **na'tive** is pronounced with a long *a* and a short *i* with the accent on the first syllable (nā'tiv) according to the following guide*:

> hat, äge, càre, fär; let, ēqual, tėrm; it, īce
> hot, ōpen, ôrder; oil, out; cup, pùt, rüle, ūse
> əbove, takən, pencəl, iemən, circəs
> ch, child; ng, long; sh, ship
> th, thin; ŦH, then; zh, measure

Syllabication

Notice that **na.tive** is broken into two syllables with a dot between. This dotted syllable division, as well as helping with pronunciation, tells where the hyphen goes when there isn't room for an entire word at the end of a line of typing or writing and part of the word has to be carried to the next line. You can break a word with a hyphen at one of these dots. Don't, however, leave a single letter dangling by itself. Break a word like **o.rig.i.nal** after the *g* or the *i* but not after the *o*. One rule about hyphenating: you can break between a double consonant except when it is part of a prefix. For example, break between the two *l's* of *originally* but not between the two *l's* of *all-inclusive*.

As a general rule, it is better to end a line a few spaces short (or long) than to break the word. Too often, typists will automatically break words without considering the overall effect and appearance of typewritten communications where every other line has a broken word. Excessive hyphenation also introduces the possibility of needless errors creeping in.

Parts of Speech

The italicized *n.* after **na.tive** *n.* indicates that this is a noun. Farther down we are given the meanings of the word when it is used as an adjective, *adj.* These abbreviations, and others like *v.t.* for verb transitive, *v.i.* for verb intransitive, and *adv.* for adverb, give the part of speech. (Can the verb *exhibit* be used as a noun also, or do we have to use the longer word *exhibition*? Check with your dictionary to find out.)

*From the *Dictionary of Canadian English.*

23

Inflected Forms

Inflected forms are those that undergo some change in grammar form. (What, for example, is the present tense of wrought as in "What wonders hath God wrought?") For irregular verbs, the forms for the past tense, the past participle, and the present participle are listed as in **blow** (blo), *v.i.* [blew, blown, blowing]. The comparative and superlative forms of adjectives and adverbs are given also when these are irregular (**well** (wel), *adv.* [better, best]).

Etymology

Etymology is the study of the origin of words. Most dictionaries include the derivation of a word (**English** (en'glish), *adj.* [ME. Englysh]. ME. is an abbreviation for Middle English, that is, English as it was written and spoken between 1150 and 1475. The descriptive *hodge-podge* derives from an Old French word, *hochepot*, which meant a thick stew of various meats and vegetables; hence, a mess.

Current Standing

Most dictionaries also include the current standing of a word to indicate whether it is standard English, slang, a colloquialism, or an obsolete form. Included in a long list of standard English meanings for *square*, you will probably find these:

n.   [Slang], a person who is unfamiliar with current fads
     [Obs.], a criterion, rule, etc.
adj. [Slang], not familiar with the current fads, styles, etc.
     [Colloq.], satisfying; substantial: as, a square meal
v.   [Slang], to bribe

Synonyms

Although a thesaurus like *Roget's Thesaurus* will give you a more comprehensive list of synonyms than most dictionaries, a desk dictionary usually includes them. Notice that, in the synonym list under the entry for *na.tive* in the sample reproduced, a distinction is drawn between the various shades of meaning. A thesaurus, generally, is a poor substitute for a dictionary, and if you know how to use the dictionary it will answer more thoroughly any questions you have about synonyms. Synonyms are words whose meanings are the same; the words are interchangeable in context. A thesaurus provides additional words of similar connotation that extend the meaning of the indexed word. The writing of a college student who faithfully uses a thesaurus invariably sticks out like a sore thumb — because subtle nuances of meaning and usage are not fully or clearly explained in the thesaurus.

24

As you write more and read more, synonyms will become a natural part of your vocabulary. And you should spend time reading your dictionary (though not during a final exam).

Spelling Aids

There is no substitute for the dictionary when you are unsure of the spelling of a word. Otherwise, reading — and reading with awareness — is the best way to improve your sense of spelling. If your own spelling sense is so poor that incorrectly spelled words don't jump out at you, you might consider a remedial spelling course. Your college probably offers one. A knowledge of the basic spelling rules is also helpful. Some of these rules that seem to cause the most difficulty follow.

Plurals

- The plurals of most nouns are formed by adding *s* to the singular.
  paper, papers
  book, books
  letter, letters
- Nouns ending in *y* preceded by a consonant, change the *y* to *i* and add *es*.
  company, companies
  city, cities
  industry, industries
- Nouns ending in *ay, ey, oy,* merely add *s* for the plural.
  day, days
  survey, surveys
  alloy, alloys
- Nouns ending in *ch, sh, s, x, z,* add *es* for the plural.
  latch, latches   box, boxes
  ash, ashes   buzz, buzzes
  boss, bosses
- Musical terms ending in *o,* add *s* for the plural.
  cello, cellos
  piano, pianos
  solo, solos
- Nouns ending in *o* preceded by a vowel, add *s* for the plural.
  rodeo, rodeos
  studio, studios
  boa, boas
- Compound nouns, pluralize the most important word.
  brother-in-law, brothers-in-law
  major-general, major-generals
  lady-in-waiting, ladies-in-waiting

- Verbs that undergo changes in the present tense usually follow the same spelling rules, where applicable, as above.

try, tries	rectify, rectifies
stay, stays	rush, rushes
catch, catches	fix, fixes

In the spelling of plurals, the trend is toward the shorter form. Although most words that end in *o* preceded by a consonant add *es* for the plural (tomato, tomatoes), new words coming into the language opt for the shorter *s* only (memo, memos), and some older words are beginning to drop the *e* (mosquito, mosquitos or mosquitoes).

To make spelling even more complicated, there are a great many irregular plurals in the English language that seem to follow no rule at all (mouse, mice; loaf, loaves; moose, moose) and there are a great many words of foreign derivation that retain their foreign plural form (analysis, analyses; alumnus, alumni). So if you are not sure of the correct form, consult your dictionary.

Past Tense and Participle

When forming the past tense (*-ed*) and participle (*-ing*) endings of verbs that end with a consonant, a simple rule is that if the final syllable of the word is stressed (o mit', oc cur') you should double the final consonant (*omitted, occurring*). If the final syllable is not stressed, then you don't double the consonant (*suffer, suffered; vomit, vomiting*). Other commonly misspelled words in this category include *focus, refer, benefit*.

Apostrophes

The apostrophe is used to denote the possessive case of nouns and pronouns (Rob's bike). If a noun can be turned into a phrase beginning with *of* or *belonging to*, then it is possessive.

    Rob's bike = the bike belonging to Rob
    this company's pension plan = the pension plan of this company

- Use the apostrophe and *s* to form the possessive of singular nouns and pronouns. The apostrophe comes before the *s*. The possessive pronoun *its* is an exception and does not have an apostrophe.
  a student's jacket
  somebody's books
  The dog hurt its paw.
- If a singular noun already ends in *s*, the second *s* should not be omitted for the possessive case if it is pronounced in speaking.
  Yeats's poems
  the authoress's signature
- Use the apostrophe after the *s* to form the possessive of plural nouns.

our friends' faults
your parents' house
- For plurals that do not end in *s*, add apostrophe and *s* to form the possessive.
  the children's playground
  the people's rights
- To form the possessive of a compound phrase, add the apostrophe and *s* to the last word.
  my sister-in-law's car (singular)
  my sisters-in-law's house (plural)
- Use an apostrophe and *s* to form the plural of words, letters, or figures used as a word.
  the *and's* in this sentence
  the ABC's of learning
  more 6's than 7's
  the 1980's
- In contractions, use an apostrophe to indicate the omission of a letter.
  it's (it is)
  don't (do not)
  haven't (have not)

Influence of the Media

Newspapers, magazines, radio, and television continue to popularize language changes that are in common use on the sidewalks long before they are officially sanctioned in the schools. Some of this, of course, is inevitable and fine. Yet, before you jump on the bandwagon of modernization, whether of spelling or ethics, you should consider that the technological advances of recent years have compressed (and continue to compress) centuries of change into a few decades. Some of this change is trendy and inelegant, to say the least.

The mass media most often do not present the language in a carefully crafted form. No newspaper or magazine, rushing to meet deadlines, is totally consistent in style of spelling or language use. And at least one influential newspaper, the *Chicago Tribune*, tried for a number of years to force spelling simplification with such "innovations" as *thru* for *through*, *altho* for *although*. Needless to say, your boss might not appreciate memos incorporating such simplified spelling. And the *Chicago Tribune*, more recently, reverted to standard spelling. Anyone who feels a great urge to revamp and "simplify" the language should read and study the writings of George Orwell, especially *Animal Farm* and *1984*.

Good taste dictates the use of accepted formal English for formal business writing and any departure from this norm would be in poor taste. You would not come to class in a bathing suit any more than you would go swimming in a shirt and tie. Dress your sentences in diction appropriate to the occasion.

Canadianisms

A number of Canadianisms have originated in this country. The *Dictionary of Canadianisms on Historical Principles* contains over 900 double-columned pages of words and expressions of Canadian origin — a much more extensive list than might have been expected. Words like *metis, mountie, pemmican* have their roots in Canadian history, while *muskeg* and *toboggan* were adapted from the Indian language.

A Final Comment on Spelling

The gist of this section has been to urge you to investigate dictionaries and then to invest in a good one. A dictionary will help you spell correctly; it also will teach you to make subtle distinctions among similar yet different words. The most important thing to know, with spelling, is how good or poor a speller you are; a poor speller who recognizes this personal limitation will present more accurate work than a good speller who fails to recognize any limitation or any need ever to refer to a dictionary. The dictionaries and other reference works listed in the bibliography should provide you with a starting point for your own investigation of the study of words.

Our language, Canadian English, has its original roots in British English, and although the American influence is enormous, the form that has evolved in Canada has a distinct flavor and direction of its own. One of the attributes of an educated person is the ability to absorb this flavor and to spell according to the accepted pattern of this time and place.

Linguistic change is a slow process but words do eventually get stripped of their superfluous appendages. The *Dictionary of Canadian English* has already dropped the *u* from *-our* words in the labor-color-honor class as the preferred spelling, and the *CP Style Book* insists on the shorter form. Mark M. Orkin drily points out in *Speaking Canadian English* that although the English profess to turn from this American practice with horror, they forget that the same development has been taking place in England since Johnson's day when *"authour, horrour* and *terrour* were so spelled."

The federal government in Canada advised its employees several years ago to use the *-or* form in the labor-color-honor class in all correspondence. If you write the civil service exams, you would be well-advised to use this spelling. Otherwise, you must defer to your employer in spelling as in other office practices.

Punctuation

There are two schools of thought on punctuation: one would eliminate all punctuation that isn't absolutely necessary, arguing that unneeded commas, semicolons, and the like only slow down the reader and retard clarity; the other school insists that punctuation can and should be used rhetorically, to shade and clarify meaning and to add texture. George F. Will, a *Washington Post* columnist, has this to say about the ongoing debate:

In an age of flaccid consensus and too much tolerance, robust prejudices are welcome. But Paul Robinson, a contributing editor of *The New Republic*, has gone too far in an essay in that journal. He has said rude things about semicolons and parentheses.

He says the period and the comma "are the only lovely marks of punctuation" because they are "simple," and the period is especially lovely because it is "innocent of ambiguity," whereas, "More than half the semicolons one sees, I would estimate, should be periods, and probably another quarter should be commas. Far too often, semicolons, like colons, are used to gloss over an imprecise thought. They place two clauses in some kind of relation to one another but relieve the writer of saying exactly what the relationship is."

Halt right there, Robinson. What is so marvelous about simplicity? Why this dislike of ambiguity?

Semicolons do, indeed, signal, rather than shout, a relationship. Therefore they require a reader to read, really read. The reader must bring an active mind to bear on what the writer is doing. A semicolon is a compliment from the writer to the reader. It says: I don't have to draw you a picture; a hint will do . . . .

Surely there is one supreme rule: That punctuation is best that best serves to make writing subtle, supple, delicate, nuanced, and efficient. Of course you can write using only periods and commas for punctuation. You can cook using only salt and pepper for seasoning. But why do it when there are so many seasonings pleasing to a mature palate?

Robinson also frowns on parentheses (and dashes — they often serve similar needs). He says they "are, of course, indispensable" but that all of them are "syntactical defeats." Indispensable defeats?

He says parentheses and dashes "generally betoken stylistic laziness," an unwillingness to present things "in the most logical order." Thus "every random thought, every tenuous analogy gets dragged in." Come now.

Of course parentheses can be used promiscuously. So can salt, pepper, dill, sage, and cloves. Parentheses are for writers (such as, I am sure, Robinson)

29

whose minds do not lumber along like a truck on a straight-away, but rather soar and swoop and change directions gracefully, like a swallow at home in the whole sky . . . .*

As a business writer, you don't want to "lumber along like a truck on a straight-away," but neither should you "soar and swoop and change directions . . . like a swallow at home in the whole sky." The whole sky is the province of the novelist or essayist, who has the time and the audience to permit subplots and graceful digressions. Punctuation, always, should be functional, and its function is to provide clarity. If this were all we wished to provide the reader, though, we might gladly agree with Paul Robinson and dismiss George Will as a romantic who wants to return to a past when people had the leisure and the time to mull over the subtle nuances of well-crafted prose.

But even in business writing, we should reach for more; and clarity does not always mean a reduction to absolute simplicity. Then the writing becomes simplistic. There is a place for texture, for rhetoric, in business writing; there is a need for you to be able to use semicolons and parentheses correctly. The rhetorical connection is obvious: punctuation, after all, takes the place of inflection in a speaker's voice. When you are talking to someone, you don't have to say "period" when you come to the end of a sentence because the listener can tell that you have rounded off a thought by the pause and the drop (or rise) in your voice.

Punctuation is necessary where a signpost is needed to point to the sense of the sentence so that the reader doesn't have to backtrack to puzzle out the meaning. A few guidelines are all that are necessary for contemporary business writing.

The Period

- Use a period to close a sentence. Make sure your sentence is a complete unit of thought and not just a fragment.

> *This:* He broke his leg playing hockey.
> *Or:* After he broke his leg playing hockey, he came to school on crutches.
> *Not This:* After he broke his leg playing hockey.

- Use a period to break run-on sentences into shorter units.

> *This:* She came back to school after being out for several years. Although she found the work hard at first, she soon adapted to a routine of regular study which helped tremendously. Then

it became easier for her.

Not This: She came back to school after being out for several years and although she found the work hard at first, she soon adapted to a routine of study which helped tremendously and then it became easier for her.

- The period is used after standard abbreviations such as Mr., but avoid peppering all abbreviations with it.

Dr. Jones is a member of the NDP.
Britain, a NATO member, devoted 4.5 per cent of its GNP to defence in 1972.

The Comma

The comma is the punctuation mark most often used. The following are guidelines for its use.

- Before a co-ordinating conjunction that joins two independent clauses. Co-ordinating conjunctions are *and, but, for, or, nor.*

Business people have had to collect sales taxes for both the federal and provincial governments for some time now, but they are not paid for doing it.

Omit if the sentence is short, unless the rhetorical pause is desired to emphasize the second independent clause.

They are instructed how to do it but they are not paid for doing it.
They are instructed how to do it, but they are not paid for doing it.

Insert in a short sentence if needed for clarity.

It is an unhealthy state of affairs, and governments are aware of this. (If this comma is left out, the reader tends to run *affairs and governments* together.)

- After a long introductory dependent clause.

When Canadians were struggling to complete their first tax returns under the new tax law, there was a loud chorus of complaints.

Omit if the sentence is short.

After he graduated he started his own business.

Don't insert a single comma between the subject and the verb. This

31

is a common error when the sentence starts with a gerund or an infinitive.

> *This:* Growing a garden in this polluted city is difficult.
> *Not This:* Growing a garden in this polluted city, is difficult.

A similar error occurs when a parenthetical phrase comes between subject and verb.

> *This:* Two other executives, Bimbo and Dimwit, resigned at the same time.
> *Not This:* Two other executives, Bimbo and Dimwit resigned at the same time.

● After a long introductory phrase or string of phrases.

> In spite of the reservations of his family and friends about his ability to run a business, he did well.

Omit if the phrase is short.

> In the beginning he did well.

Insert if needed for clarity.

> *This:* With her, life and literature are one.
> *Not This:* With her life and literature are one.

● To separate words and phrases in a series.

> It has an effect on their cost of living, the productivity of the businesses for which they work, the creation of stable jobs in the country.

Note: The serial comma preceding the conjunction at the end of a series is not used as regularly as it once was, yet no writer or publication is consistent in not using it. Often, too, when the comma is missing the meaning becomes garbled.

> *This;* The emphasis is on creative thinking, speaking, and writing for contemporary situations.
> *Not This:* The emphasis is on creative thinking, speaking and writing for contemporary situations.

Without the serial comma in this example, that part of the sentence following the single comma appears to be a clarification of the first

32

part of the sentence. One wonders whether that comma really shouldn't have been a colon. This can be termed the "peanut butter and jelly" (or "peaches and cream") rule: if you don't use the serial comma you are suggesting a special relationship between the last two items in the series that doesn't actually exist. There is a difference in meaning between these two sentences:

We ate steak, potatoes, peas, peaches, and cream
We ate steak, potatoes, peas, peaches and cream.

The second sentence suggests a relationship between the last two items in the series — the two combined become one item, *peaches and cream*, and, if this is what is meant, the item should be preceded by *and*:

We ate steak, potatoes, peas, and peaches and cream.

- When a series of adjectives precedes a noun and each adjective is modifying (describing) the noun:

  He wore a wide, striped tie

  In this instance, the tie is both wide and striped. If the sentence reads:

  He wore a wide striped tie.

  the *wide* modifies *striped* rather than the tie, and the tie, for all we know, might have been narrow and quite out of fashion.

- To separate parenthetical words, phrases, clauses from the rest of the sentence. Note that two commas are needed, one each side of the interjection.

  This assignment, I know, is difficult.

- With non-restrictive clauses.

  This man, whose name I don't know, is back again.

No commas are needed with restrictive clauses. Clauses that "restrict" the meaning of the noun modified can't be left out without changing the meaning of the sentence.

All who have jobs after school may leave now.

(Leave out the restrictive clause and see what happens to the meaning.)

The Semicolon

The best way to understand the use of the semicolon, besides reading the excerpt quoted at the beginning of this section, is to remember that punctuation is rhetorical and that it substitutes for the inflection of the spoken language. A semicolon is a pause — of greater emphasis than the comma, of less emphasis than the period. Often, this pause is between two independent clauses (i.e., clauses that could stand on their own as complete sentences); sometimes it is between the parts of a series (or list), when items in the series are lengthy and contain commas or when each item requires a more careful look than the brief pause of a comma would provide.

The Dash

The dash is showing up more and more often in contemporary writing, frequently replacing a semicolon or a comma. The dash can be used for variety, interest, or emphasis. If it is used too often, however, it can give the writing a sloppy appearance. Use the dash:

- For emphasis or suspense.

  We are totally unprepared to comment — we fear the worst.

- To set off parenthetical expressions.

  Two others were employed — one in government and one in industry — before their academic training was completed.

The Colon

The colon is used to alert the reader that a list, a series, or an explanation follows.

Qualifications for this position are as follows:
— two years of business education
— two years of varied office experience
— ability to write clear, concise reports

- The colon is used after the formal salutation of most business letters.

  Dear Ms. Johnson:

Conclusion

The handbook at the back of this text discusses some of the most common problems in writing and lists commonly misunderstood and misspelled words. As with spelling and writing in general, the best way to improve your skill and your feel for punctuation is to write often and to read a lot. But don't ever assume that style and usage are correct just because something is in print.

Mass education and media influence have had a pervasive influence on English usage. Just as much of the popular media are rightly accused of aiming their message at the "lowest common denominator," so too is their use of language an attempt to simplify sometimes complex (and subtle) style that has developed and been proven effective over the past several hundred years. Language and its use are never static but always in a state of change. Yet the writer — of business reports or of novels — who accepts all current trends is in danger of clouding rather than clarifying meaning. You may find some of the reference works in the bibliography to this book helpful as you explore the use of punctuation and other questions of style. Fowler's *Modern English Usage*, though first published in 1926, is still the definitive work on the subject.

Exercises

1. Find dictionary definitions for the following Canadianisms:
   Aberhartism
   beaver currency
   Brule
   draegerman
   Franglish
   geddie
   grog-boss
   high-grader
   Indian list
   mug-up
   pike-pole
   rawhiding
2. Find three words in the *Dictionary of Canadianisms on Historical Principles* that are not in any other dictionary.
3. What are the differences in meaning between artificial, counterfeit, ersatz, false, and synthetic?
4. What are the plural forms for: memo, tax, A, attorney general, crisis, grouse, church, dairy, hero, class, radio, topaz, subsidiary, wharf, radius?

5. What year did each of the following die: Albert Einstein, Louis Riel, Eleanor Roosevelt, Johann Sebastian Bach?
6. What is the past tense for each of these verbs: burst, dive, do, rise, set, sink, spring, swim, wring, can, can go?
7. What is the past participle of each of these verbs: beat, build, catch, do, eat, get, go, rise, ride, run, see, steal, swim, write?
8. How do you pronounce a propos? bilingual? germander? schizoid?
9. Change the following *of* or *belonging to* phrases into the possessive:
   the office of the boss
   the meeting room of the Board of Directors
   the policies of the steel companies
   boots belonging to them
   the laws of the country
   the new car belonging to Mr. Jones
   the collar belonging to it
   the uniform of the commander-in-chief
   the work of someone else
   the dresses of the bridesmaids
   rights of women
10. Punctuate the following paragraph, supplying capital letters where necessary.
    big government is strikingly different from big business in these areas the amount of money at its disposal the use of that money and accountability when government becomes involved in a losing game an unnecessary airport a heavy water plant or a local initiative program it does not have to extricate itself the normal response of government is to pour good money after bad on the other hand a business corporation is disciplined by the harsh realities of the market place when it has made an investment in a product a new line of automobiles for example it must be prepared to cut its losses a company whatever its own feelings of pride or sentiment must know when to let go
11. Discuss the content of the above paragraph. Is this an objective statement of differences between government and business? What assumptions are not supported in the paragraph?
12. Rewrite the following sentences, correcting the punctuation where necessary. State your reasons for each correction.
    a. If business persons were really interested in government improvements could be made.
    b. The qualifications are as follows, ability to get along with other people, administrative experience and knowledge of more than one language.
    c. When he lost his coat he did not miss it immediately; since it was

a warm day and the others were not wearing coats, he thought he had left it home.

d. Mary Kostach, the company president has the quality of all successful career persons the quality of high motivation.

e. He could not complete his report of course because he had not received the work of his subordinates.

f. Do not quote figures from a risky unconfirmed source.

g. This book, *The Risk Takers* explores the world of seven of Canada's entrepreneurs, their dreams, their efforts and their successes.

h. Rapidly rising prices for food, energy and related products were the main contributors to inflation initially.

13. Supply commas where they are needed in the following sentences. State your reason for each insertion.

a. Until the government replaces its indexing mentality with balanced fiscal and monetary policies the basic problems of inflation will persist in Canada.

b. Company president George Anderson said yesterday that he expects this year's net profit to exceed last year's.

c. The public's image of big labor she said is of an organization that has clearly understood motives and considerable power.

d. In this instance the solution was simple and those who had worked on the problem were relieved.

e. Choosing a career for today's complex and rapidly changing world is becoming more difficult than ever.

f. After he had passed his courses were easier the following year.

g. These figures which are mentioned for some reason at the end of the annual report are disturbing.

Part Two
Letter Writing

Letter Styles and Mechanics

Types of Letters

Chapter Three

Letter Styles and Mechanics

There are two aspects to every piece of writing — form and content. Up to now, as we explored the principles that work together to mature your writing into distinctive prose, we have been discussing content generally. The next step is to apply the principles to specific kinds of communication and, starting with business letters, to choose the form that will hold your efforts.

A well-developed letter deserves a form that will set it off at its best. All of the following details, each one seemingly trivial in itself, add to the overall effect when executed with care. Any one of them, if neglected or done carelessly, can spoil the effect and leave a bad impression on the reader.

Stationery

The first thing your correspondent is aware of, consciously or unconsciously, is the color of the paper. Most business firms are partial to white stationery. If color is used, it is used sparingly and only in the letterhead, although green stationery would be appropriate for a florist or orange for an interior decorator. With some recipients, however, colored stationery has the same effect as bragging does — it arouses resistance because of the flamboyance. On the other hand, if you are after a dramatic effect and need color for a special reason, go ahead.

Avoid flowered, heavily bordered, or lined paper. An appalling number of answers to want ads are submitted on lined pages torn out of scribblers. For a business letter of any kind, select a good grade of typing bond, 210 mm by 297 mm. Good quality paper is not only attractive, it permits easier and neater typing. The price is nominal — two or three cents a sheet. Do not use erasable bond; the type on this paper can smudge easily and the paper itself doesn't last as long. This is an important consideration since most business communications are kept on file for a long time. Instead, use non-erasable typing paper and make corrections with correcting tape or fluid.

Appearance

The next consideration, because it is noticed next, is the arrangement and spacing of the words on the page. Your letter should look like a picture in a frame. Centre the contents so that there is a neat border approximately 4 cm at each side with a deeper border top and bottom. Leave extra lines between the letterhead and the date, and between the date and inside address. This will give your letter a better balance.

Almost without exception, business letters today are typed. Even if you are answering a career ad which says, *write to box* _____, it does not mean handwrite. If an employer wants a sample of your handwriting, the ad will state this explicitly. So type your letter if you can. For placing the letter on the page, there is a chart converting words to centimetres. If you are unfamiliar with it, type your letter once, then retype it to please the eye. There should be no erasures or crossouts. And, of course, no mistakes in spelling or grammar. In the business world you can stay up front, in the preliminaries at least, by seeing that the appearance of your letter is attractive and that the mechanics are correct. Indeed, without an attractive appearance and correct mechanics your letter probably won't be taken seriously or receive the desired response.

The Parts of a Business Letter

1. *Letterhead.* The letterhead is an organization's identification. It is made up of the company name and address, phone number, and perhaps a logo and slogan or descriptive line telling what the company does. Letterhead stationery speaks with the company voice. Therefore, if you are already working you will not use company stationery when writing for another job somewhere else.

Some day you may be designing a letterhead for your own business. Remember to keep it simple and easy to read. The worst fault of many letterheads is that they contain too much information. Keep yours uncluttered and it will serve as a better ambassador for you.

2. *Date.* Date everything you send off in business, from memos and work orders to letters and reports. It is frustrating to locate an important piece of correspondence and find it undated, particularly if you need the date for reference. The date should always be written out in full.

Does 3/2/74 mean March 2, 1974 or the 3rd of February, 1974? You may know but your correspondent may not. In order to avoid any ambiguity use the full form. This includes spelling the month out in full also (January 5, not Jan. 5).

3. *Inside address.* This is the full name and address of the person or firm you are writing to. Copy the name or names exactly as they appear in previous correspondence or letterheads and don't use any abbreviations unless they are part of the company trademark (e.g., Vickers & Benson, Ltd.). If you don't know the exact spelling or wording of the firm name or of some person within the firm, phone and ask the switchboard operator. Be sure to ask for the correct spelling. This is one detail to check out thoroughly. A careless mistake in the spelling of a person's name can provoke an unfavorable reaction, to say the least. This is a sensitive area because if you destroy a person's name you attack that person's identity and therefore diminish his or her sense of self-importance. We all like to think we are important to some degree, and, of course, we are.

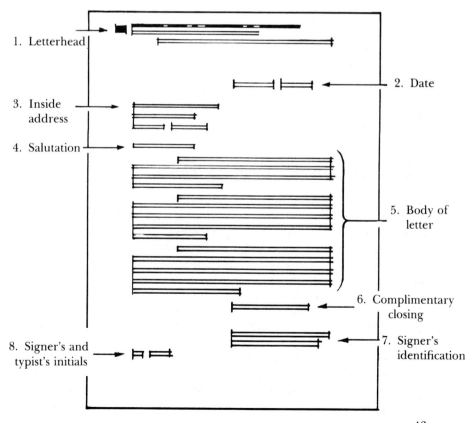

1. Letterhead

2. Date

3. Inside address

4. Salutation

5. Body of letter

6. Complimentary closing

7. Signer's identification

8. Signer's and typist's initials

4. *Salutation.* The salutation is the opening or greeting that precedes the body of the letter. Like the hello that opens a conversation, the salutation is virtually meaningless in itself, but it does help to establish tone. By moving gracefully toward the introductory sentence, *Dear Mr. – – – – – – –* avoids a too-abrupt beginning. The salutation also helps establish a certain rapport between writer and reader. It could be omitted except that custom dictates its continued use. This is probably why the simplified letter form, which leaves out the salutation, has not caught on to any greater extent in spite of its greater economy in the matter of non-essentials. The preferred salutations are:

Dear Mr. Brown
Dear Miss (or Mrs.) Brown
Gentlemen (*never* Dear Gentlemen)

and these should agree with the first line of the inside address.

Miss Arlene Scofield   Eastern Mining & Smelting Ltd.
279 Skyview Avenue   P.O. Box 5000
Regina, Saskatchewan   Bathurst, New Brunswick

Dear Miss Scofield: Gentlemen:

The correct salutation for a company is *Gentlemen.* For a woman *Ms.* is becoming a more common and acceptable title for either *Miss* or *Mrs.* since it obviates the question of whether or not she is married. If you are writing to a group where all the members are women (Chrysler Girls' Club), the salutation is *Ladies.* Whenever possible, write to a person within a company instead of merely addressing the company. Avoid *Dear Sir,* which is impersonal and extremely formal, and address the person by name. Sometimes you can't find out the name of the person you want to write to. For example, if the company is halfway across the continent and you don't have the money for a long distance phone call to ask the name of the individual,* then you will have to use *Dear Sir.*

Personnel Supervisor
Eastern Mining & Smelting Ltd.
P.O. Box 5000
Bathurst, New Brunswick

Dear Sir:

*Public libraries have directories of business and industry — often with the names of key people in each company.

44

The salutation *Gentlemen* is always used when writing to a box number in a newspaper ad.

Box 2729
The Globe and Mail
Toronto, Ontario

Gentlemen:

5. *Body.* Single-space the lines of your letter with double-spacing between paragraphs. If you think of your letter as a picture in a frame, see the paragraphs and the spaces around them as the lights and darks. Be an artist with paragraphing, arranging for balance and interest. Break the body of the letter into three or four paragraphs because a densely crowded letter repels the eye and is more difficult to read.

A paragraph in a letter can — and frequently should — consist of only one sentence. In a literary work one-sentence paragraphs are the exception, but in business letters, as in newspaper writing, the reverse is true. Too many short paragraphs, though, suggest shallow, undeveloped thinking. And remember to limit your letter, if possible, to one page or less in length.

It is helpful to think of the body of the business letter as consisting of three paragraphs or main sections — an introduction, a middle, and a conclusion. The first paragraph states the purpose of the letter, what the letter writer wants or hopes to achieve by this communication. The middle paragraph (or paragraphs) explains why this purpose or desire should be met. Here the facts of the argument are presented. If the letter is of some length, the final paragraph will summarize what has been discussed in the middle paragraph(s). In any case, the concluding paragraph should suggest what you want the reader to do and should make it easy for the reader to take this action. Remember that a business letter is not sent willy-nilly into a void — it has a definite purpose that should receive a response of some kind.

6. *Complimentary closing.* Several phrases in common use are suitable for signalling the end of your letter. The one that hits the right note most often is *Sincerely* or its other form, *Sincerely yours.* This is the standard closing for any business letter. The *Yours truly* type of closings now sound as stilted and old-fashioned as *Dear Sir* so you will want to avoid these. Business acquaintances, especially those on a first-name basis, might choose *Cordially yours,* although this is also becoming dated. *Warmest personal regards* is preferable. But neither of these is appropriate for a letter of application.

Even though the complimentary closing is a formality, it can contribute to the overall tone of the letter and should be in keeping with the salutation. Try out some closings of your own to match the tone you are establishing. *Hopefully yours?* Too timid. *Yours for a quick reply?* Too presumptuous. How about taking a line or a phrase from the last paragraph of your letter and using that as the closing? For example,

Looking forward to meeting you,

Robert Langlois

Robert Langlois

7. *Signer's identification.* Your written signature goes above your typed name and under this your business title if you have one. Sign your name as legibly as possible even though the typed spelling goes underneath. Why on earth anyone should take pride in an indecipherable scrawl is beyond comprehension, since writing is supposed to be a form of communication.

Your signature (with the typed spelling) requires nothing further than your full name. No *Mr., Miss, or Mrs.* A businesswoman who happens to be married does not need to include her married name, though she may, thus: (Mrs.) Laura Findlay. The name by which she is known professionally, followed by her title or department, is sufficient, however:

Alice M. Hayes
Sales Manager

Always sign your name in ink, never in pencil.

8. *Signer's and typist's initials.* It is customary to include the initials of the dictator of the letter in capitals and the typist's initials in small letters, as in AMH:bj. If you type your letter yourself, no initials are necessary.

9. *Postscript.* Business letters, and certainly letters of application, should not include a postscript (or p.s.), which creates a chatty, oh-by-the-way tone to a letter. If you find yourself wanting to attach a postscript at the end of your letter, you need to start over and reorganize the body of the letter to include what you were going to tack on as an afterthought. Generally, postscripts are only used in unsolicited letters advertising new products or special deals, and they create a kind of informality that is often jarring and offensive. Close business associates who are personal friends might use postscripts in their correspondence, but then the correspondence naturally would have

the kind of personal informality that most business writing tries to avoid.

Troublesome Details

Attention line. This line is sometimes added when the letter is sent to the company as a whole but directed to the attention of a specific person, perhaps one who is familiar with the problem of the writer. It is also used when the writer wants the letter to reach a particular department but doesn't know the name of the person in charge. When the attention line is used it comes between the inside address and the salutation and is preceded and followed by two spaces.

The Robert Sampson Company Ltd.
Place Ville Marie
Montreal, Quebec

Attention: Mr. Richard Marin, Manager

Gentlemen:

The attention line creates a problem in consistency. In principle the salutation *Gentlemen* has to be used to agree with the first line of the inside address. But the letter is intended to reach Mr. Marin. It looks as if the writer can't make up his mind whom to address his letter to. If the letter is intended for Mr. Marin it is better to say so in the first place. However, the attention line is acceptable in the following instance:

The Robert Sampson Company
Place Ville Marie
Montreal, Quebec

Attention: Small Motors Repairs Department

Gentlemen:

Enclosure notation. When something is being enclosed with the letter — a cheque, a résumé, etc. — the word *Enclosure* is typed below the typist's initials. (In this instance you can use your initials if you type your own letter.) The enclosure notation reminds the typist to make the enclosure and it alerts the reader to look for it.

File number. Frequently, particularly in ads inserted by management consultants, you will come across lines like these:

Reply by letter with a comprehensive résumé to our Vancouver office, 1112 West Pender Street, Vancouver, B.C., and refer to file 4591.
STEVENSON & KELLOGG, LTD.

Management consultants frequently handle personnel recruitment for clients. Sometimes the consulting firm is asked to choose the successful candidate, or else the top two or three applicants are sent on to the client for the final selection. An ad like that above from the *Globe and Mail* may bring anywhere from 20 to 100 answers a day from all over Canada. Since management consultants usually run ads for more than one client at a time, the file number is used to identify the position and the client.

This number can be the most important detail in the ad, for if you omit it the firm won't know which ad you are answering. Like other special subject lines, the file number normally appears in a letter of application between the inside address and the salutation on the left-hand side, but to give it added prominence you can centre it on the line.

July 11, 1973

Stevenson & Kellogg, Ltd.
Management Consultants
1112 West Pender Street
Vancouver, British Columbia

Your file 4591

Gentlemen:

Punctuation

For punctuating the body of your letter, follow the guide in the chapter on punctuation, conforming to modern English usage. But for the other sections of your letter — the date line, the inside address, the salutation, the complimentary closing — there are departures from the usual rules. The standard pattern illustrated here is used for most business correspondence today.

Besides the standard pattern, which is most commonly used, there is the closed pattern that requires some punctuation mark after every display line. The open pattern, which uses almost no punctuation except in the body of the letter, is gaining wider acceptance, particularly in the simplified letter. The style of punctuation should match the style of letter.

Letter Styles

The letter styles seen most often in business correspondence are the modified block, the full block, and the semiblock. You will also find, but

48

less frequently, the simplified form and the hanging-indentation form. These are illustrated for you on the following pages. No one style is intrinsically "best." After you start working you will be expected to conform to the company preferences in letter styles as in other details. Even though you have learned a modern style — the simplified form, for example — you won't be encouraged to use it in many firms.

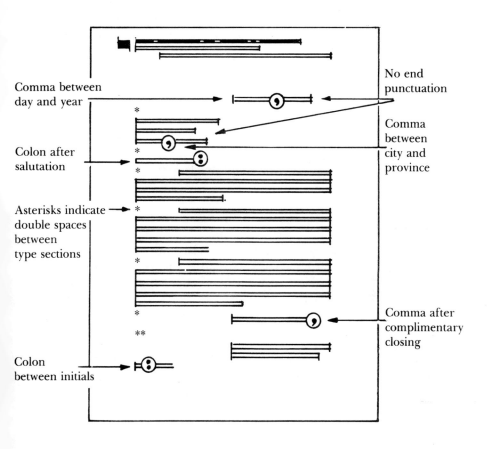

Comma between day and year

No end punctuation

Colon after salutation

Comma between city and province

Asterisks indicate double spaces between type sections

Comma after complimentary closing

Colon between initials

November 4, 1980

Ms. Pauline Gorski
34 Homedale Avenue
Wood Mountain, Saskatchewan
SOH 4LO

Dear Ms. Gorski

This letter is typed in the full block style,
which is the most modern of the preferred
Canadian styles. You might want to use this
setup, with its open punctuation, for your own
personal business letters.

In this style each of the sections is arranged in
straight-sided blocks with no indentations.
Because every line begins at the left margin, this
style is fastest to type and has an asymmetrical
appearance which is not unpleasing to the modern
eye.

Note that I recommend placing the writer's
address directly under the name if this style is
used for a letter of application. This is a
departure from the usual placing of the address
just above the date.

Sincerely

Ronald A. Amberley

Ronald A. Amberley
7259 Spruce Street
Vancouver, British Columbia
V6E 9S9

Full Block Style

2999 24th Avenue, N.W.
Calgary, Alberta
T2N 1N9

December 21, 1980

Mr. Gary Goodwin
34 Fairview Crescent
Brampton, Ontario
L6T 9Z9

Dear Mr. Goodwin:

This letter is typed in the modified block style.

In this letter style, as in the full block, each
of the sections is arranged in straight-sided
blocks with no indentations. Note that the
modified block varies from the full block in that
the date and the closing sections are lined up to
start in the centre of the page.

The style is simple and attractive. It is also
easy to type. It is probably the most widely
used in business because, while modern in
appearance, it is not too extreme for the average
business person.

If you wish, you can place your address under
your name if you use this style for a letter of
application.

Sincerely,

Margaret Wilson.

Margaret Wilson

Modified Block Style

229 Poplar Avenue
Kirkland Lake, Ontario
P2N 2N9

January 28, 1981

Miss Mary Wenzel
718 Melvin Avenue
Sudbury, Ontario
P3C 2X8

Dear Miss Wenzel:

This letter is typed in the semiblock
style, with the first line of each paragraph
indented five spaces. Some typists even indent
ten spaces.

The semiblock style is an older, more
conservative form of business letter. It is
still widely used, and many employers prefer
it.

One advantage of this style is that it
most clearly indicates paragraphing. Especially
with longer typewritten communications, such as
reports, the paragraph indentations make for
a more attractive format.

Yours sincerely,

Roger L. Morrison

Roger L. Morrison

Semiblock Style

June 22, 1980

Mr. Dennis Quinn, Manager
Prairie Sales
Brandon, Manitoba
R7A 5Z5

THE SIMPLIFIED LETTER

This letter style, Mr. Quinn, was designed by
the National Office Management Association (NOMA)
to be as streamlined as possible. Based on the
full block form, it carries efficiency several
steps further than the other letter styles.

1 Open punctuation is used throughout.

2 A subject line is typed in capitals with a
   blank line above and below it.

3 The salutation and the complimentary closing
   are omitted.

4 Usually, the addressee's name is used in the
   first sentence to add warmth.

5 The writer's name and title are typed in
   capitals and appear four spaces below the
   body of the letter.

Although this letter style has not gained wide
acceptance yet, it has several advantages. For
one thing, it saves the typist about 19 strokes.
Note, however, the desperate attempt to reclaim
the greeting in the first sentence.

RUTH CARSTAIRS, CORRESPONDENCE DIRECTOR

Simplified Style

53

August 10, 1980

Mr. Murray Lander
2049 Maple Street
Kingston, Ontario
P9N 1A7

Dear Mr. Lander:

If you are after a slightly different style of
   letter for sales or advertising, this one
   will interest you. The hanging-indentation
   style is the reverse of the semiblock in
   that all lines but the first of each
   paragraph "hang" five spaces in from the
   left margin.

Key words can thus be emphasized by placing them
   at the beginning of each paragraph. By
   typing key words in capitals you can give
   them even more emphasis.

Typists find it too awkward and time-consuming
   for daily correspondence so you won't find
   this style in common use in business offices.

                          Sincerely,

                          Dana Bormann

                          Dana Bormann
                          Sales Manager

Hanging-Indentation Style

54

Addressing the Envelope

The last step before getting a letter off in the mail is addressing the envelope and placing your folded letter in it. For a business envelope, single space the address beginning on line 14 slightly to left of centre. Type the postal code underneath the name of the city to which the letter is addressed. Type your return address in the upper left-hand corner about 1½ cm in from the edge.

Marion Lovell
Central Office Supplies
425 Clearall Avenue
Toronto, Ontario M8Z 2X9

17
Canada

Mr. Sneed Hearn, Office Manager
Motor City Sales
7423 Cameron Avenue
Windsor, Ontario
N9B 1Z9

Exercises

1. Write a letter to the editor of the "Letters-to-the-Editor" section of your newspaper. Write about a topic of current concern. Be sure to use the most suitable form for this type of letter.
2. Using the modified block form, write a letter to a friend telling him why you like college better than high school.
3. Bring to class examples of letterhead stationery and be prepared to evaluate them.
4. Assume that you are the office manager at Moore Electric Company located at 1206 Oakton St., Kingston, Ontario, L3P 9H3. Write a letter to your Business Communications instructor using the letter format you consider most attractive. Describe your reasons for having chosen it, and discuss the importance of writing business letters that are attractive to the reader. Address a business-size envelope and submit the letter to your instructor.

Chapter Four

Types of Letters

Some business correspondence can be handled by form letter, but most of it still needs personal attention. If you keep the Five C's in mind, letter writing need be no more intimidating than any other kind of communication. In addition to the Five C's, the letter writer's code below should help you become a good or even an excellent letter writer.

The Letter Writer's Code

- **Be prompt.** If at all possible, answer letters the same day they are received. The longer you put off answering, the harder it becomes.
- **Be tactful and considerate.** The long-range purpose of all business letters is to create and maintain good will. Be considerate of the feelings and point of view of the recipient.
- **Be friendly.** Remember that the reader is a human being and not a cold statistic.
- **Be sincere.** Avoid statements you can't back up.
- **Be yourself.** No one can write a better letter for you than you can write for yourself, because no one thinks or talks exactly the way you do.
- **Be brief but not curt.** Try to avoid writing a two-page letter about anything. Put lengthy detail on a separate enclosure.

Favorable Tone

Tone, you remember, is the writer's attitude toward the reader. Most examples of poor tone, in letters as in any other kind of communication, result from the inability of the sender to perceive the position of the other person. Try putting yourself in the recipient's place. Ask yourself: how would I feel if I received a letter like this? Keeping the other person in mind is sometimes called the "You-attitude." If you truly consider the feelings and point of view of your correspondent, your letter is bound to be more courteous and considerate. Give some thought, then, to the tone you want to achieve in your letter. The right tone will go a long way toward putting your correspondent in a favorable frame of mind. This is especially important because, just like when you meet someone in person, you want to make a good first impression with your letter, and a letter with a favorable tone can promote good will.

Since tone is the sum total of the words you choose, there are a few *don'ts* to observe. Don't use angry or insulting words, or arrogant or fawning ones. In fact, avoid extremes of all kinds in business correspondence. Don't reach for unfamiliar words, stilted phrases, or weak ones like "I hope" and "I wish." Use a positive voice. It isn't necessary to apologize for taking the reader's time. To achieve a distinctive tone as well as a favorable one, be friendly and sincere. Writing a business letter is not like writing to a pen pal or to your grandmother thanking her for a birthday present, but a business letter need not be stiff and wordy. The formality of a business letter is simply the formality of speaking to someone in the presence of others. If you have some business experience, then you know that this means being yourself, being human, and letting the best of what you really are be that which impresses people.

Specific Types of Letters

There was a time when letters were necessary for conducting any business transaction, but today they constitute only one of the kinds of interchange available. Requests for payment, for example, used to require seven collection letters starting with "a friendly reminder that your payment is overdue" and working up to "we regret that we must now turn your account over to a collection agency." Most requests for payment have been streamlined now into stickers that can be attached to the statement. Or, the computer that prints your statement also prints on it an overdue notice — of increasing severity depending on how overdue your payment is.

Similarly, the ordering of merchandise on forms provided by the wholesaler makes a letter unnecessary. Also, direct mail selling is usually handled by advertising firms who specialize in high pressure campaigns. The only sales letters most career persons are apt to write are letters of application in which they are selling their services, and these letters are handled in detail in the next section. To some extent, though, all letters are sales letters in that the writer wants the recipient to buy something — a product, a service, an idea, or a point of view.

In any such situation, if you can handle the matter over the telephone, do so. But we have all known the annoyance at being called to the phone at an inappropriate time to listen to a sales pitch for a set of encyclopedias or an auto club membership. In this case the caller loses not only the sale but the good will of the customer. A letter would have been preferable.

A Sequence of Collection Stickers*

Letters of Inquiry

The letter of inquiry or request is one of the most frequently written business letters. If you are seeking information, ask for it clearly and concisely. (The Five C's again.) To make it easy for the other person to answer, indent and number your questions (or the items of information you require) if there are two or more of them. Remember that you are more apt to get an answer, especially if you are conducting a survey, if you include a self-addressed stamped envelope.

Outline for a Letter of Inquiry
First paragraph
1. Explain why you are writing to this particular person or company.
2. State your request.
Middle paragraph(s)
1. Explain why you need the information.
2. If the inquiry is a survey, state where the results will be published

*Courtesy New England Business Services, Inc.

or offer to send a copy of the results.
3. Point out how the recipient will benefit from the results.
Last paragraph
1. Thank the recipient or express appreciation for whatever help you
   might receive.

Dear Mr. Brown:

As Member of Parliament for this riding, you
undoubtedly know what government help, if any,
is available for new companies. We want to apply
for such a grant or loan to open a toy
manufacturing plant here in Westfield.

There are three of us in on the venture. We
each have $5000 to put up and enough experience
to convince ourselves that we can make a success
of it. All three of us worked at Hargreaves
before its closure. We believe that as a small
company we could compete more effectively in the
marketplace than Hargreaves.

The marketing surveys we have done look good and
we have hard evidence of cost and revenue
projections. Suitable quarters are available at
very reasonable rent. In fact, everything looks
favorable if we can raise the necessary capital
to open.

We would appreciate your putting us in touch
with any government agencies that could help.

Sincerely,

Claim Letters

Angry complaints about products and services have become so common in our society that some newspapers now operate an ombuds-
man's column on behalf of their readers. Many consumers simply do
not know how to go about seeking redress. Besides furnishing such
information, these columns are run on the assumptions that the airing
of justifiable complaints about unscrupulous practices will, if nothing
else, warn the public, and that legitimate businesses shun adverse
publicity and will do everything possible to adjust valid claims. Often

all that is needed by a claimant is a letter to the right department.

Tone is important in any communication, but is doubly so in a claim letter. Poorly written claim letters often convey pointless threats and spiteful comments that do nothing but alienate the recipient. Such letters are apt to delay rather than facilitate settling the claim. If you have a valid complaint, be firm but reasonable. Include in your letter the exact amount of your loss and the inconvenience you have suffered. Refer to any contract clauses that cover your loss. (Note that valuable documents seldom should be included except in facsimile.) State what you consider a fair settlement or suggest a solution to resolve the differences between you. Don't threaten to sue — at least, not in the first letter. If you don't receive satisfaction, you can be more demanding in subsequent letters.

Gentlemen:

A year ago Acme Appliances, your dealer here in Westfield, installed your Arctic Cooler air conditioner model 419 in our office. It worked fine at first, but broke down this year on June 2.

In response to our call, the Acme service man came out, examined the machine, and went off to get some part or other. We have not seen him since. The manager of Acme Appliances is never available when we phone and our calls have not been returned.

Meantime, we are into the longest heat wave on record. My secretary is threatening to quit. The office boy has monopolized the water cooler. And my temper is reaching the boiling point. We need that air conditioner -- fast.

A copy of the warranty is enclosed. I am sure a word from you to Acme Appliances will get things moving again so that we can all cool off around here.

Sincerely,

Bertram Gough

Bertram Gough

Responses to Claim Letters

There are two basic responses to claim letters. Either you agree with the writer or you do not. In the first instance, if you or your company is at fault, you apologize and agree to take care of the matter at once. Explain how the mistake occurred and try to get the other person to see your side of it. Since you are accepting the responsibility, explain what will be done by way of compensation. Express sympathy for the correspondent's problem and for any inconvenience that has been experienced. And, of course, promise to do what you can to see that the mistake is not repeated. If you are sincere in your apology, you can probably restore a good relationship.

Remember, however, that as you accept some or all responsibility for the claim, you are the one to determine how and to what extent the claim is to be satisfied. Also, unless you are very sure that you have accurately "read" the tone of the claimant's letter, you should not apologize directly or profusely. "Settle the problem" to satisfy the customer or to solve the "misunderstanding that has arisen"; don't state flatly that your company is to blame and at fault. In this latter case, the customer may still not feel satisfied and his or her lawyer would be only too happy to see your written admission of absolute fault and your detailed account of how you goofed.

The following answer to a claim letter perhaps is too direct for the good of the writer's company. Mr. Gough just might not have cooled off, and he might be the sort of person who takes legal action whenever he can. Perhaps he didn't mention in his claim letter, above, how his business has lost man-hours and thousands of dollars because of the broken air conditioner. In most instances, though, such a letter as this would be perfectly acceptable.

Dear Mr. Gough:

I don't blame you for being upset when your Arctic Cooler broke down during a heat wave. You have been remarkably patient, considering the circumstances.

Our regional service manager tells us that he has no record of the order from Acme Appliances for a condenser for your machine. Acme, however, insists that they did order the part and have produced the carbon copy of the order dated June 2. Obviously, the order did not reach its destination.

This whole incident has exposed a weakness in our communication methods. We have instructed our dealers to order parts in future by telephone.

Yes, Mr. Gough, we do honor our guarantees. We have instructed Acme Appliances to install a new Arctic Cooler in your office immediately at no cost to you. In fact, by the time this letter reaches you, everything should be working comfortably again. We have also suggested to Mr. Cascadden, Acme's manager, that in future he be more available to take phone calls.

Please accept my personal apology for the inconvenience you and your staff have experienced. I can safely promise you it will not happen again.

Sincerely,

Letters of Refusal

Not all disputes between business persons can be settled satisfactorily for all concerned. Sometimes it is necessary to refuse to accept responsibility for a claim. You may not be at fault. Similarly, occasions may arise when you will have to turn down a request for confidential information or will have to refuse someone a favor. Letters can say "no" gracefully but firmly and still leave the reader in a friendly state of mind providing the letter is written with tact and shows concern for the person making the request. Tone, again, is very important.

Too many letters of complaint are written in the heat of the moment — the writers want to let you know just how angry they are. Usually they tell you what they think of you at the same time. You do not reply in kind. No one gains in an exchange of angry letters. In your answers you want to be able to say "no" and keep the customers' good will at the same time. This is a large order, but it can be done. If you have to say "no," tell the reader why you are refusing.

Dear Ms. Bowers:

We have been in touch with Westfield Audio Repair Shop on your behalf. It seems your machine requires a flywheel. The part has been shipped by air freight to Westfield and your machine should be as good as new in a day or two.

Perhaps I can modify your opinion of our
Electraphonic tape cartridge player somewhat,
even though we cannot assume responsibility for
the repairs.

If you will read your warranty carefully, you
will note that the guarantee applies to the
first year only. Since you have had un-
interrupted playing pleasure from your machine
for three years, a breakdown at this time,
though annoying, is not unreasonable.

I am sorry you have experienced this difficulty.
Your rebuilt player should give you many more
years of trouble-free listening from now on.

Sincerely,

Letters of Persuasion

There will be times during your career when you will be writing what
amounts to a sales letter even though you may never be involved in
a campaign of direct mail advertising. Any letter that attempts to
persuade the reader to "buy" a proposal of some kind is, in effect, a
sales letter. Such letters are a test of the writer's ingenuity. Consider
the daring involved in the following example. The young man printed
his message in letters one metre high on a public billboard.

MARY, I LOVE YOU.
WILL YOU MARRY ME?
JOHN

John didn't waste words. His message was clear, concise, and convincing; the method of getting it across was unusual. (P.S., Mary said
yes.) You would have to know your reader rather well, though, to use
a method this startling. And do remember that once an approach like
this has been used it loses much of its advantage. Originality counts.

Well then, what can make your letter different? Go back now and
re-read the letter writer's code, noting particularly the two tenets, *be
friendly* and *be yourself*. If you apply these, your own personality will
give your letter the touch of originality no one else can give it. Don't
try to create a literary masterpiece. Just write the way you talk to

people in formal situations. That way you will come across as sincere and as yourself.

The object of the letter of persuasion is to convince your reader to do something you want him or her to do. You may not be able to sell the reader with as few words as John used above. You will probably need more room to structure your thoughts into a cohesive argument. The basic steps for a letter of persuasion can be incorporated in four paragraphs:

1. Catch the reader's attention with your opening sentence.
2. Explain your proposal.
3. Show how the reader will benefit.
4. Clinch your proposal. Make it easy for the reader to respond.

Dear Ms. Roberts:

Would you be willing to share the success story of your rise to the presidency of Fairview Enterprises?

Our college paper, VIEWPOINT, is preparing a series of articles featuring top executives in this area. As a reporter for VIEWPOINT, I would like to interview you for the lead story for the series. The way you have overcome obstacles in your career should be an inspiration to our readers, many of whom may someday face similar problems.

Do say yes. I've enclosed a stamped self-addressed envelope for your reply. I can come whenever it is convenient for you.

Yours sincerely,

Letters of Resignation

Some day, for any one of a number of reasons, you may decide to resign. It may be because you have found a better job, or perhaps because you have been unfairly treated or did not get the raise you asked for. Or you may resign over a policy disagreement that cannot be resolved. Never write an angry or accusing letter of resignation if only because you may need a recommendation from the company later on. The writer of the following letter decided to resign to take a job with more challenge. He included these points in his letter of resignation:

- an expression of gratitude to his present employer for past benefits
- his reasons for resigning
- effective date of resignation
- an offer to train his replacement

Dear Mr. Linton:

As you know, I have been with Benoit's for three years now. On the whole they have been rewarding ones for me. I am grateful for the challenges and opportunities afforded me while working for so large and prestigious a firm as Benoit's.

However, I feel that it is time for me to move now into other areas of experience, to accept other challenges. I have been offered the position of sales manager with a small company just starting up in Westfield. Since this means getting in on the ground floor of a new venture, I have decided to accept.

My resignation will take effect at the end of this month. In the meantime I will do whatever I can to help transfer my present responsibilities to the person who will be taking my place.

Sincerely,

Exercises

1. Assume you are working in your profession. Write a claim letter about a piece of office equipment you ordered that did not arrive on schedule. Explain the inconvenience you are experiencing because of the delay.
2. A man you did not know gave you a lift to school several days ago. You left your books in his car. Since he lives out of town, he mailed the books to your home. Write a letter telling him how grateful you are to have the books back. Include some mention of the value of the books to you.

3. Write a persuasive letter to your favorite rock group asking them to perform at a college benefit. Since you can't offer them a fee, what arguments can you muster to persuade them to come?
4. Rewrite the answer to a claim letter on pages 61-62 so that your company is less likely to be taken to court by Mr. Gough.
5. You are a management trainee in a trust company, and you are interested in working in Quebec. Of course French is required, but your high school French is pretty rusty. Write a letter to Beavertail College inquiring about a French course for business persons. Ask for all details you consider relevant.
6. You recently ordered some promotional matchbooks to give out to your clients. Owing to faulty printing, some of the letters are too faint to see — your slogan "If it is Simons, you can be sure!" now reads "If it is Simons, you can   su e!" Write a letter to the printing company.
7. You are the owner of a small restaurant. You have been having trouble with your dishwasher and two servicemen have come to look at it. The first one reported that the gazingus wire was shot but since he didn't have one with him he would have to go back for it. He never returned. Another call brought a second repairman who declared that the dishwasher was beyond repair. Write a letter to the president of Sterikleen Washers, asking for some clarification.
8. You are the business manager for Synthetic Dirt, a punk rock group, and have received a letter from a concert promoter in Halifax demanding that you pay $18 500 to cover damages caused during the group's recent visit in Halifax — they painted the motel room black and broke the television and furniture; as part of their act, they broke the sound equipment provided by the local auditorium; their food and beverage bill from a local catering service far exceeded what the promoter expected to pay. You may or may not have a contract that anticipated some of these problems. Write a response to this claim letter.
9. Exchange the letters you wrote for nos. 1, 3, 6, and 7 with a classmate and write responses.

Part Three
The Job Application Package

The Résumé

The Letter of Application

The Interview

Chapter Five
The Résumé

Many of you who are just starting your college career will one day make it to top management positions in business and industry. If your job objective is already in line with this goal and if you are willing to do the spadework necessary to put you there, these next few chapters can show you how to get your start. The background preparation that led you to this point in the text has been designed to develop your writing skill for better business communication. Knowing the principles of good writing prepares you to put together a better job application package.

Applying for a job requires research, a written application, and, if the first two steps are successful, a personal interview. The written application is a two-part document made up of a letter of application and a résumé. It requires that you have a good understanding of yourself, both your strengths and your limitations, and that you are comfortable with whom you are. The written application also demands that you have some knowledge of the company to which you are applying for a job. Taken together, the application letter and résumé can have as far-reaching an effect as any document you will ever put your signature to. You should prepare a résumé before writing any application letters, so we will begin with this important advertisement of yourself.

What's a Résumé?

A résumé is a concise summary of all the information about you that will interest an employer — education, job experience, personal details. If you try to include all this information in a letter, it can become so unwieldy and stretch over so many pages that the prospective employer will throw it down impatiently before finishing reading it. *Never write a two-page letter or memo in business* if you can help it. Reports are an exception to this, and a résumé is a kind of report. So the résumé may go more than one page, but the accompanying letter most often should not. The function of the letter of application is to introduce you to the employer with a brief handshake, so to speak. The résumé delivers the rest of the goods. Although the prospective employer will read the letter and then the résumé, you will want to prepare the résumé first since the letter actually depends on information in the résumé.

Competition today is so keen and good jobs so scarce that employers don't have time to interview all the candidates who are qualified. Those who can write a better letter and résumé will find the inner doors swinging open for them, while other applicants never get past the secretary. Since the résumé is so vitally important to your personal success, it is worth putting a good deal of thought into organizing and highlighting the best features of it so that it will do a top-notch job of self-selling for you.

Your Career Goal

The first major category on your résumé is your job objective. If you haven't yet sorted out your goals in life, it's time to do it. This may take some time. And don't be afraid to change your mind. If in the process of examining your life you decide you are slotted into the wrong niche, there is always time to change your mind. It's your life. What do you want to do with it?

This would be a good place to tell you about Tom Caulfield. Tom was a first-year student in one of my Business Communication classes several years ago. When I asked the class to list their career objectives, Tom didn't have one. He was enrolled in the business administration course for lack of other motivation.

"No job objective?" I asked.

Tom shook his head.

"What are your interests? What about hobbies?"

Tom merely shrugged, scrunching farther down in his seat and sprawling his long legs farther out into the aisle. His friend sitting next to him tapped him on the arm.

"You played in *The Crucible* last year."

"That was different."

It sure was. A few more questions finally drew out of him the information that the theatre was his overriding passion, but that he felt he didn't have a great deal of acting talent. In spite of his high school performance, he had failed to land even a bit part when he tried out for the college play.

I started him on a clipping file of careers related to theatre but exclusive of acting. He took on a publicity campaign for the drama club and conducted it so successfully that the club had its best financial year to date. At the end of the first term his professional file was bulging with clippings about the theatre arranged under headings like Favorite Actors, Plays Seen, Reviews. One significant subsection was titled Theatre Management. He continued working with the drama club and although he never did get to perform on stage in college, when he graduated he had a portfolio of impressive accomplishments to show employers.

Tom dropped in to see me a few years ago. He had been working with a local performing arts group in Windsor along with his regular job as manager of a downtown theatre. He had just accepted the position of assistant manager at the Civic Auditorium Centre in a large Canadian city. He is headed for a fascinating career combining his business training with his hobby.

Sell Your Strong Points

Everyone has something he or she can do well, or has qualities that some employer, somewhere, will value. Before you can do an effective job of self-selling you have to sort yourself out, decide what you want to do and what your strong points are. What do you have that an employer wants? In what way do you stand out from the other applicants?

Stop for a moment and look at your classmates. Really look at them. Each one has a different appearance, no two are the same height and weight, no two have hair and eyes exactly the same color as anyone else's. Personality differences are even more striking. What traits and interests distinguish you from the others in the class? List what you consider your outstanding characteristics and emphasize them in strong positive language. Are you aggressive and outgoing? Confident of your ability to sell igloos in the Arctic? Are you a self-starter? Extremely efficient? A hard worker? Write down your positive points and decide where you want the accent to fall. If you are too modest to write out your own best qualities, don't be. False humility and lack of self-knowledge have no place in the business world.

Accomplishments

The two things about you that will interest an employer most when experience isn't the only criterion are personality and achievements. Some of you already have part-time jobs to your credit that will look good on your résumé. But you need more than this. Resolve now that when you graduate you will have one positive accomplishment from your college career that you can emphasize. Join something: the Marketing Club, the Debating Society, the hockey team. Do more than join — accept some responsibility. Whatever you take on do it so well that you can make it a focal point of your self-selling campaign after graduation.

Every year the top graduates of the community colleges and universities are picked up by representatives of business and industry through interviews right on campus. You can be sure these graduates have something on the record besides marks. Get your name into the student newspaper now and save your clippings. They will be a solid addition to your job package portfolio. Most employers are looking for leadership potential. A record of extracurricular achievement alongside a B- average can make as strong a recommendation as straight A's. Not that there is anything wrong with A's, unless you run up against an employer who considers them the product of an anti-social personality.

The all-around experience of college life is just as valuable as good marks, and you are cheating yourself if you don't take advantage of some of the extras available. Any of the extracurricular activities you get involved in may eventually steer you toward a different career than the one you originally planned. And your résumé will continue to change along with you as you mature in personal growth and experience. Ten years from now no employer is going to care what marks you made in college, but he or she is going to be interested in what you have done in the meantime.

Résumé Form

Any employer could tell you that the form the résumé takes varies widely from one applicant to another. Qualifications and experience being equal, the best résumés are those presented in a concise, attractive, tabulated form. This form can be either loose and chatty or tight. A loose form assumes that the application letter will be quite brief; a tight form demands that the letter highlight and expand upon data in the résumé. Regardless of the form you use, the résumé should contain the cumulation of your qualifications. The details should be presented in a clear and easy-to-read outline.

The following discussion details the loose form, with some comment on the tight form. Bear in mind that there is no correct or incorrect form *per se*. For example, if you use an elite typewriter, you may want to use capital letters for your headings; with a pica typewriter, full capitals may not look as attractive as upper and lower case underlined. Never, by the way, use a typewriter that types only script or italic. The résumé begins with your name and address:

RÉSUMÉ

YOUR FULL NAME   Your marital status
Your home address   Number of dependents
Your home phone number   Height and weight
                                  Health status

Your name goes at the top left-hand corner. You don't have to list your age or sex unless you want to. And don't go into details about your health. If you have a serious problem you can bring it up in person during the interview where you can explain that it doesn't interfere with your working ability. If you can't truthfully list your health as excellent, list it as good and omit references to defects.

Job Objective

The first heading on your résumé, after your personal identification, is your job objective. Be as specific here as you can, listing your immediate goal, not a pie-in-the-sky future presidency. If your eventual goal is related to the job you are applying for, you can add it immediately underneath.

JOB
OBJECTIVE: Accountant

                  with the aim of an eventual role
                  in financial management

Whatever you do, don't put down *Job Objective: anything*. Not even if you are desperate for work and are willing to start anywhere from the janitor's job on up. (Janitorial work requires special skills and therefore requires a serious and separate job application.) Avoid any smart-aleck quips. The employer will expect, at the very least, a professional attitude on your part.

Education

Put the name of the most recent school you attended at the top of the list and work back. The dates should be inclusive, starting with the year you enrolled and ending with the year you graduated. If you are currently taking courses toward a degree, you would put this at the top of the list.

Include your departmental major and other significant courses you have taken. And don't forget to mention awards and scholarships, if any. Be sure to include here any out-of-the-ordinary achievements

73

such as editor of the campus newspaper, an office held in student government, any clubs you belonged to, or any clubs you started while in college.

EDUCATION: SENECA COLLEGE OF APPLIED ARTS
              AND TECHNOLOGY, Toronto, Ontario

1980-82   Diploma in Business Administration
              with a major in accounting. Minor
              in data processing. Graduated
              with grade point average of 3.5.

Experience

Include all your summer jobs and part-time jobs, putting your most recent first and working back as you did for your education. Your most recent experience will probably be the most relevant to the job you want after graduation, so if there is any special training you received, talk about it here.

Never falsify any of the facts. If employers are seriously interested in you, they are going to scrutinize your résumé carefully and will check out items like references and past employment. If you leave out a job you were fired from, or worse still, if you move the starting date of your next job to try to cover up, the discrepancy will come to light in a check of your employment history. A small lie can lose you a big opportunity.

While describing your job experience emphasize the scope of your responsibilities rather than just listing the duties of the job. Employers know what these are anyway. They are more interested in how you did what you did and what you accomplished.

EXPERIENCE:

January to   WILLIAMS, BROWN & FILBERT,
May, 1982   Chartered Accountants, Ajax,
               Ontario.

               As part of a co-op program through
               Seneca College, I worked part-time
               in the offices of Williams, Brown
               & Filbert during my graduating
               year. I worked under Mr. Willwood's
               supervision on several auditing
               engagements and thus was able to

74

put my formal training into
practice as I received it.

May to August, 1980 and	ARGUS CONSTRUCTION COMPANY, Scarborough, Ontario.
May to August, 1981	Timekeeper. I was able to save enough of each summer's wages to finance my following year of college.

A Word on Chronology

Most job application forms require that such information as education
and work experience be presented in reverse chronology, with the
most recent experiences listed first. The examples given above follow
this order. This is logical, in one way, because the employer is most
interested in what you have been doing lately, not five or ten years
ago. In another way, though, a straight chronology is more logical,
and you might want to consider it for your résumé.

With a straight chronology, employers are forced to read all of what
you have done. They cannot so easily look just at your most recent
experiences and achievements. In other words, the straight chronology (beginning at whatever point in time seems appropriate) forces
the reader to see you as a total person, where one job or educational
level logically led to another. This organization can effectively show
that you are (and have been) growing and developing. It does not rip
you out of a time continuum, so to speak, and freeze you in the present
moment. If there is a real sense of growth and development in your
work and education experiences, if the past truly has brought you to
the present and is significant to you, then you will want to consider
using a straight chronology in your résumé.

Personal Background

This area is extremely sensitive: personal accomplishments that may
impress one employer will be of little interest to another or may actually
offend someone else. Employers are forbidden by law to discriminate
against you on the basis of race, religion, sex, etc. But you are not
forbidden to identify yourself in these ways if you have reason to
believe such personal characteristics may carry an advantage.

It is not possible to produce guidelines for you that will cover the
range of tastes, interests, and prejudices you are likely to encounter.
Your summary of your interests is going to create a general impression
of the sort of person you are — athletic, community-minded, church-

oriented, good with children, artistic, brilliantly mechanical, or whatever. If you feel a particular hobby or interest demonstrates certain skills or qualities, you will usually need to point this out. For example, if you have worked one summer as a camp counsellor it will not be obvious that you are good with children — you should add some commendation you have received. On the other hand, if you were hired as a counsellor for three consecutive years that record is its own advertisement of your capability and you don't need to add to it.

It is probably to your advantage to keep your summary general rather than specific. You paint; you have travelled; you play hockey. This is better than to say you paint posters; you have been to Norway, Sweden, Spain, Portugal, and the London airport; you play defense for the St. Mary's Angels. A general summary suggests that these interests could expand to include other artistic activities, company business out of town, other sports.

PERSONAL
BACKGROUND:
Toronto is my home town. I grew up here, attended Dougall Avenue Public School and Stephen Leacock Collegiate. Have always been active in sports. Made the hockey team in high school. Also enjoy golf, ice-fishing. Taught Sunday School for several years and currently am a Big Brother.

Wrote a weekly sports column for the student newspaper in my second year at Seneca. Am also interested in furniture refinishing. Currently refinishing an old desk bought for $1.

Salary

If you are applying for your first full-time job, your salary expectations may be out of line with what the employer is prepared to offer. Better leave this item for the interview where you can work it out between you. Even if you are answering an ad that says, "State salary expected," don't do it. A quality product will sell itself without a sale price tag, and your inexperience on the job market may lead you to underestimate your market value as easily as you can overestimate it.

References

Include the names and addresses of three people who will give you a good recommendation and ask their permission ahead of time. If you are a student or a recent graduate your teachers will be glad to do this for you. One teacher to a résumé is usually enough. Don't ask friends or relatives because their opinions are apt to be lop-sided. No interviewer will attach any weight to your uncle's praise of you. If you have had some work experience, a former or present employer is the best source for a recommendation.

Other Categories

As you grow professionally, you will want to add categories to your résumé, such as Professional Meetings, Reports, perhaps even Publications. Other categories you might want to include now are Honors and Societies, Extracurricular Activities, Major Term Papers and Reports, and Coursework.

Scholastic awards, such as being on the Dean's List or receiving a scholarship, and professional and campus organizations, including any offices you held, are to be included under the Honors and Societies heading. If the "honors" part of this heading doesn't apply to you, then the "societies" should be subsumed under Extracurricular Activities, which should include all *organized* activities you have participated in during high school and college. Again, if you have not been a joiner of clubs or a member of athletic teams, then Extracurricular Activities should be omitted and replaced by Special Interests. Under this category you can list, in brief tabulated form, some of the information you otherwise would include in the Personal Background section.

During your college career you may have written term papers or reports that bear directly on your job objective. If so, and if you did well on these papers or reports, list the titles under a separate heading. This is just the sort of thing that can catch the eye of a potential employer, and, in an interview, is something you could talk about intelligently. For example, if you wrote a research paper titled "Will Communications Technology Make the Secretary Obsolete?" or "The Potential for Energy Conservation in Small Business," a job interviewer likely will find this of considerable interest.

Once a job applicant has successfully gotten past the initial screening of applications, most employers will automatically contact the applicant's college to get a transcript of grades and courses. Some small companies, however, might not, especially if they require extensive on-the-job training. These employers will be more interested in an applicant's personality and motivation, and in the fact that the applicant has completed his or her studies with distinction. Besides, a computer-printed transcript with its inevitable abbreviations often is not the easiest thing to read. Thus, unless your grades have been mediocre or worse, you probably should include a category titled Coursework in Major Field(s) of Study. This is a courtesy to the employer; it also tells more about you and what you know and can do. Of course, include the grades you earned, but as important as grades are the course titles themselves. These give the employer or interviewer more information about you, and any interview questions that arise from this information should be ones you can handle with ease.

The Completed Résumé

To sum up: your résumé should be clear, condensed, and interesting. The format you use will depend upon a number of variables: the typewriter you use, the application letter you write, the achievements you have accomplished, the interests you have, the job you are seeking. The following are examples of résumés, one in the loose form and one in the tight form, for the hypothetical graduating student we have come to know in this chapter.

RÉSUMÉ

Christopher T. Scott	Age: 22
6609 Billings Street	Single
Scarborough, Ontario	5' 10", 165 lbs.
(416) 452-9999	Health: excellent

JOB OBJECTIVE:	Accountant
	with the aim of an eventual role in financial management.
EDUCATION:	SENECA COLLEGE OF APPLIED ARTS AND TECHNOLOGY, Toronto, Ontario
1980-82	Diploma in Business Administration with major in accounting. Minor in data processing. Graduated with a Grade Point Average of 3.5 out of a possible 4.0.
1976-80	STEPHEN LEACOCK COLLEGIATE INSTITUTE, Scarborough, Ontario
BUSINESS EXPERIENCE:	WILLIAMS, BROWN & FILBERT, Chartered Accountants, Ajax, Ontario
January to May, 1982	In conjunction with Seneca's policy of "hands-on" learning, I worked part-time in

the offices of Williams, Brown & Filbert during my graduating year. I worked under Mr. Willwood's supervision on several auditing engagements and thus was able to put my formal training into practice as I received it.

May to August, 1980 and May to August, 1981	ARGUS CONSTRUCTION COMPANY, Scarborough, Ontario Timekeeper. I was able to save enough of each summer's wages to finance my following year of college. I was offered year round employment with Argus but turned it down to finish my education.
PERSONAL BACKGROUND:	Toronto is my home town. I grew up here, attended Dougall Avenue Public School and Stephen Leacock Collegiate. Have always been active in sports. Made the hockey team in high school. Also enjoy golf, ice-fishing. Taught Sunday School for several years and currently am a Big Brother. Wrote a weekly sports column for the student newspaper in my second year at Seneca. Am also interested in furniture refinishing. Currently refinishing an old desk bought for $1.
SALARY:	Open
REFERENCES:	Mr. Elwin Sneed Business Division Seneca College of Applied Arts and Technology Toronto, Ontario Mr. Anthony Argus, President Argus Construction Company Scarborough, Ontario Mr. Otto Willwood, C.A. Williams, Brown & Filbert Chartered Accountants Ajax, Ontario

Christopher T. Scott
6609 Billings Street
Scarborough, Ontario
(416) 452-9999

Age: 22
Marital status: single
Height: 5' 10"
Weight: 165 lbs.
Health: excellent

Job objective

Accountant, with the aim of an eventual role in financial management

Education

1976-80: Stephen Leacock Collegiate Institute, Scarborough,
          Ontario -- grade 13 certificate

1980-82: Seneca College of Applied Arts and Technology, Toronto,
          Ontario -- Associate of Accounting Degree

Honors and Societies

Honor Roll, Stephen Leacock Collegiate, 1980
Class President, Stephen Leacock Collegiate, 1978-79
Hockey Team, Stephen Leacock Collegiate, 1979-80
Dean's List, Seneca College, 1981-82
Accounting Club, Seneca College, 1980-82, secretary-treasurer, 1981
Debating Society, Seneca College, 1981-82

Work experience

Summer, 1977-Summer, 1979: Lifeguard, Smedley Pool Services, East
          York, Ontario
May-August, 1980: Timekeeper, Argus Construction Company,
          Scarborough, Ontario
May-August, 1981: Timekeeper, Argus Construction Company,
          Scarborough, Ontario
January-May, 1982: Apprentice Accountant, Williams, Brown &
          Filbert, Chartered Accountants, Ajax, Ontario

Coursework in Major Field (Seneca College)

Business Communications 75
Introduction to Accounting 85
Introduction to Computer Science 70
Computer Programming 75
Sales and Marketing 70
Corporate Business 65
Tax Law 70
Accounting II 80

Reports and Term Papers

"Reasons for Man-Hours Lost: A Statistical Analysis," report to
          Anthony Argus, president, Argus Construction Company,
          Scarborough, Ontario, August, 1980

"The Potential for Energy Conservation in Small Business," term
paper for Corporate Business class, Seneca College, 1981

"Pre-planning and Organization: The Key to Small Business
Accounting," report for Accounting II class, Seneca College,
1982

Other Activities and Interests

Sunday school teacher, Little Trinity Anglican Church, Toronto,
Ontario, 1976-82
Big Brothers, 1981-82
golf (3 handicap)
ice-fishing

References

Mr. Elwin Sneed
Business Division
Seneca College of Applied Arts and Technology
Toronto, Ontario

Mr. Anthony Argus, President
Argus Construction Company
Scarborough, Ontario

Mr. Otto Willwood, C.A.
Williams, Brown & Filbert, Chartered Accountants
Ajax, Ontario

Application Forms

Many large firms require you to fill in their own application forms whether or not you have already forwarded your résumé to the personnel manager. Some firms mail these forms out on request, and some ask you to fill them in during an interview session.

Always take a duplicate copy of your résumé with you to an interview. Having already worked out the information you will gain confidence transferring it to the application form and you won't leave out, through an oversight, some detail you meant to include. Also, you won't be so apt to stumble around and spoil the form and have to ask for another one. If the interviewer is present when you fill in the company forms, he or she will note that you made this kind of advance preparation.

To fill in an application form in the company's offices:

- Take a copy of your résumé with you.
- Take a pen along.
- Read all the instructions and all the questions before you start to write.
- Plan your answers before you write.
- Answer all the questions. If a question does not apply to you, write N/A or "not applicable" in the answer space.
- Answer as honestly as you can.
- Review the whole thing when you are finished.

Exercises

1. Prepare your résumé, basing it on your present educational attainment, work experience, etc.
2. Discuss the differences in form and style of the two résumés in this chapter. For example, why doesn't the tight form use the word "I"? Can you combine features and headings of the two forms to create a résumé form uniquely suitable to you?

Chapter Six
The Letter of Application

Now you have your career objective firmed up and you know the type of job you want when you graduate. To get that job, you probably will need to write a letter of application, and even if you get what you consider a good job at graduation, you likely will be back on the job market within a few years. Statistics indicate that the average worker changes jobs four times in the first ten years of his or her working life. A number of factors can contribute to this turnover pattern — disillusion with a current job, desire for a more stimulating career, or simply a need for more money. Quite often, factors beyond an employee's control — the phasing out of a job or the closing down of the company — will send the employee into the job market.

The Letter

Each time you apply for a position with another company you have to write another letter of application, particularly if no job opening has been advertised. You may get your first job by telephoning for an interview, of course, or by applying in person unannounced, but the better the position you are after the more apt you are to have to send in a written application.

If you aren't convinced you might have to write that letter, consider the case of Bob Borowsky, which is by no means unusual. Bob, as the ads put it, is an "ambitious, highly motivated super-salesman with managerial talent." In the two years he has been with his present company he has shot up from stock boy to assistant sales manager. Now he wants a crack at running the whole sales operation. But the sales manager likes it where she is, shows no signs of moving on, and is a long way from retirement. So Bob's ambition for advancement is blocked unless he applies for the position of sales manager with another company. The chances are he will sit down one night soon and answer one of the ads in the career pages of the *Financial Post* or the *Globe and Mail*. He wants a better job.

To most employees, a better job usually boils down to one thing: more money. Although a member of our materialistic society, you might resist the concept that making money is the most satisfying goal in life. You can make more money on an automotive assembly line than you can as junior clerk in the purchasing department, but if you have had a taste of assembly-line work during your summers, you know what that kind of monotony can do to a person. Perhaps that is why you've decided to continue your education. A job with challenge, with opportunity for advancement and personal growth, is far more gratifying in the long run than the size of the pay cheque. Not that money isn't one of the necessities in our society, but all too often payday becomes the goal itself instead of reasonable reward for a job you enjoy doing.

The sales manager, of course, achieves greater financial reward than the assistant does. But the higher the salary, the greater the responsibilities. Scan the double-columned ads on the career pages of your local newspaper. Notice how often phrases like "decision-making" and "managerial ability" appear. Read the career sections of the leading newspapers until you find an ad describing the job you will want eventually. Clip this ad and put it in your professional file under CAREER OBJECTIVES. Resolve to become the trained, responsible person who can land and hold that particular job.

Answering a Career Advertisement

Read over the ad you clipped and find the word to describe its tone. Tone, you remember, has to do with the writer's attitude. In answering this kind of ad, adopt the same tone the writer used. If you don't like the writer's attitude, why go after the job in the first place? You probably wouldn't be happy if you landed it. Your goal ad must be one that you can answer with sincerity.

If you feel that your best qualification is a quiet reliability, this kind of ad will appeal to you:

ACCOUNTANT

required by small but growing Canadian manufacturer to handle accounting position. Duties include general ledger, statement preparation, and other general and cost accounting work.

Experience in a manufacturing environment desirable but not essential. Applicants who are willing to enroll in the R.I.A. program preferred. Excellent opportunity for a responsible individual.

Full fringe benefits. Salary open. Please submit résumé detailing personal data and education to:

Box 254, this newspaper

Presume you are a year or two into the future and have graduated. In your search for a job you have come across this ad and it interests you. (If you aren't an accountant, translate the terms of the qualifications into your particular career language.) Read between the lines of the ad. "Salary open" means a low starting salary if you don't have actual working experience. This company probably will offer you much less than another firm would be willing to pay for experienced help. "Small but growing" probably means the company is just getting on its feet and may not be able to afford executive-type salaries yet. If you are willing to settle for a low salary in order to get your start, you could quite conceivably interest this employer — provided, of course, that you have the other qualifications asked for. This is how one applicant answered the ad:

Gentlemen:

Your ad in Thursday's GLOBE AND MAIL indicates that you want a dedicated person for your Accounting Department. You will find that I fit this requirement and that I really enjoy working with figures. My interest and abilities in accounting are borne out by the following:

> Last year at St. Clair College I campaigned successfully for the position of Treasurer of the Students' Administrative Council (SAC). While in office I streamlined the book-keeping system and set up a completely new set of books.

> This new system resulted in lower auditors' fees. It also brought to light several ir-regularities which the new executive council was able to eliminate. This effected a further saving in SAC expenditures.

The enclosed résumé details this along with my other qualifications. I would welcome the opportunity to go over them with you. You can reach me at 728-9022 to arrange an interview.

Yours sincerely,

On the other hand, if you are an ambitious person with lots of drive and if one of your strong points is your ability to cope with a variety of situations, you might keep your eyes open for a job like the following:

86

The energetic tone of this ad demands a distinctive and creative answer. And the ad itself requires a close analysis. The company, for example, is "large but aggressive and highly motivated . . . ." Read one way, this means the company is strong, successful, growing; in short, a wonderful place to work. Now read it more closely: what does the seemingly insignificant "but" suggest? First, it implies that the company is not content merely to be "large," that is, it is growing and highly competitive. Second, the "but" implies that *they* (the company and its personnel consulting firm) think most "large" companies are content with the status quo. But this one is not. It is "aggressive and highly motivated." "Aggressive" has obvious connotations, which do not conjure up images of gentleness, love, or consideration for others. "Highly motivated" is a less than honest way of saying "highly competitive," both within the company and within the industry. You either perform at a high level or the company (and possibly the industry) will chew you up and spit you out.

So, now that you have looked at the ad closely and know something about the company, do you still have "flair"? Are you prepared to temper your "creative talent and vision" in the fire of a highly competitive and aggressive organization? If you are a self-starting, self-confident extrovert, then give it a try.

```
Gentlemen:

Have flair, talent, vision, and would like to
meet you.  Résumé enclosed.

You may phone me direct at _____.
```

Sincerely,

You have to be very sure of yourself and even a bit daring to take a chance on a letter this short. If this is your style, you might be ahead of the game to send a telegram, indicating that a letter and résumé are in the mail. This way, you catch their attention and then follow up with something more substantial. Or you could phone, and then follow that with the more conventional letter and résumé.

In any case, you need to read the job advertisement closely and use the same tone in your answer as that used in the ad. If the tone of the ad is not *you*, then you shouldn't apply. Even if you got the job, would you be comfortable with it? Probably not.

The Unsolicited Letter of Application

Classified ads and career pages of newspapers are not the only places to look for a job. Personnel managers of large firms seldom have to advertise in the newspapers for applicants to fill junior office positions. They have a wealth of likely candidates to choose from whose application forms are already filled in. You can submit yours for the files along with an appropriate letter and if you are fortunate you may be called in for an interview. On the other hand, you may not want to work for a large company. You may prefer a small local firm or office. The Yellow Pages of the telephone books are likely places for such prospects. So are the pages of business journals. The list at the end of this chapter suggests other employment sources.

So don't wait for the job to come looking for you; go out after it. Many employers expect job applicants to contact them around graduation time and they may have job openings that haven't been advertised. You can be more selective in your preferences when you canvass firms where no openings have been published. Look for organizations that fit your goal and job objective and for whom you really want to work. Remember that you are offering a unique product and somewhere there is an employer looking for your particular combination of skills and attributes. The employer needs you as much as you need him or her. Don't lower your standards when you make up your job prospect list.

When you apply in writing for an unadvertised job, your immediate competition is much less. If your letter arrives on an employer's desk without rivals, he or she is more apt to give it undivided attention. An unsolicited letter of application calls for a little different approach than an application which has been invited. As a graduating student you will have three main categories you can present attractively to a prospective employer. These are:

- *Your Education.* The strong selling point as far as a college student or recent graduate is concerned is education. If your grades were good stress your grade point average or the fact that you were in the top half of your class. If your grades weren't uniformly good you can emphasize the subjects you did do well in, or any options or electives you took that tie in with the job you want. And, of course, you should point out the related achievements of your college career.
- *Related Experience.* You may feel at a disadvantage in the job market if you have little or no actual experience. I have found that most young career persons do have some working experience somewhere along the line and this can be used to emphasize character regardless of the importance or unimportance of the job. If you were a newspaper

carrier for any length of time while in grade school or high school, for example, this says a great deal about your dependability.
- *Personal Qualities.* The preliminary self-analysis you did for your résumé will help you to emphasize your positive qualities. Employers respect sincerity, honesty, enthusiasm, and the ability to get along with others. You can include here any activities or offices held — class representative for a student organization, for example — that indicate acceptance of responsibility on your part. Or simply state that you like to work and have never backed off from a difficult job.

Let the Facts Speak for You

Employers will be mainly interested in two things about you — background and personality — and neither is your unsubstantiated opinion of yourself. It is better to let the facts speak for you so that you can avoid either of the extremes of overconfidence or underconfidence. Avoid bragging. You can as easily wipe out your chances by going overboard on your own worth as you can by being so self-effacing that the employer doesn't even see you. Of the two alternatives, however, it is better to err on the side of enthusiasm. At least you will be displaying confidence in your own abilities. Self-assuredness especially is important if you plan a career in marketing or advertising. Most employers in these fields expect some evidence of the hard sell.

In stating your qualifications, use a straightforward record of the facts with a little justifiable pride showing through. Avoid using the passive voice ("It can be shown that I . . .") because it tends to wordiness and is less direct. Likewise, don't use an impersonal tone, as if someone else were doing the talking, because this is artificial and doesn't allow you to come on strong enough. A good application letter impresses the reader by setting out facts in a clear and logical way. Most often, this is done by using clean, expressive prose and keeping catchy gimmicks and stylistic flair to a minimum. Again, and I can only repeat, the application letter should suit both the job and the applicant.

Sample Letter of Application (Unsolicited)

Mary Forrestal was aware of the above points as she prepared to apply for a secretarial position with a small advertising agency in Vancouver. She had no idea whether a job opening existed or would exist soon in this particular office, but she started sending out letters of application shortly before the end of her secretarial course at the local community college. The Arner Agency was one of the places where she wanted to work. After examining her own aspirations and abilities she drafted this letter:

89

Mr. Harold Arner
Arner Advertising Agency
Canada Building
Vancouver, B.C.

Dear Mr. Arner:

Will you have an opening in the near future for
a secretary who can handle correspondence
creatively? Who can come up with that extra
touch when needed? ·

If you are interested in this kind of assistant,
these are my qualifications. I will be graduating
in a few weeks from City College where, in
addition to my secretarial subjects, I took
courses in Contemporary Literature and Creative
Writing. The following are on my record:

. Typing speed of 75 w.p.m. (with complete
accuracy)
. Second highest Grade Point Average in my
class
. Winner of the President's Medal for this
year

Last summer I worked in the offices of Harbour
Master Sales filling in for each secretary in turn
as she went on vacation. This gave me excellent
insight into all phases of office duties. I was
offered a permanent position with Harbour Master
at the end of the summer but turned it down to
finish my schooling.

I would welcome the opportunity to talk to you
and tell you why I was awarded the President's
Medal. You can reach me at _____.

Sincerely,

Mary didn't try to cram all her credentials into the letter. In keeping
one of her aces — the reason she was awarded the President's Medal —
in reserve, she was hoping to arouse the employer's curiosity and give
him an additional reason to want to call her in for an interview.

Ordinarily it isn't wise to play games in a letter and you have to judge how far you can risk departing from accepted practices. Mary's approach might not work with the personnel manager of a large corporation. In fact, it might have just the opposite effect from the one she is hoping for. But because she wants a little different tone in keeping with the kind of job she is applying for, she has decided to risk it.

Give Your Letter an Individual Touch

Employers receive too many application letters all written according to the standard textbook formula beginning,

Dear Sir:

I would like to apply for the position of secretary (or data processor or salesperson) advertised in today's paper ...

and all of them hopelessly, needlessly dull. The letter that is refreshingly different often has a greater chance of achieving its goal. Employers get tired of reading letters that all sound the same, just as teachers get tired of marking essays that all sound the same. You know what happens to those few that stand out from the rest.

Lynn Patterson wanted her letter to stand out. Way out. She also applied to the Arner Advertising Agency. Here's how she drafted her letter:

Dear Mr. Arner:

I've finished my secretarial training and can

. write a letter of application and a résumé
. list my credits and accomplishments
. present my best qualities attractively

and I'm ignoring all of it.

I am telling you, instead, how much I'd like the chance to create with Arner Advertising.

How about my coming in and talking it over with you? Say when. 969-4401.

Which one of these approaches would you use for an application letter? It depends on your own personality and on the type of job you are applying for. No one way is best for all situations, and quite possibly a more straightforward, conservative letter that shows a greater understanding of the job itself will be the most convincing. The positive, confident tone of the following letter from Pat Smith just might win the job.

Dear Mr. Arner:

Are you looking for a secretary with unique qualities? I am a fast, accurate typist and am competent with both shorthand and dictaphone. You will be more interested to learn that I enjoy the challenge of meeting close deadlines, the stimulation of working for creative people, and the responsibility of keeping confidentiality.

Dealing diplomatically with ruffled and excitable people is one of my strong points, as perhaps you can infer from my experience in professional theatre. I believe you would appreciate the role I could fill in your reception area.

My résumé is enclosed. May I meet with you soon to discuss the possibility of my working for you?

Sincerely,

A New Letter for Each Application

Everything discussed thus far suggests that for each job application you must write an entirely new letter. In theory, at least, this is true. But the extent to which this should be the case depends on (1) how specific your training is, and (2) how much you have narrowed your career choice. For example, if you have trained to be a legal secretary and are determined to accept no other position, then your basic application letter will remain the same.

Even in this situation, however, some adaptation of the letter will be needed. The opening paragraph should refer specifically to the company you are writing to and why you think the employer might be interested in hiring you (newspaper ad, a friend told you there might be an opening, etc.). Similarly, in the next-to-last paragraph you should speak specifically to your interest in working for that particular company. This is where your research into the company first comes into play. (Your knowledge of the company also will be helpful during the job interview.) Finally, your letter will be shaped by the tone of the career advertisement you are responding to, if in fact you are writing in response to an ad.

On the other hand, if you are writing to quite different companies for positions that might entail rather different tasks and responsibilities, then the application letter should be a new one each time you write. Different aspects of your résumé will need to be highlighted, depending on the kind of job you are applying for.

Paragraphing the Contents

If you are unsure of how to begin your letter of application or what to include, there is a formula you can follow. But avoid sounding like a letter copied from a textbook. Canned writing, besides being unimaginative, tells nothing about your personality. The guide offered here should be fleshed out in your own words. The following are merely the details that need to be included in a letter of application written in answer to an ad.

The First Paragraph

The first paragraph should be short, frequently as short as one sentence. In principle it should be designed to attract and hold the reader's attention. The technical points to include are:

- the purpose of the letter *(In reply to your ad . . .)*
- the date and place the ad appeared *(in the Brantford Expositor, January 22 . . .)*
- some mention of your qualifications *(you will find that I fit the requirements because . . .)*

Thus, as in any business letter, the opening paragraph clearly states what the writer wants — in this case, a job.

The Middle Paragraphs

The second paragraph should pick up and expand the last sentence of the first paragraph. No more than two middle paragraphs are necessary to develop your statement of your qualifications. Remember that the résumé does a complete job for you. All your letter is designed to do is to interest the employer by highlighting your best qualifica-

93

tions. The second paragraph should expand on your opening statement by mentioning:

- your education
- your experience
- other important qualifications

In other words, the middle paragraphs of a business letter explain
why the writer wants what is stated in the opening paragraph — in
this case, why you think yourself to be qualified for the job.

The Last Paragraph

The purpose of the letter of application is to get you an interview.
Therefore, make it as easy as possible for the employer to reach you
to arrange one. The last paragraph winds up your letter with these
details:

- a courteous request for an interview
- the time you will be available
- your phone number

Like any business letter, then, the final paragraph of the application
letter suggests the action you want the reader to take.

The "You-Attitude"

One other observation. Don't sprinkle your letter too liberally with
I's. Notice how Mary Forrestal started her first paragraph by asking,
"Will *you* have an opening . . ." rather than "*I* would like to apply . . ."
Keep in mind the employer's viewpoint and interests. Naturally you
can't avoid the big *I* altogether in a letter of application when you are
talking about yourself, but work the word *you* in as often as you can.

How Long Should the Letter Be?

You probably have asked this question several times when instructors
have given written assignments: "How long does it have to be?" As stated
previously, a general rule for an application letter is that it shouldn't
exceed one page. But length will depend in part on your résumé. If you
have chosen a loose form, which includes full sentences, then the résumé
is doing some of the work that the letter otherwise would do. This choice,
for the résumé, will depend largely on how much you have accomplished.
If you have little work experience and are simply an average Joe Good-
guy, then your résumé likely will be in the loose form. Your application
letter, consequently, will not go beyond one page. By contrast, if you are

older and have accomplished more, then your résumé will be more tabular and more tightly organized. And your letter of application might extend to a second page. If your letter has a mind of its own and wants to sprawl onto a second (or third!) page, you should (1) use an elite typewriter if you haven't already, and (2) extend the margins slightly. If this doesn't bring the letter to one page, have a friend who knows both you and the English language well make deletions. And if this doesn't work . . .

Write a two-page letter. You won't be the first person to have gotten a good job with a two-page letter of application, and you won't be the last. Especially if you are applying for a high-paying, prestigious job, and if your qualifications are considerable, a letter of more than one page might be preferable. The same is true if you are applying for a job that emphasizes communications skills, or for an advertised job that has involved a national (or international) search.

In short, a one-page letter is usually best, but there always are exceptions. And as you advance professionally a longer application letter probably will be in order, just as your résumé grows with you.

Write Your Own

After you have studied the letters in this chapter I have to tell you in all seriousness, forget them. That's right. Wipe their phrases and their diction right out of your consciousness. The reason is this: If an employer receives several dozen letters all sounding like one of the models in this chapter, yours has lost its advantage. Employ the principles but not the wording and your letter will come out alive and distinctively your own.

Telephoning to Request a Job Interview

Some career advertisements include a phone number rather than a box number, in which case you may be telephoning to request a job interview insteading of writing a letter of application. Some employers prefer to screen job applicants over the phone but these are usually for the smaller offices. The larger the firm, the more prestige it has, the more apt it is to insist on a letter of application.

If you are considering applying for a job with a firm where no opening has been advertised, should you write or phone for a job interview? A good rule of thumb is, if the company is large enough to have a personnel manager you should approach this person by letter. Next in preference is the telephone call. Whatever you do, don't just drop by. Secure an appointment first.

The Best Time to Phone

There is no really "best" time for an unsolicited phone call as far as employers are concerned since individual working habits vary. But some hours are worse than others. It would be bad timing on your part to call during the lunch hours between 12:00 and 2:00. Also, the hour immediately preceding or following the lunch period is bad as this time is usually given over to meetings or appointments. No manager wants to be held up on the phone just before heading for a committee meeting or a tour of the plant with an executive from the head office. In fact, your phone call won't be put through and you will be wasting your time and the secretary's. Psychologically the best time for you to phone is in the morning shortly before 10:00. You will be at your freshest and the employer will be at his or her least frazzled.

Sample Telephone Call Requesting an Interview

Gary Brightmore has phoned the Midland Manufacturing Company at 9:45 and has asked to speak to the office manager, Mr. Bigbee. (Gary found out ahead of time that the company has no personnel manager. Mr. Bigbee hires his own office people.) The secretary puts the call through and Mr. Bigbee answers:

"Bigbee speaking."

"Mr. Bigbee, my name is Gary Brightmore. Thank you for taking the time to talk to me."

"That's all right, young man. What can I do for you?"

"I'll come right to the point, Mr. Bigbee. I'm looking for a job and I'd like to work for you. I'm a graduate of Goodgoal College. Majored in Business Administration."

"Goodgoal, eh? I've met your president. What's he up to now?"

"Right at the moment, I'm not sure. He's had some good ideas in the past. I interviewed him several times while I was editor of the college newspaper last year."

"Now that's interesting. Editor, you say. Hmm. Tell me, how were your grades at Goodgoal?"

"Graduated with a B average, Mr. Bigbee, with some A's. I believe I could have made straight A's but the paper took a great deal of my time last year. I consider the school paper important."

"So do I, young man, so do I. How would you like to come in and talk about it further?"

"Anytime you say, Mr. Bigbee."

"Let's see . . . hmmm . . . looks like I'm free at 3:30 tomorrow afternoon. Come in then and bring some copies of that paper you edited."

"Yes sir. I'll be there, Mr. Bigbee — 3:30. And thank you again for talking with me."

96

"It's been my pleasure, Gary. Goodbye for now."

Now let's look at this imaginary conversation by considering each of Gary's six speeches during the phone call.

1. Several things are important in Gary's opening words. He addresses the employer by name, not only here but several times during the conversation. (Remember? A person's name is important to him.) Gary had taken the trouble to learn the manager's name ahead of time. Also, Gary introduces himself immediately. And he thanks the employer for giving his time.

2. Gary has mastered the 5 C's. His sentences are clear, concise, and courteous. He comes to the point right away and states the purpose of his call. He keeps to the you-attitude with "I'd like to work for *you*," not stopping with "I'm looking for a job."

3. Gary has detected a slight edge to the manager's tone when he mentions the college president. There is a temptation for Gary to curry favor by siding with the manager in some way and agreeing with a disparaging remark but he doesn't do it. Whatever you do, don't say anything derogatory about your present superiors, teachers, administrators, or employers. Never. In fact, Gary uses this occasion to put in a word in his college president's behalf. (Prospective employers are impressed by fairness and loyalty to a present boss.) Gary further seizes the opportunity here to bring up his strongest selling point — he was editor of the school paper for a year. He doesn't mention that he has no previous business experience — not unless he is asked about it directly. He saves as much information as possible for the actual interview.

4. Gary is able to voice his opinion of the college paper with enthusiasm. Who needs a guy who is wishy-washy about his own interests? That kind of person would probably be weak in other ways, too. Note: Gary didn't bring up his editorship by accident. He had found out, through an article in a business periodical he had been reading, that Midland's parent organization was planning a company magazine and he rightly supposed that the branch plant where he was applying would need someone to write up articles and news items for the company magazine. He hoped that Mr. Bigbee didn't have anyone definite in mind to do that job.

5. Notice that the employer by this time is interested enough in Gary to take the initiative in asking him to come in. Gary lets the employer set the time. Actually, Gary had tickets for a baseball game the next day but he says nothing about it. At this point the job is more important to him.

6. Gary thanks the employer again and repeats the time for the interview to be sure he heard it correctly. Notice the tone Gary maintains throughout this whole conversation. He is enthusiastic without being overbearing. He is confident that his accomplishments are worthwhile, but he is not arrogant or boastful. On the other hand, he is not so bashful and self-effacing that he neglects to press his strong points. You have to try to hit this happy medium.

Where to Look for Employment Opportunities

Don't give up because you don't connect with a suitable job on your first few tries. If you know the kind of job you want and have itemized your qualifications there are plenty of employment sources to explore. You will be amazed at the large number of jobs available once you know where to look. I have already mentioned three logical places, and Employment Canada offers, in addition, these suggestions:

- Check the help-wanted ads in your local newspaper every day. Don't be afraid to answer ads if your qualifications do not fit exactly. And be prompt. Many employers stop processing applications once they have a number of reasonably qualified applicants.
- Trade publications and professional journals generally feature career ads within their own fields. If you are not a subscriber, copies are available in libraries.
- The Yellow Pages of your phone book list phone numbers and addresses of companies, which may have work you would be able to do. You may want to copy these down and use them as a master list.
- Employment Canada Centres provide a description of the services they offer.
- Provincial and municipal government employment services are another possibility, and your elected representative can advise on these. Government is the biggest employer in the country and usually many hundreds of jobs are available.
- Private employment agencies listed in the Yellow Pages. Bringing employers and employees together is their business.
- Your college placement office.
- Former employers. Depending on the reasons you left, they may be very glad to welcome you back.
- Help-wanted notices posted in public buildings (post offices, tax offices, and other government buildings in your area). Somebody will get these jobs — why not you?

- Plants and factories in industrial parks. In one day you may be able to cover a dozen or more prospective employers.
- Professional, commercial, or industrial associations.
- New office buildings and factories. They all need workers, from typists, clerks, and stenographers to executives. There may be three or four jobs that you could do in one building alone.
- New shopping centres and new branches of department stores.
- Your friends, relatives, and neighbours. Ask them if they know of job openings in their own or other companies. Renew old acquaintances and develop all the contacts you can.
- Teachers and former teachers. Teachers in community colleges often have professional connections that may prove helpful to a good student.
- Religious, welfare, and veterans organizations.
- Public libraries. They have directories of business and industry, often with the names of key people in each company.

Employment Canada also suggests that you think about going into business for yourself. In many cases you don't need a lot of money or even an office. In fact you may be able to set up shop for little more than the cost of printing business cards or putting classified ads in the papers. And a lot of careful thought and organization. There are many opportunities for people with initiative. A bright idea on your part, plus a local need for services, plus your skill training could set you up in a business of your own. Government grants are available for persons with initiative. Phone or write to your local Member of Parliament and ask what these are. The grants change from time to time as new programs are added and old ones dropped. You may be eligible for one of these grants.*

Exercises

1. Assume you will be graduating in a few weeks. Find an advertisement for a position that you would like to apply for. Answer the ad using your own background.
2. Find an ad for a position you would like but don't have the job experience asked for. Answer the ad, persuading the employer that your other qualities compensate for your lack of experience.
3. Draft an unsolicited letter of application to Maritime Industries Ltd., P.O. Box 5600, Saint John, New Brunswick, requesting an interview.

*For a thorough and up-to-date discussion of federal and provincial sources of support to small business, see Raymond Kao, *Small Business Management: A Strategic Emphasis* (Toronto: Holt, Rinehart and Winston of Canada, 1981).

4. You have read in *The Financial Post* that the Waymore Corporation is planning to open a branch plant in your area in the near future. Write and ask if they can use a good accountant (or whatever your career specialty is) when they open.
5. List at least five situations (type of job and type of applicant) where a two-page application letter might be preferable.
6. Ask at least three people how they got their current jobs and report your findings in a class discussion.
7. Discuss the three examples in this chapter of an unsolicited application letter and explain why you prefer one over the others.
8. Prepare a brief report for class presentation on using one of the following:
   a. Canada Employment Centre
   b. college placement service
   c. employment agency
   d. provincial apprenticeship training
   e. management/sales trainee program

Chapter Seven
The Interview

"Why do you want to work for this company?" The personnel director of one of Canada's largest and most respected manufacturing concerns, one that grosses over a hundred million dollars worth of export business annually, was telling me that this question is one that throws most job applicants.

It didn't throw Ed Carlyle, though, during his initial interview with this same company. (Ed is now one of the personnel director's assistants.) His answer came back like a shot:

"Because I've wanted to work here ever since high school — because you are the only company I've applied to so far — because I admire your approach to environmental pollution. Your president said in a recent interview that he wondered if the new stack filters you are installing will do the job. I can tell him they will. There's a company in Akron, Ohio, that has been using these filters for over a year now with very good results . . ."

Ed's answer was spontaneous, enthusiastic, and honest. He really did want to work for that company. At that point, although he had just risen to leave, he sat down again eager to talk about pollution and the latest smoke abatement methods. He was aware, just through his reading of the daily newspapers, that the company presented a corporate image of good citizenship and this he sincerely admired. Also important, Ed's interest in the environment was genuine. (He had mentioned in his résumé the work he had been doing as a member of Pollution Probe.) He knew a great deal about the company's pollution control program. Furthermore, in the time between the mailing of his letter of application and the phone call inviting him in, he had done a considerable amount of further research to find out everything he possibly could about the company. He had done his homework well.

Prepare Ahead for the Interview

Ed simplified his job-hunting problem with an intensive campaign aimed at getting a job with this one company. You probably won't want to limit your field that drastically, but you will improve your chances of a job offer if you concentrate on a few choices — at least at first — and go after those places with foresight and determination. If you are faced during an interview with the question Ed was asked, how will you answer it? An inane "because I need a job" isn't apt to impress hardnosed employers. They aren't interested in your problems — they want to hire someone to help take care of their problems. If you have anticipated the interview session and prepared for it ahead, you will be able to take this question and others like it in stride. If you don't plan ahead you will be running around like a rat in a psychology experiment with the interviewer calling all the shots.

Research the Company

The employment interview is one of the most important events in the average person's experience, determining as it does in many cases the entire future course of his or her life. Yet a surprising number of candidates show up for an interview without knowing anything about the company they say they want to work for. As a job applicant you need to have a clear picture of the company and its products and services. If you know something about its organizational structure, this will help, too. You should be aware also of the company's growth pattern over the past few years and its potential for the future. You can get some of this information from the library, some from the company's promotional literature, and some from its employees.

Another good source of information, if the company is a sizable one, is the annual report that contains valuable facts about the company's financial standing, assets, and subsidiary holdings. In addition, these reports usually contain profiles of key executives. You can get a copy of the report from the library or from a stockbroker. If there is time you can write to the company or phone and ask to have one mailed to you.

Any or all of this will help you form the picture of the company that you need. (You will certainly be investigated before you are hired — turn about is only common sense.)

Find out, also, whatever you can about the person who is going to interview you. If your appointment is with a large company you may not know who will be assigned this task as it is usually taken care of initially by Personnel Services. But if it is a small office or local retail shop you will be interviewed by the owner or manager. Here is where your research can pay dividends, particularly if you have discovered your prospective employer's tastes, interests, or hobbies. Knowing about the interviewer beforehand will establish a ground of common interests for discussion if the opportunity presents itself. Keep your knowledge in reserve and if the chance for an opening appears you will be ready.

It happened that way with a former student of mine, Ron Crawford, while he was being interviewed by his future employer. Ron had found out ahead of time that this man was a golfing enthusiast and had, in fact, won an all-city trophy. Ron had been a caddy at a local golf club, although not the one the employer belonged to, and was able to comment knowledgeably on the recent tournament when golf was mentioned. Ron got the job. He had other things going for him, of course, including a good college record, but so did most of the other candidates. Sometimes, as in Ron's case, a discussion centred on a seemingly irrelevant topic seals an interview in an applicant's favor when all the candidates are more or less equally qualified.

Let the employer introduce these extraneous subjects unless you can do it unobtrusively. You can be too blunt and obvious with your comments if you aren't an experienced conversationalist. Don't do as I did one time. I was applying for a position as a doctor's receptionist. The doctor was an elderly man and I was very young, just out of business college. On the doctor's desk there was a recent photograph of him with two small children.

"Are those your grandchildren?" I asked.

"Those," he said, "are my children."

I was so embarrassed at my own tactlessness that I blew the rest of the interview and, needless to say, I didn't get the job.

Imagine Yourself in the Interviewer's Place

Look at the interview from the employer's point of view. What does the employer expect from the interview? Primarily he or she wants to know what kind of person you really are underneath. The employer wants truthful responses to the questions. If you and the employer will be working together in a small office, he or she is going to want to know if your personality will be congenial in such a situation. The task of choosing suitable employees is a nerve-wracking one. A wrong choice can be costly. It's worth reminding yourself again that if you are the person for the job, the employer needs you as much as you need him or her.

On your first job-hunting expedition you are apt to be too timid rather than too arrogant. Muster a little pride and sense of your own self-worth. Good interviewers seek to put you at ease and to infuse

103

the meeting with a feeling of mutual understanding. They may open the conversation by complimenting you on the way you are dressed or on some aspect of your letter.

If it is a large company, the personnel office will screen the original applicants before sending candidates on to the destined department for final interview. The personnel director will be looking for the right person for the organization as well as for the job, and the applicant's personality will be every bit as important as an ability to do the work. If you have more than one interview, the first one will be with an experienced interviewer.

Professional interviewers are trained to check your appearance, your attitudes, your mannerisms, and the time of your arrival. They watch how you react to stress situations; they are alert for any hedging; they assess your reactions to the questions, probing for weaknesses and testing for strengths. Their questions are designed to show up any unfavorable characteristics. On the positive side they are looking for evidence of:

- alert and relevant responses
- spontaneous and enthusiastic replies
- a relaxed manner (smile, don't frown)
- a clear voice free of mumbling and stumbling
- a sense of humor
- ability to think on your feet
- ability to speak well of others
- honest answers

The interview is not the only method the company will use to find out what kind of person you are. They know that any applicant who is wise to the ways of interviews can fake his or her way through them by coming up with the right type of answer. But you can't fake hard facts. Your credit rating will be checked and so will your references. If you are a poor credit risk it will tell heavily against you. A police record needs no comment except to say that it will prevent your being bonded and this can keep you out of a number of careers. You can't hide unfavorable facts of this kind. The best you can do is explain them. Don't under any circumstances lie.

Anticipating Interview Situations

Although the majority of interviews are conducted in a pleasant atmosphere, you may run up against some unusual situations where things don't go at all as you expected. The prospective employer, as an interviewer, may be no more experienced at interviewing than you are at being interviewed. In this case, problems may arise out of quirks in the employer's personality. He or she may be arrogant and argumentative or may exhibit overt prejudice. He or she may do all the talking or may say next to nothing so that long stretches of silence follow each question and answer. If you anticipate each of these situations you can act accordingly.

Be a good listener. Most likely the interviewer will do the initial talking and if so you won't want to interrupt. Let the interviewer talk until a question is asked or until there is an expectant pause. Then, when you do talk, try to strike a balance between short, clipped responses and rambling, digressive conversation. Most of all, be aware of the interviewer's response to you and to what you say. Don't bore the interviewer with long digressions, but also don't leave the interviewer's comments and questions less than fully answered. You are, after all, a social animal, and one consequence of your social nature should be an ability to gauge how you are being received. The interviewer will set the tone of the interview (quick, brief questions and short answers; or slow, thoughtful questions and longer answers), but your personality also will (or should) have some effect on how formal and tense or casual and relaxed the interview is.

Personality Testing

If you are asked to take a written personality test, you will, of course, comply. Usually it isn't too difficult to see what the questions on such tests are designed to find out. For example, a personality test for sales might contain a question like the following in which you check the most appropriate answer:

On a long train journey, do you
 ☐ Head for the club car for a drink
 ☐ Look out the window at the scenery
 ☐ Engage in conversation with the person next to you
 ☐ Read a good book

Obviously, this question is designed to test your social response. For a job in sales the answer wanted is the third one, which reveals a social nature. Such tests actually prove little since the answers can be slanted; as with other parts of the job application process, the best answer is the honest answer. For insight into personality testing read the appendix in William H. Whyte Jr.'s *The Organization Man.*

Sample Interview Questions

Almost all interview questions fall into one of two basic classifications — (1) the job and (2) your personality — and each of these can be subdivided into a number of other categories. If you can fit the question into the right category and are prepared to talk in that area, you will probably be able to answer any variation of the basic question the examiner can come up with. If you don't know the answer to a technical question, say you don't know but that you are willing to learn or that you learn fast. This is preferable to stumbling over question after question about a machine or a system with which you are unfamiliar. The secret of turning a question with a negative answer to your advantage is, "No, but . . ." and then getting in there with a positive personal compensation.

You will be asked obvious questions, of course, about your training and experience. The interviewer will probably have your résumé at hand, but even so, have a copy with you and be thoroughly familiar with it. Job applicants have been known to forget what they wrote in their own résumés. In general the employer will be seeking answers that reveal drive and personal ambition, ability to think on your feet and to plan ahead, willingness to assume responsibility. Interview questions, categorized for you here, might include any of the following:

On Your Career
- Why did you decide to make data processing (or marketing or whatever) your career?
- What do you expect to be doing in 10 years? (or 5 or 15.)
- What do you think should determine promotion in the business world?
- How much do you expect to be making in 10 years?
- Do you prefer working with others or by yourself?
- What kind of boss do you prefer? What kind do you dislike?
- What opportunities exist in your career field?
- Do you prefer to work in a large city or a small one?
- Do you prefer to work for a large company or a small one?

On Your Education
- Why did you choose the college you did?
- What was your grade point average last year?
- Tell me about your extracurricular activities.
- What courses did you like best?
- What courses did you dislike?
- Did you earn any of your own expenses while in school?
- Did you enjoy college?
- Do you plan to take any further courses?

- Do you consider a college education valuable? Why?

On Former Employment
- What did you do on your last job?
- Why did you leave your last job?
- Did you train your replacement?
- Have you ever trained anyone to do a job?
- What do you think of your former employer? (Never make a slighting reference of any kind to any other person or company.)
- How did your previous employer treat you? (Same comment as above.)
- Can you give me three additional recommendations?

On the Company You Are Applying to
- Why do you want to work here?
- What do you think of this company?
- What do you know about our business operations?
- What job would you choose if you were qualified?
- Are you willing to start in another position than the one you applied for?

Salary
- What did you make on your last job?
- What salary do you expect on this job?
- Are you willing to work for the minimum wage to start? (Don't register shock. Most graduates without experience overestimate their earning power. Before you keep your interview appointment investigate the salary range for the job. You can find this out from Employment Canada or from the salaries offered in the classified ads. Decide ahead whether you are willing to work for the minimum wage or whether you will hold out for a higher salary.)

Self-evaluation
- What qualities do you have that compensate for your lack of experience on the job?
- What do you consider more important: money or service to others?
- Do you object to routine work?
- What type of worker do you object to most?
- How do you get along with others?
- Define success.
- What do you consider your greatest strengths?
- What do you consider your greatest weaknesses?

Personal Life
- How do you spend your spare time?
- Do you live at home?

- What does your father do?
- What does your mother do?
- Are you married? Planning to marry?
- If married, does your wife/husband work?
- What debts do you have?
- Do you have a bank account?
- How do you keep in good physical condition?
- What is your favorite sport?
- Have your ever had a serious illness?
- What books are you reading at the present time?

Current or Controversial Issues
- What do you think of the last election?
- What do you think of Women's Lib? (Watch out for the what-do-you-think-of type of question. The employer may merely want to know if you read the papers, or may be testing you for prejudice, or may want to see if your ideas mesh with his or hers. Absolute honesty is best. If the employer is strongly prejudiced against, say, your religion, you wouldn't want to work for that person anyway.)

Your Questions

The employer will usually ask, toward the end of the interview, if you have any questions. This is the time to bring up legitimate queries about fringe benefits, working conditions, company training program, or any other points that weren't covered in the interview. You have a right to know how much the job pays, what your promotion chances are, and when you can expect a raise. But avoid giving the impression that you are more interested in getting than in giving. Any questions that reveal a genuine interest in the company will be welcome. Have them written down ahead of time in a notebook.

Final Preparation

It goes without saying that you should dress neatly and that your hair, fingernails, teeth, and clothes should be clean. Don't wear new clothes if they are uncomfortable and do keep accessories, perfumes, and lotions to a minimum. If you want a job in a downtown office, don't show up in sweatshirt and jeans. Beyond this, your style can be your own. One job counsellor suggests dressing as if you already had the job you are applying for,* and this advice is about as good as you can get.

*Richard A. Payne, *How to Get a Better Job Quicker* (New York: Taplinger, 1972).

108

The last important detail in preparing for your interview is timing your arrival. Program yourself to allow for emergencies — buses get caught in traffic jams, cars have flat tires, people lose their way in strange cities. If you are unfamiliar with the location where your interview is to take place, drive over the night before and check it out. Then allow yourself ten or fifteen minutes leeway the next day. If all goes well and you arrive early for your appointment, you can probably find a cup of coffee or a coke somewhere nearby and use the time to run over in your mind the points you want to cover.

Take with you in a notebook or small pad the questions you have thought out ahead about the company and the job. You will need a notebook and pen, too, for jotting down other questions that occur to you during the interview. You may need them also for noting the time of a second appointment or for other information. The interviewer will certainly think you are better prepared if you have these essentials with you than if you have to ask him or her to write down names or dates for you on a slip of paper.

You can expect to be a little nervous. You wouldn't be normal if you weren't. If excessive nervousness is a problem with you, though, read the tips in Chapter Seventeen on how to control it. Maintain a comfortable eye contact (not a stare-down) with the interviewer and determine to be your best self, poised and quietly confident. Above all, be yourself. Nothing contributes more to nervous strain than trying to maintain a false image.

Overcoming the Brushoff

By the end of the interview you should be able to tell intuitively what your chances for the job are. If you can't you can ask. But before you allow yourself to be knocked out of the running, try some of the following suggestions if the situation applies in your case.

Situation: You have a two-year community college diploma, and university graduates with four-year degrees have applied for the same job as you.

Suggestion: Stress your practical training and "hands-on" experience. Many community colleges arrange actual working experience in business and industry for their students and this in many cases is preferable to a university degree.

Situation: You have plenty of theory courses but no practical experience.

Suggestion: Stress your education, your grades, your training. Point out how valuable theory is. (See Chapter One.)

Situation: The employer seems doubtful that your skill training is adequate

109

for the job. You have had no training on the business machines in use in the office.

Suggestion: Offer to take a skill test anyway. A reasonably bright student can apply what has been learned on one machine to a similar one.

Situation: The employer is firm about wanting a more experienced person for this particular job.

Suggestion: Ask if there is another job in the firm that you can fill.

or: Ask if you can work as assistant to the person who does get the job.

or: Ask if you can apply again at a later date.

Analyse the Interview

If you weren't the right person for the job, it's probably a good thing that you didn't get it. Perhaps you have been trained for a different vocation or perhaps you haven't advanced enough yet. If you have just recently graduated as a bookkeeper, for example, a controller's position at this time is out of the question. But don't rule out applying for a job that asks for more experience than you have. Maybe none of the other applicants has any more than you. There is challenge in growing along with the job. A challenging position is one thing, but if you bluff your way into a job that you really can't handle, you'll be struggling every minute. If the job is over your head, you'll go under. Believe me, it isn't worth it.

But it's a different matter if you miss out on a job that you know you could have handled. If you have the sinking feeling after you have been led to the door that this was a don't-call-us-we'll-call-you brushoff, don't bury the experience as an unfortunate one and proceed to forget it. Analyse it to see where you went wrong. If you missed a tough question, make a note of it immediately after the interview and resolve that you will be able to answer it if it comes up again. Analyse your general attitude. Were you too forward? Too timid? Were you too stiff? Too relaxed? Go over the interview, asking yourself at each step what you could have said or done differently.

The Follow-up Letter

Unless you were refused employment outright, the interview should be followed up the next day with a letter thanking the employer for his or her time and letting that person know you enjoyed the meeting. The follow-up letter consolidates whatever gains you made in the interview and shows your continuing interest in the company. Such letters are particularly effective if your job-seeking program was carefully planned and executed to begin with.

In the follow-up letter you have a further opportunity to stress the strong points of your résumé. You might include also some reference to a part of the interview that went well or to some special consideration given you, such as a tour of the premises or an explanation of some part of the company's operations. Thus, the letter serves to recall you to the employer's mind and to impress you on his or her memory.

The follow-up technique is better used in a letter than over the telephone. If you call at a time that is inconvenient for the employer you will create an unfavorable impression — which is the opposite of what you want. Even a pleasant telephone conversation sandwiched into a busy schedule can be easily forgotten, whereas a letter is a tangible record, when it is filed along with your résumé, of your interest in working for the company. You can adapt the follow-up letter below to your own interview.

Dear Mrs. Benson:

I sincerely appreciate the time and effort you spent on my behalf yesterday during our interview. Now, more than ever, I would like that job in your sales department.

It was kind of you to take the time to show me around. I was impressed with your modern facilities, especially the showroom, where I know it would be a pleasure to work with your Mr. Montrose.

You will remember from my résumé that my summer job last year with Gregory & Forest Inc. included contacts with a number of firms who are customers or potential customers of yours. I am sure my sales experience here would be profitable for your company.

Once more, thank you for your time yesterday. I look forward to hearing from you again about the job.

Sincerely,

Perhaps you weren't granted an interview in the first place but were merely sent application forms in the mail. Then what? Must you just sit and wait? Not at all. You can write or phone in a week or so, remind the employer who you are, and emphasize that you are still interested in working for the firm. Your application will be updated. Don't, however, make a nuisance of yourself by telephoning too often.

The Commercial Videotaped Interview

A new twist to the interview game has come on the scene lately with the advent of commercial videotaping in which a professional interviewer prescreens graduates on videotape for showing to employers anywhere across the country. Since these interviews are intended to be shown to a variety of employers, the interviewee has no focus for his or her job talents. Such interviews are basically personality tests employing three or four types of questions. The first question is usually a softening-up process to get the interviewee to start talking and get his or her voice under control. The second question is intended to produce a stress situation requiring the applicant to think quickly. Still another ploy is asking about a controversial issue to see how the person's thought processes work. The questions have no right or wrong answers. As long as the applicant can think clearly, it doesn't matter what conclusions are drawn. According to one videotape interviewer, as long as the interviewee is honest and spontaneous some firm will be interested no matter what is said. A recent poll of employers, however, reveals that few are in favor of this kind of interview. Most prefer to participate personally by doing their own interviewing.

Exercises

1. Answer the interview questions listed in this chapter.
2. Take each of the roles in turn of interviewer and interviewee using the career ads you brought in for the exercises at the end of Chapter Six.
    a. You are the employer. Interview the student who answered the career ad you brought in.
    b. You are the job applicant being interviewed for the career ad you answered.
3. Write a follow-up letter to the employer who interviewed you in 1. above.
4. You have been awarded a bursary donated by a local firm. Employing the same principles used for writing a follow-up letter, write a thank-

you letter to the firm. Use this letter as a door-opener for a job application later.

5. Choose a company you would like to work for after graduation. Write a letter introducing yourself and asking what career opportunities with this company exist in your field. Include in your letter:
   - the program you are enrolled in
   - the courses you are taking
   - electives or options you are taking

   (One student of mine mailed the letter he wrote for this class exercise to an employer. It was such a good one that the employer came out to his house and wanted to hire him on the spot.)

Part Four
Research Methods

Library Research

Field Research

Chapter Eight
Library Research

The one word that describes today's business world more aptly than any other is change. Many of the facts and even some of the skills you are mastering now in college may be outdated in the next few years. Once you are out on the job, however, you can keep up in your particular field in a general way by reading current materials relating to your business interests, by taking courses to update your skills, or by attending conventions to exchange information with other members of your profession. But when you need specific information in a hurry, when your boss says, "Get me a report on that," you have to know how to go about getting the facts and getting them fast.

Knowledge does not mean memorizing data and storing them in your head for instant playback. Computers can do that better than you can, and anyway, as already pointed out in the preceding paragraph, facts change and proliferate too rapidly for the human brain to encompass all the knowledge in even one area. Instead, knowledge implies (1) knowing where to go for the information you need, and (2) being able to sift quickly through masses of irrelevant information to discover what is relevant. In other words, you need to know what isn't worth knowing.

The proliferation of information in today's world does not necessarily mean that people are more knowledgeable than ever before. They aren't. It only means that there are more people, and that the technological dissemination of information has developed greatly. Statistical "facts" about sales and marketing of a product or a politician can be interpreted in various ways, for example. And most of these interpretations will have little to do with any essential, universal truths. As an educated person, then, you should become able to discern among the right, the wrong, and the irrelevant. In a society of specialists and technicians, you need to have the broad education that permits you to select from the explosion of information that

117

which is meaningful and useful. One of the educational goals of your college is to teach you where to find facts and then to weigh and evaluate them so that you can come up with an informed opinion of your own.

Collecting facts involves research. In the business world this means either secondary (library) research using material from published sources, or firsthand (field) research. Very often a combination of both is necessary.

Secondary Research

You will find, of course, that most of the secondary material needed in research comes from the library. One mistake in starting in a research project is failure to take advantage of the different libraries available in the area. Most colleges, besides having libraries of their own, are located in or near large cities that have a choice of libraries. So the first step before starting a research project is to decide which libraries will benefit you most. You may need to consult more than one.

Kinds of Libraries Available

- **Public Libraries.** The public library is probably the one you are most familiar with. If you are new to the city, familiarize yourself with both the main library and the branch nearest to you. Your student I.D. card is usually identification enough for obtaining a public library card.
- **College Library.** You probably have been introduced to your college library through an orientation course, and you will use this library most because it is closest to you.
- **University Library.** Although you won't be allowed to borrow books from the university library unless you are a student there, nearly all university libraries co-operate with the community to the extent that you will be allowed inside the doors, that is, into the general reference rooms. The university libraries usually have the largest collections of periodicals in the city and you may consult these for research.
- **Newspaper Library.** Most daily newspapers have a library open to the public. Back issues of the newspaper are kept on microfilm and items of current interest are indexed. Because of the index, this is your best source of information about recent events and people in the news.
- **Company Library.** A company library is semi-private but is available for the use of company personnel. If you have a part-time job now, don't overlook the company library and the company magazine for timely articles.

118

- **Other semi-private Libraries.** Professional associations such as the Law Society and the Medical Society in your region have large libraries for the use of their members. Students enrolled locally in community colleges or universities can obtain special permission to use these libraries in conjunction with their studies.
- **Your own personal Library.** Begin now to build a library of your own. You have already made a start with your pocket dictionary and the textbooks you bought for your courses. You should plan to spend from five to fifty dollars a month on additional reading material as your term progresses. Keep your textbooks. Don't resell them at the end of the year. You will be surprised how often you will want to refer to them after you graduate.

Library Facilities

College libraries are being referred to more and more frequently as resource centres because of the variety of hardware and software they handle in addition to books. The bulk of library holdings is still made up of hardcover books, of course, but a growing range of related educational aids is available to you in the audio-visual field. Libraries now carry records, films, tapes, microfilms, and all the apparatus necessary for viewing or listening. A librarian will help you investigate the mysteries of these resources. Your library card permits you to borrow most of the items for home use.

Don't overlook the interlibrary loan service if your library doesn't have a book you need. You might come across the title of such a book in a bibliography when doing research. Specialized books or other library materials not available in your city can be located and borrowed for you from other libraries across the country.

Reference Materials

The reference room of your library contains books and other materials which do not circulate because they are not read in the usual sense of reading a book. They give you facts about particular items so that you need to refer only to parts of them for information. These books are kept available for all users. The following is by no means a complete list but contains suggestions of those reference sources that will be useful to you as a student.

- **Encyclopedias.** Encyclopedias contain anywhere from one paragraph about a person, place, event, or idea to several pages of information in the form of an article. They also contain illustrations and bibliographies to further sources. Either of these can be a starting place for a class essay:

119

The Columbia Encyclopedia
Encyclopedia Britannica
- **Clipping File.** If your public library has a clipping file, it will contain items clipped from local and out-of-town newspapers and filed in folders under subject headings. This is a quick and ready source of information on recent events and people in the news.
- **Almanacs and Year Books.** The *Canada Yearbook*, published by Statistics Canada, contains statistical information on such things as population figures, resources, and industries. An almanac is the place to look for information on average weather conditions or lists of colleges or universities. These two books will be helpful to you for reports:
Canada Yearbook
Canadian Almanac and Directory
- **Directories.** All public libraries carry a city directory, and the main library has telephone directories for major Canadian cities. You will be able to get information on major businesses and industries from these two directories:
Dun and Bradstreet
Poor's Register of Corporations, Directors and Executives of the
*   United States and Canada*
- **Indexes.** Periodical indexes are particularly valuable because they list recent articles under subject headings and they tell you where and when the article appeared. There are a number of these indexes but the three you will find most helpful are:
Business Periodicals Index
Canadian Periodicals Index
Readers' Guide to Periodical Literature
There is also the *Applied Science and Technology Index* for those taking technology courses.

How to Use an Index

Trying to find articles for a research project by leafing through magazines without using an index is comparable to trying to phone someone by dialing numbers hit and miss without looking up the number in the telephone directory. The subject index gives you the titles of the articles that have been published on your topic during the past month. It also gives the name and date of the magazine where the article appeared, the page numbers, the name of the author, and other information. The entries are in coded or abbreviated form but the code symbols are listed for you along with a sample entry at the beginning of the index. The following article on Investments is decoded for you here.

Sample Entry from *Canadian Periodicals Index*, reprinted by permission of the Canadian Library Association.

The College Research Paper

Before the specific details of a research paper are set out for you, you will want to have a clear idea of the nature of this kind of writing. A research paper is argumentative — that is, you have an idea or thesis that you set out to prove in your writing. The object of library research in connection with such a paper is to use relevant information that has already been published or gathered by someone else. You must, however, credit the original source of material that you borrow.

Plagiarism

No more than a quarter of your text should be quoted or borrowed from other sources. There is nothing wrong with using support from other sources for your paper; in fact, it is to be encouraged, provided it is relevant and you acknowledge the original. If you use someone else's words or ideas and pass them off as your own, you are plagiarizing. This is not only dishonest, it is illegal. Authors and publishers have been involved in lawsuits for using published material for which permission to reprint has not been secured. And penalties for student plagiarism range from automatic failure on the assignment to failure in the course. Writing your own material is more stimulating and more satisfying and you will learn more in the long run.

Notecards

Periodicals and reference works are not the only places you will find materials for a research paper. Other library materials, particularly books, will yield information you can use. Radio and television documentaries are good sources of information and so are personal interviews with knowledgeable persons. Whatever the source of your material, you will want to take notes so you can find the material again when you need it. You will also need the information if your written project is to have a bibliography and you will certainly need it for footnotes. For each article or book you refer to, make a separate bibliography card. Then, when taking notes, you can use the author's last name and the title to identify each note at the top of the card.

One 7.5 cm by 12.5 cm card for each item of information you may use is handiest for this purpose. On these cards you record all the detail you will need for the bibliography for your paper — author, title, publisher, and date of publication. For an article you will record also the name and volume number of the periodical in which the piece appeared and the page numbers. Then you summarize the material or facts you intend to use. If you use the exact words of the author, enclose them in quotation marks. Write only one note on a card, no matter how short the note or quotation is. And be sure to indicate on your notecard the page where the information appeared.

> Moore, "Canada's Perverse Oil and Gas Policies," 28
> "proven reserves of gas in the western Provinces are sufficient to meet existing export commitments and Canadian demand until 1990."

The bibliography card should look like this:

> Moore, Milton. "Canada's Perverse Oil and Gas Policies," The Canadian Forum, 53 (June - July, 1973), 27-29.

Filing

While you are gathering the information you will need for your major report, you have to arrange your notes in some way so that you can locate the sections you want to work on later without going through a disorganized mass of material. Whether you are filing facts gathered from the library or from your own interviews and surveys, the information has to be arranged and kept in order. Alphabetical filing is a systematic method of keeping track of names or facts so that they can be located easily when they are needed again. A filing cabinet is one piece of equipment all businesses require in order to operate efficiently. For the purpose of organizing your notes and bibliography, a small file box or even a shoe box will do. Each notecard should be given a general subject heading to facilitate filing and, later on, the organization of your report. In the above example, a likely subject heading would be "Gas reserves."

The starting point for all filing is the alphabetical arrangement of names. Most office filing systems are set up similar to the system used for listings in the telephone directory. These are the filing rules, with perhaps some minor variations, that you are most apt to encounter in a modern office.

Filing Rules

• File alphabetically, last name first.

Armstrong, James
Baldwin, Jasper
Carter, Margaret

• Surnames, when used alone, precede the same names with first names or initials. In filing, nothing comes before something.

Behrens
Behrens, M.
Behrens, Margaret J.
Behrens, Margaret Joan

• Disregard *a, an, the* where they appear in a company name. Disregard titles like *Dr.* or *Mrs.* and enclose in brackets after the name.

House of Lee (The)
Howard, Alice H. (Mrs.)
Howith, Edward M. (Dr.)

• Surname prefixes like *Mc, Van der, De, Des, Le, La,* etc. are considered part of the surname. They are indexed as one word and filed exactly as spelled.

123

Des Rosiers, Doris
Le Mire, J.H.
MacDonald, Marvin L.
Van der Hoven, Peter

- Treat *St.*, as in *St. Pierre*, as if it were written out in full. Richard St. Pierre would be filed before George Smith, for example.

St. Pierre, Richard
Smith, George

- File by word, rather than letter by letter.

North American Life Insurance Co.
Northabbey, Marlene

- Ignore the apostrophe in proper names and file as one unbroken word.

Oberon, Margaret
O'Brien, Michael J.

- Ignore hyphens and & signs. Treat hyphenated words as two separate words.

Canadian-American Insurance Co.
Canadian American Record.

- Names consisting of capital letters only are placed before all other names beginning with the same letter.

ABC Nursery (The)
Abbott, George

- Treat numbers as though written out as words. File *1867 Restaurants* under the *E's*, *20th Century Plastics* under the *T's*.
- Where a firm has adopted a proper name as its title, leave the words in their original order.

Hiram Walker & Sons, Ltd.
Laura Secord Candy Shops

- Where names are identical, use the street address to determine the order of indexing. File by street name, alphabetically.

Robertson, John, 29741 Lincoln Road
Robertson, John, 17 McDonald Drive

Library Indexing

The library system of alphabetizing differs in some respects from the telephone system or office filing system we have been discussing. While

124

doing research for your project, you will find some names listed in the card catalogue of the library in different order than in a telephone directory. Major differences are:

- Names beginning with *M'*, *Mac*, *Mc* are all indexed as if spelled *Mac*.

  McAleer, Pauline
  McDonald, B.J.
  MacDonald, Raymond

- Foreign prefixes are disregarded. Peter Van der Hoven would be filed under the *H's*.

Footnotes

Material taken from other sources and used in your text is acknowledged by means of footnotes. The word "footnote" means a note found at the foot of the page. Today, however, in books, professional journals, and even research papers, common practice (and common sense) calls for notes to appear in a separate section after the text. Only when an occasional note appears, as in this book, should it be at the foot of the page. And if your research paper has but a few notes, then it isn't really a *research* paper. Put the notes at the end, between the text and the bibliography.

You put as much information in the note as the reader will need to look up the original source. Various styles are used, especially with more complicated bibliographic entries (e.g., government documents; an article by Joe in the second edition of a book edited by Mary in a series edited by Phil). The main concern is consistency. The first note for material from a book will include (1) the full name of the author with first and last names in normal order, (2) the title of the book underlined to indicate italics or else capitalized, (3) city and date of publication in parentheses, and (4) the page number. For a note referring to an article, the title is enclosed in quotation marks and if the article appeared in a periodical the volume number and full date of the issue are given. Notes are numbered in order of appearance. Entries are single-spaced.

1. Ralph Nader, *Unsafe at any Speed* (New York: Grossman, 1965), 58.
2. Robert Page, "The Image of the North," *The Canadian Forum*, 53 (June-July, 1973), 8.

If the author of the article is unknown. For an unsigned newspaper item simply list the title or caption first, followed by the name of the newspaper, then the place of publication and date in parentheses, and finally the page number. Radio or TV documentaries or newscasts are cited this way, too.

The Use of Ibid. Ibid., italicized and used with a period, refers to a note immediately preceding. It means that all the information in this note is the same as in the previous one. If you wish to refer to a previously cited source and other notes intervene, the author's last name and the title or a short title followed by the page number is sufficient. If, in the example above, you want to refer to Robert Page's article again, and following that to Ralph Nader's book for the second time, the notes appear as follows:

2. Robert Page, "The Image of the North," *The Canadian Forum*, 53 (June-July, 1973), 8.
3. *Ibid.*, 9.
4. Nader, *Unsafe at Any Speed*, 65.

Social Science Annotation

Additional examples of style can be gotten from any handbook on style. Several of these are listed in the bibliography at the end of this book. In your research you may encounter what is commonly called the *social science style of annotation,* which includes parenthetical references in the text (e.g., Nader, 1965: 58), and a bibliography in the following style:

Nader, Ralph
   1965 *Unsafe at Any Speed.* New York: Grossman.

This form of annotation and bibliography is preferred by some instructors and by some consulting firms, but generally it should not be used unless required. The social science style encourages excessive paraphrasing (as opposed to direct quotation) and excessive and non-specific citations. A researcher who fails to analyse and synthesize the research data can often be found lurking behind the plethora of paraphrases and vague references that this style fosters. Besides, the parenthetical citations in the middle of the text get in the reader's way and break the flow of the writing.

Bibliography

All the sources referred to in your text or in the notes are listed again in a *Bibliography* at the end of your paper. For a research paper of some substance, you will have consulted books and articles you did not specifically cite in the paper but which nonetheless are germane to the topic.

These should be included in the bibliography. If, in fact, your bibliography only includes works you have cited in your notes, then it properly should be titled *Works Cited* or *List of Works Cited.* The items in a bibliography are arranged in alphabetical order with the last name of the author first, which is the reverse of the footnote form. Note, too, that parentheses are dropped for book references, and inclusive pagination is required for articles. Bibliography listings are not numbered.

Meadows, Donella H., and others. *The Limits to Growth.* New York: Universe Books, 1972.

Style and format for research papers may vary depending on the style book you consult and the intended destination of your finished product. It is becoming quite common, for example, for titles of books to be printed in all capitals, but this would not be allowed for a scholarly dissertation submitted for a university degree. The standard authority is the *MLA Style Sheet,* but your teacher may prefer you to follow the procedure outlined in another manual.

Sample Research Paper

The sample pages taken from a student's research paper and reproduced on the next pages should give you a model to follow.

THE ENERGY CRISIS: AN OVERVIEW

BY

MARY CARTER

PREPARED FOR

BUSINESS COMMUNICATION LS101

ST. CLAIR COLLEGE

NOVEMBER 18, 1973

Title Page of a Library Research Paper

THE ENERGY CRISIS: AN OVERVIEW

The terrifying possibilities predicted a few years
ago in The Limits to Growth[1] appear today as
realities after the lightning course of fuel shortages that zigzagged across the United States in the
summer of 1973. Whether the fuel shortages were
artificially imposed at that time or not, some gas
stations were shut down because of a lack of supplies, and a fuel shortage in the United States has
serious consequences for Canada any way we look at
it. The purpose of this paper is to re-examine
the energy crisis and to suggest a possible course
of action for Canada in the face of the American
appetite for oil.

Oil is a non-renewable resource. Even the most
optimistic reports see our reserves becoming
depleted sometime during the next century. Even
without taking into account the expected increase
in consumer demand between now and the end of the
century, our reserves in the Western Provinces are
expected to last only until 1990.[2] And even if

1. Donella H. Meadows and others, The Limits
to Growth (New York, 1972), 142-45.

2. See Milton Moore, "Canada's Perverse Oil
and Gas Policies," The Canadian Forum, 53 (June-
July, 1973), 28.

1

First Page of a Library Research Paper

BIBLIOGRAPHY

"Arab Oil Talks avoid Israel Policy," The Globe and Mail, Toronto (September 5, 1973), B2.

Dack, W. L. "How U. S. Energy Study can affect Canada's Plans," Financial Post (February 24, 1973), 1-2.

Lepkowski, W. "Special Report: Will Petroleum Interests Dictate U. S. Energy Policy?" Science Forum, 6 (February, 1973), 10-11.

Meadows, Donella H. and others. The Limits to Growth. New York: Universe Books, 1972.

Moore, Milton. "Canada's Perverse Oil and Gas Policies," The Canadian Forum, 53 (June-July, 1973), 27-29.

Wilson, J. T. "Selling Today What We'll Need Tomorrow," Maclean's (March, 1973), 24-25, 84-85.

Bibliography Page of a Library Research Paper

Exercises

1. Your office manager, who is new to the city, has a luncheon date with the mayor next week, and wants to be briefed on the mayor's background and current involvements.
   a. Collect this information using your library facilities.
   b. Prepare a five-minute oral summary of your findings.
2. Research project (to be continued in Chapters Twelve and Thirteen). Choose a topic related to an interest that has grown out of your clipping file.
   a. Starting with the indexes, prepare a preliminary list of recent articles relating to your chosen topic.
   b. Prepare the notecards to go with your list.
   c. Prepare the tentative bibliography.
3. Prepare a bibliography of at least fifteen items on one of the following topics. Include at least five magazine or newspaper articles. Indicate where you obtained the titles.
   a. legalization of marijuana
   b. nutrition for pregnant women
   c. surviving economic disaster
   d. selling real estate
   e. religious cults
   f. the literacy crisis
   g. improving cardiovascular fitness
   h. buying a used car
   i. making wine at home
4. Arrange the following names in alphabetical order for filing according to the usual office procedure:

Kaiser Wilhelm	The UAW
Jack Armstrong	Dr. A. Armstrong
The U-Principle	K-Mart Department Stores
The 49-90 Club	Mr. Armstrong Thompson
The A-1 Fitness Salon	Absenteeism
Johns, A.R.	Mr. Arnold St. John
Allan Jones	Mr. Anderson J. Smith
Miss L. Armstrong-Jones	Ms. R. Ala
Dr. I.R. Abalone	Al's Gas Station
Anderson's Stationery Store	Robert McGraw
St. Aiden's Church	S. MacPherson
The AAA Driving School	John Van Winkle
Miss Alice D'Arcy	

Chapter Nine

Field Research

Most of the material you gather for an actual report in business won't come from library books. Once you know how to use the card catalogue and the indexes, the library will provide you with printed material on a subject. Some of this material will prove useful as supplementary data, but most of the information for business reports comes from firsthand observation. After you begin working in an office you may be asked for a progress report on your accomplishments since joining the firm. Or you may be assigned to investigate a company bottleneck and recommend a course of action. Or you may be involved in marketing research. Gathering firsthand information for any of these or similar projects, making your own observations, formulating your own conclusions and recommendations — all this is primary or field research.

Business reports involving primary research are not very different from the term projects you do as a student if your topics are "My First Term at Cordon College: A Progress Report," or "The Parking Problem at Cordon College," or "Physical Distribution, M. Larkin & Company: A Marketing Report." Personal observation coupled with a creative conclusion is more important in these cases than library research material. When you turn in a report involving primary research, your employer or teacher wants the facts you have gathered, your conclusion or recommended course of action, and your reasons for choosing it.

Creative Investigation

Suppose you have been elected to the Student Activities Council, which has been asked to investigate student apathy at your college. For instance, yesterday the president of the college attended an afternoon performance of a play presented by the drama club. The president liked the

132

play and wants to know why the performance was so poorly attended by the student body. The activities council asks you to find out why the students aren't supporting college activities and to suggest a solution for student apathy. Where do you begin?

Preliminary Investigation

Try first of all to keep an open mind and get rid of preconceived opinions. There's no point in going down a highway with blinders on — you won't learn much about the country around you and you might miss the best route altogether. Student apathy, in our project above, may not be the problem. Think about the situation. All you know for sure is that attendance at this play was poor. This is your starting point. Your task is to find out why more students didn't attend. You can begin your investigation by talking to people and interviewing some of the students who missed the play. Eventually you will want to interview many of those who were connected with the situation, but you can start with the potential audience. A little preliminary questioning is a good idea. You can talk to a cross section of students in the cafeteria. Your question, "Did you see the school play yesterday? Why not?" elicits the following responses:

"I gotta job after school."
"I have a four o'clock class."
"Would've missed my ride."
"Had hockey practice."
"What play?"

Defining the Problem

This preliminary questioning in the cafeteria will give you some leads. Let's look at the answers you got. There seems to be a variety of quite valid reasons, centred mainly on the time of the performance, as to why the students did not turn out yesterday. And don't overlook the answer from the student who didn't even know a play was being presented. Train yourself to see the big picture before isolating one segment of it. The problem in this particular study appears to be a complex one involving a conflict of student activities, timing, and publicity. In any of these, student apathy may or may not be a factor.

Gathering the Facts

You have no road map to guide you from here on in. This is where ingenuity of approach in tackling the problem will help you to get the information you need to solve it. One thing you can do after you have isolated the problem is to contact other persons who have experienced the same situation and request information on their handling of the problem. In this case you could write to other colleges and ask how and when they make student activities available to the student body and if apathy is a problem. In the meantime, while you are waiting for the replies to come in you can go on with your interviewing.

You can talk to others who were connected with the play: the actors, the director, the producer. Ask the standard newspaper questions: *who, where, when, what, why.* Why was this play chosen? Was the choice a good one? Who was in charge of publicity? What kind of publicity did the play receive? Where was the play presented? Were the physical facilities attractive? Is there an auditorium or is the building program incomplete on your campus? Why was the play presented when it was? Why 4 p.m. instead of an evening performance? Are students unable or unwilling to return for evening activities? Perhaps the producer did not have funds for a full-scale evening production.

The time factor seems to be the major stumbling block as far as attendance is concerned. The answers to your preliminary questions have revealed that the students are actually involved in a number of afternoon activities including after-school jobs. You should be able to ascertain how many other students have part-time jobs. If your investigation is thorough you will be able to turn up all kinds of interesting and relevant data.

The Questionnaire

You might decide, now, to ask the students what activities they would be interested in if time were available for them. If so, a printed questionnaire that can be distributed to a large number of persons with relative ease will serve your purpose better than oral questioning, a slower process. Questionnaires allow for greater uniformity and they keep your respondent on track.

You will find people are usually willing to co-operate in a survey if you explain the purpose of it and if all they have to do is answer prepared questions. So create a friendly atmosphere with a brief explanation of your task and remain courteous, conversational, and unbiased. In any opinion poll your respondents will answer more freely and fully if you put them at ease. Have a few clear questions prepared and never show surprise or disapproval at the answers you get. Above all, keep all answers for later analysis.

Whether you decide on oral questioning or a printed form when doing field research, prepare your questions carefully in advance. There are two kinds of questions: (1) *fixed-alternative,* in which the responses to the questions are limited to stated alternatives (Which do you prefer to attend: a basketball game or a creative writing workshop?) and (2) *open-ended,* which are designed to permit a freer response (What activities would you like to participate in if they were available for you?). Here are the preliminary steps for preparing a questionnaire:

- Decide what information should be sought. To do this, you have to be sure you know what the real problem is.
- Formulate the precise questions to be answered. Keep the Five C's in mind.
- Decide which style of questioning — oral or printed — is most appropriate for the data you are collecting.
- Write up a first draft and then go over it and revise, aiming to keep all your questions right on topic. Ask yourself, is this question necessary? Just how will it be useful? Does this question duplicate any other question?
- Waken your respondent's interest without being controversial. Start with simple questions and work up to those that are more personal.
- Pre-test the questionnaire. Try it out on two or three respondents before having a large number of copies printed.
- Now edit it for usable size. A few clear questions giving you the leads you need are better than several pages of irrelevant probing.

Analysing the Problem

After you get your questionnaires back you have to correlate the findings. You can then sit down and combine your information with the facts you gathered from other areas. When analysing your problem be alert for the moment of insight. Your questionnaires reveal that the students are interested in a variety of activities but many of them are tied up after classes with previous commitments. It might occur to you now in a sudden flash of inspiration that what the college needs is one free period during school time — a Common Hour — when no classes are scheduled so that students are free to support an activity of their choice.

Actually, if you had sent a questionnaire to other colleges and universities asking them what they were doing to promote student involvement, you would find that many of them have already adopted the Common Hour as the answer. This idea, originally, was the result of creative thinking on the part of someone.

The Solution

Now you have all the information necessary to prepare a report with a creative recommendation. You decide that the solution to the problem is a Common Hour and you recommend that this be implemented.

135

Your report will include a further recommendation for a centrally located bulletin board listing the various student activities available and giving the time and place where each one is held.

Scientific Investigation

The foregoing discussion has outlined the scientific method of investigation. Briefly put, such research includes five steps: (1) stating a problem to be solved or an hypothesis to be tested; (2) pre-field preparation; (3) collection of data; (4) synthesis and presentation of data; (5) conclusions, which may include new, untested hypotheses.

Hypothesis

The hypothesis, or problem, is a statement of what you seek to solve in the course of your research. Normally, it is like the thesis statement in an essay, and it presupposes that someone else has done similar research or at least stated what the problem seems to be. In the case above, for example, someone might want to test at a later date the hypothesis that a Common Hour is the answer to poor student attendance at campus events. Note that this is only an hypothesis — it never was or could be tested until it had been used at that college for a while. The hypothesis for that bit of research was that student apathy toward college-wide events was a problem. As it turned out, if the study were to be proven valid, that original hypothesis was not valid.

Pre-field Preparation

This is probably the most important step in scientific research. Pre-field preparation requires that you develop a methodology for your research. This should include: the number and types of sources needed (interviewees, questionnaire respondents, print sources); the preparation of questionnaires and interview questions and the pre-testing of these; methods to be used for recording information (tape, dictation, notes, photographs); library research to familiarize yourself with the topic; and, perhaps most important of all, a realistic estimate of the time you will need for each step of the research. Don't establish a research task and methodology that requires at least a month when you only have a week to complete the report.

Collection of Data

Now you are in the field, so to speak, are familiar with the topic, and know how you are going to collect the data and how much time you

136

have to do it. Even the best pre-field preparation, however, can't take into account the problems that might occur: your questionnaire is not getting the specific information you need; a key informant is hospitalized or out of town or won't talk; your tape recorder breaks down; you get the tape recorder fixed and then accidentally erase an important interview; the postal service seems to have lost many of the questionnaires you sent out because you've gotten so few responses; it takes six hours to transcribe an hour of audio tape, not two hours as you had mistakenly figured; the data you are collecting suggest that your initial hypothesis was ill-conceived and begged the question.

Don't panic; just remember that your estimate of time needed should include some calculation for unforeseen problems, and also should include a long-range forecast of possible problems and how you would handle them. Consider the potential problems listed above — what would you do in each case, or what should you have done before they happened? If your preparation has been adequate, then most likely the data will be collected easily and quickly.

Synthesis and Presentation of Data

Some of the synthesizing and analysing of data will occur while you are collecting it. You are not, after all, a census taker merely gathering information for someone else's computer. In your planning, however, don't cut yourself short of time for this important step. Organizing and presenting the information, that is, writing your report, requires at least as much time as collecting the information.

Conclusions and Hypotheses

Your conclusions are part of the written report, and are based on the hard evidence you collected and presented. But few research projects are so exhaustive that the conclusions are absolutely irrefutable. In essence, your reasonable, thoughtful conclusions are hypotheses that you, or someone else, might want or need to test at some time in the future. The methodology for that testing might be quite different; the focus probably would be more specific; in fact, your methodology for collecting data might be questioned by another researcher. Conclusions and recommendations are educated guesses derived from the collection and analysis of information. In the conclusion to the report, you also might want to make suggestions or hypotheses that can't be supported by your data but which seem to fit. These, of course, would need testing to be proven or disproven, just as the success of the Common Hour in the previously discussed example can't be known until it has been tried.

Exercises

1. Conduct a fact-finding investigation into a trouble spot at your college.
   a. Suggested areas:
      - the cafeteria
      - student parking facilities
      - the book store
   b. Prepare a printed questionnaire to accompany the investigation.
2. Gather material for a code of Student Rights and Responsibilities.
3. Research the question of student loans at your college.
4. The annual office barbeque is traditionally a disaster. As this year's social organizer, you are determined to turn this situation around. Give at least five steps you will take at the planning stage to ensure a successful event.
5. Interview a successful business person in your career field. Prepare a printed interview sheet containing questions similar to those in the sample interview sheet below and adding a question or two of your own. File your completed interview in your personal clipping file.

SAMPLE INTERVIEW SHEET

Interview conducted by _____(your name)_____ Date _____
Purpose of interview: To help me make a wise career choice.
Name of career person interviewed _____
Vocation of person interviewed _____
Where employed _____ Years of experience _____
1. What are the principal satisfactions to you personally as a practising ____?
2. What new trends are developing in your career field?
3. What do you consider the main problem in your career area?
4. What professional associations do you belong to?
5. Would it be permissible for me to attend a meeting?
6. What is the name of the leading professional journal in your field? Do you subscribe to it?
7. What do you consider the most valuable asset a beginner in your profession can possess?
8. What do you consider the worst?
9. If you had it to do over again, would you still choose the same vocation?
10. Why or why not?

Part Five
Report Writing

Graphic Simplicity

The Memo

The Short Report

The Long, Formal Report

Chapter Ten
Graphic Simplicity

The plant supervisor of a large Montreal manufacturing company tells this story. One of his foremen sent him a rambling six-page report on why a certain machine had to be replaced. The written description was so confusing that the harried supervisor could make nothing of it. Calling the foreman in he said, "Draw me a diagram of what you are trying to say." The foreman did and had no trouble outlining his needs in the sketch. "Now," said the supervisor, tearing up the typewritten effort, "I know what you are saying. You have given me the whole thing in the diagram."

The prime objective of better business communication is to transmit information in as clear, concise, and interesting a manner as possible. Succinct prose, as outlined in Chapter One, is one way to achieve this objective. Visual communication is another. If the most attractive features of each of these two kinds of communication are combined, a graphic simplicity can be achieved. This kind of directness marks the best contemporary business communication.

To dispel the impression that graphic refers only to the use of graphs, a rundown of denotations included in the term is probably in order here. If you look up *graphic* in your dictionary, you will find that its meanings include (1) vivid or life-like (a graphic description of a car crash), (2) referring to diagrams of all kinds (a graphic record of progress), (3) referring to drawing, painting, engraving, or etching (the graphic arts). If we combine these meanings we have the definition for graphic as used in the term *graphic simplicity*.

Graphic Presentations

Graphic presentations using charts, diagrams, or drawings have been used for some time to supplement — and shorten — the text of printed reports. (Again the old adage: one picture is worth a thousand words.)

Almost everyone is familiar with the chart that depicts the ups and downs of the economy. Facts and trends can usually be seen more quickly and more vividly through pictorial means than through verbal descriptions alone. If this could be kept in mind and a pictorial approach conceived in the first place, a great many long-winded reports could be enhanced as well as condensed.

Reports and presentations take many forms. The sophisticated presentations necessary to keep a business competitive today combine three kinds of communication and a great deal of psychology. If a planning and consulting firm has been granted a half-hour interview to outline a proposal to a client you can bet your last pen that every minute of that time will be planned ahead for maximum effect. The consulting firm will be represented at the interview not by one representative but by a team who will bring with them such audio-visual aids as overhead projectors and one-metre color charts. Their proposal will be outlined verbally and visually before the written version is placed on the client's desk at the end of the interview.

Closely printed material alone can bore the average person. We have been so conditioned by color television, films, comic strips, picture magazines, and audio-visual teaching aids that we expect visual interest in business reports as well as in leisure entertainment. The salesperson who ignores visual and graphic aids does so at his or her own risk. Advocating graphic simplicity, however, is not to suggest replacing the printed word with pictography. I have too much respect for the power and beauty of the printed word to advocate its overthrow in favor of an aid. Pictorialization should be seen for what it is — a valuable supplement, not a replacement.

Just as a well-planned line drawing makes a visual impression that remains with the viewer, business writing presented with a graphic approach will imprint its message more clearly in the reader's mind. Commercial layout artists mastered the principles of visual simplicity long ago. It is no surprise, then, to find the leaders of the contemporary business-writing scene making more use of graphic devices and actually using some of the techniques of the commercial artist. The last few years have seen a tremendous evolution in this direction in the business world.

Career ads are a good example of this evolution. In the following examples you will see an ad as it might have appeared in the newspaper sixty years ago and as it actually appeared recently. If you compare the two layouts you will see that the wording in the ads is identical. Only the spacing and type size are different.

FINANCE
Our expanding Lending Operations require managerial candidates for a career progression program in Commercial Lending. THE CHALLENGE:

The program covers job rotation and specific assignments in our Head Office and selected branches. Initial duties include industry studies, analyzing loan accounts and performing research assignments. THE CANDIDATES: The successful candidate must possess up to 5 years' business experience, a Bachelor's degree with concentration in Finance, ability to analyze and interpret financial statements, ability to relate effectively with the public, ability to write a clear and concise report. Candidates will commence employment at our Head Office in Montreal with subsequent placements in major Canadian centres. Relocation expenses will be absorbed by the Bank. Send your resume in strict confidence, including detailed information of your education and major business accomplishments to . . . .

143

What makes the layout of the second ad so much more eye-catching than the first is its graphic approach. Let's look at this second one analytically to see just what features add up to commercial appeal. All of the following principles are applicable to business report writing as well as to ad layout.

Spacing

The main difference between the two ad arrangements is the use of space. In the second one, just as in a well-planned letter, the content is arranged creatively to look like a picture in a frame. Instead of attempting to cram as many words as possible into the perimeter of one small area, space itself has been used as one of the live elements in the ad.

Paragraphing

Again, as in a letter, breaking your content up into several paragraphs per page makes the reading of the text easier. The first arrangement repels the eye with its denseness while the second one pleases because of its light texture. And don't forget that indenting a whole paragraph can give it added emphasis and eye-interest.

Variation of Type Size and Color

Vary the size of the type. Note in the Bank of Montreal ad how the main headings are larger than the print in the body of the ad. Use capital letters for headings. White lettering on a dark background (reverse heading) is another effective variation.

Use of Headings

Notice how key words have been turned into headings. This is one of the most important aids. Headings and subheadings pinpoint and summarize ideas for easy absorption by the reader. Whatever you are preparing in business communication, break your text up into short units topped with suitable headings or titles. Clue your reader in right away with your headings.

Dots and Dashes

Finally, itemize points wherever you can. There are several devices currently in use for drawing attention to a list of points. Notice how effective the long dashes are in the Bank of Montreal ad. Where steps are listed in order of sequence or points in order of importance, the numerical system is preferable. Where the points are of more or less equal importance, there are a number of attention-getters to choose from. These are some of the usual devices for emphasizing listed points:

•	●	■	— 1
•	●	■	— 2
•	●	■	— 3

Don't, however, go overboard and start peppering dots and dashes too liberally through your text or the devices will appear gimmicky. Save these attention-getters for highlighting important points. As all artists know, a highlight is most effective against a shadow. Lights and darks, dots and dashes, used with discrimination will give your work an attractive appearance and aid reader comprehension.

Graphs or Charts

Graphs or charts — the two terms are virtually interchangeable — are visual aids that convey statistical information concisely and vividly. There are three basic kinds: the line graph, the pie chart, and the bar graph. If you can use these three and their variations, you can present almost any kind of statistical information in its most compact and interesting form. Since graphs deal with statistics, the reader will expect your graphs to be accurately scaled and pertinent to your report.

The Line Graph

The line graph is generally used to plot trends or show periodic changes. The vagaries of the stock market, for example, as presented in the financial pages of most daily newspapers are drawn on a line graph. The vertical axis marks volume and the horizontal axis depicts time. Line graphs can be used to show relationships between variables by using more than one line. It is best, however, not to use more than three or four lines to one graph.

The Pie Chart

The circle graph or pie chart is a circle cut into wedges whose total represents 100%. You have probably seen it used to show the distribution of a dollar in some relationship — the tax dollar, the educational dollar, the sales dollar. In the pie chart, the wedges are usually arranged clockwise with the largest segment starting at the top (12:00) and moving around in order of decreasing size. Like any graph, the pie chart should be plotted accurately. Use a compass or protractor to divide the circle into the necessary wedges.

145

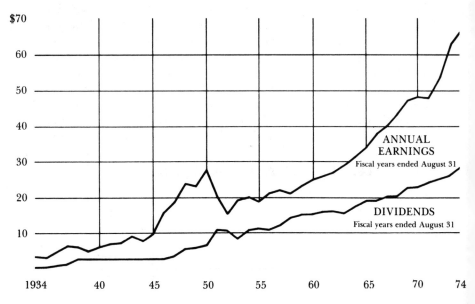

MILLIONS
OF DOLLARS

$70

60

50

40

30   ANNUAL
            EARNINGS
            Fiscal years ended August 31

20

            DIVIDENDS
            Fiscal years ended August 31
10

1934   40   45   50   55   60   65   70   74

Reproduced courtesy of Hiram Walker-Gooderham & Worts Limited.

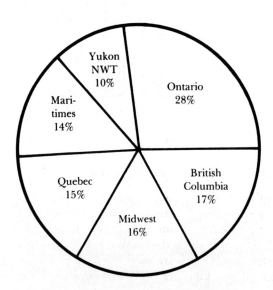

Yukon
NWT
10%

Ontario
28%

Mari-
times
14%

Quebec
15%

British
Columbia
17%

Midwest
16%

Sales by Geographical Area

The Bar Graph

The bar graph is a grouping of uniformly placed bars running either horizontally or vertically. Bar graphs emphasize differences in amounts rather than trends or distributions. Each bar represents one quantity with the length of the bars indicating the comparative size of each quantity. Bar graphs are probably the most effective way of making comparisons where a number of units are involved — differing costs in the various departments of a company, for example. By adding a differently colored or shaded bar for each variable within the unit, bar graphs can become as complicated as the size of your paper allows.

Earnings Before & After Income Taxes

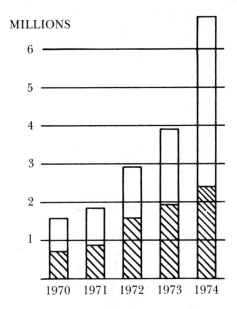

Reproduced courtesy of WAJAX Limited.

Diagrams, Drawings, Maps, Photographs

Diagrams and drawings that accompany your report should be as clear and simple as possible. For most reports, any illustrations required can consist of uncluttered line drawings although photographs also can be used. Add only those details that relate directly to the material you are illustrating. If maps are used, they can be stylized. Illustrations or visual aids of any kind are more effective placed throughout the text where references to them occur rather than grouped together in an appendix. In a research paper or report, all of these visual illustrations normally are called figures, and are labelled Figure 1, Figure 2, etc.

Tables

Graphs and charts present numerical, statistical data visually. The visual dimension of these figures necessitates a simplification of the data being presented. In other words, these illustrations give the reader *a rough idea* of the relationship among various quantities of something (manufactured goods, profits, sales, production, consumption, population, etc.) over time or space. Tables also illustrate relationships by offering comparative numerical data, yet they differ from figures in that they are not visual and consequently can be specific and explicit.

Tables present the hard data to the last decimal point, so to speak. They are especially useful when the exact numbers and statistics should be shown, which is much of the time. Does the reader, the audience, want to know only of trends and tendencies, or will the detailed statistics help to prove your point or show what you want to show? This question should be considered when you prepare figures and tables, and sometimes you might want to use both a figure and a table to illustrate the same data. Generally speaking, tables can present more complex data. It would be difficult to present the data from the following table in a figure.

Effect of Maturity Structure of Debt on Return on Equity
(Millions of dollars)

	Conservative	Average	Aggressive
Current Assets	$ 50.00	$ 50.00	$ 50.00
Fixed Assets	50.00	50.00	50.00
Total assets	$100.00	$100.00	$100.00
Short-term credit (6%)	—	25.00	50.00
Long-term debt (8%)	50.00	25.00	—
Current ratio	∞	2:1	1:1
Earnings before interest and taxes (EBIT)	15.00	15.00	15.00
Less interest	4.00	3.50	3.00
Taxable income	$ 11.00	$ 11.50	$ 12.00
Less taxes at 50%	5.50	5.75	6.00
Earnings on common shares	$ 5.50	$ 5.75	$ 6.00
Rate of return on book equity (%)	11.0	11.5	12.0

From *Essentials of Canadian Managerial Finance*, by J. Fred Weston, Eugene F. Brigham, and Paul Halpern. Copyright 1979 by Holt, Rinehart and Winston of Canada, Limited. Reprinted by permission.

Exercises

1. Without changing any of the words, rewrite the following ad to give it more graphic appeal.
   Personnel. To $20 000. Our client, a large manufacturing company in northern Ontario with international affiliations, requires an assistant manager. His responsibilities initially will include recruiting, personnel administration including the preparation of statistical reports and wage and fringe benefit research, analysing hiring practices, conducting testing programs, and co-ordinating programs geared to maintaining sound employee relations. With experience he will become involved in industrial relations and training. This position will appeal to an ambitious person having a minimum of four years' experience in management who wishes to extend his experience, with the longer term expectation of heading up the entire company. University or college training desirable but not essential. Reply in confidence to file #728. Galt & Wilson, Management Consultants, St. Clair Avenue East, Toronto, Ontario, M5S 1S6.

2. Using information from the weather report in your daily paper, keep a record of the daily highs and lows for your area for one week. Draw a line graph with one line for the highs and one for the lows to cover the seven-day period.

3. Draw a pie chart showing the distribution of a typical college student's dollar (meals, clothing, books, transportation, recreation, etc.). Use your own figures or make them up.
4. The Maple Mountain Hunting and Fishing Lodge derives its income from a variety of sources. These sources include housekeeping cabins (30%), food and beverages (40%), boats and canoes (12%), outboard motors (10%), miscellaneous (8%). Construct a bar graph showing this income breakdown.

Chapter Eleven

The Memo

A memorandum or memo is a hybrid that has resulted from crossing the letter with the report to develop a short interoffice communication. Like the letter the memo is brief, sometimes extremely so. The main difference between these two short vehicles of communication is destination — the memo is intended for a person or persons within the organization, the letter goes outside. Like the report, the memo can contain a directive or it can communicate company policy and decisions. Or, like the letter, its subject matter can be about almost anything.

The operative word in the definition for the memo is *short*. If your memo covers more than one page it probably is on its way to becoming a report. The amount of paper work involved at management levels in most organizations is one reason business personnel haven't the time to digest more than one page at a sitting. *Concise*, the second of the Five *C's*, is the watchword for memo writing.

When to Send a Memo

If you can phone your colleagues instead of sending a memo, do so. Don't add to the paper explosion if you can avoid it. However, there are times when a memo will serve your purpose more efficiently than a phone call will. Send a memo:

- to reach a group of people with the same message (for example, to announce a meeting). This is preferable to a string of messages.
- to reach someone who is difficult to contact any other way. If you have phoned repeatedly trying to reach someone who is always out of the office, a memo can save you time. Furthermore, a busy superior might not want to spend the time taken up by an office appointment

or a phone call for a matter that could be handled more efficiently in a memo.

- to provide a record, not only for the recipient but also for yourself, of dates, changes of procedure, etc.
- to transmit complex data, such as figures and dates, that can easily be garbled or misunderstood in oral transmission.

Keep a carbon copy of all memos you send out. This provides a record of dates and a verification of just who said what in case an original is misplaced or differences arise. You will need two folders in your filing cabinet for memos — one for those you send out and one for those you receive. Some offices use memo forms in triplicate — one copy for the recipient, one for your files, and one for the head office.

How to Plan a Memo

Memos generally reflect the pressure that produced them and the speed with which they were written. Too often this results in messages that are incomplete or confused in thought. Ideally, you should plan your memos as carefully as you do your letters. Keep your purpose in mind, decide what you want to say, the order you want to say it in, and the tone you are going to use. In other words, think ahead.

If the writer of the following memo, the chief inspector in a Calgary factory, had stopped to think about the purpose of his memo and emphasized that first, he could have come up with a clearer and more concise message. He had received complaints from the front office that his inspection crews, the quality control inspectors, were messing up production by trying to tell the machine operators what to do. Some of these inspectors evidently thought they could improve the company's product. To reach the inspectors on all shifts, the chief inspector wrote a memo to them rather than trying to contact them individually or in groups. He wanted each of them to understand clearly that the interference had to stop. Unfortunately, his memo was anything but clear.

To: ALL DEPARTMENT SUPERVISION AND QUALITY
      CONTROL INSPECTORS

Subject: INSTRUCTIONS

Various irregularities have been observed in the routine inspection of operational products.

Inspectors have been defining by instructional opinions to production personnel what to do with

152

machinery, etc., to improve the product.

Effective immediately quality control inspectors
will refrain from informing Supervision set-up
men or operators what improvements to implement
for operational products.

It is the prerogative of the production department
to initiate methods and procedures with proper
instructions to obtain acceptable quality products
and under no circumstances will the quality control
inspectors give directives to production personnel
at any time. This procedure must be followed
that unnecessary conflictions be eliminated.

In the rewritten version below, the statements have been rearranged
and the duplications eliminated but the original diction has not been
altered. The tone still leaves much to be desired, at least partly because
in a case such as this involving interpersonal relations the memo should
be replaced or at least preceded by personal interviews.

Effective immediately, quality control inspectors
will refrain from informing set-up men and machine
operators how to improve the product.

Initiating improvement and instructions on how to
achieve it are the prerogative of the production
department. Conflicting instructions given by
some Inspectors have resulted in confusion on
the production line.

Under no circumstances will quality control
inspectors give directions to production
personnel at any time.

Tone

The memo is the most frequent channel of written communication within
the organization. In the press of getting a message out fast, the writer
too often neglects or ignores the tone of it. Yet this is the most important
aspect, next to clarity, of this little missive, since the right tone will
facilitate the desired action, while the wrong tone, if it arouses resentment, may actually impede implementation. Because the memo is so

closely related to the letter, the letter writer's code is applicable to both. The memo writer needs to keep in mind that the recipient is a human being as well and not just a cog in the company machine.

Note the tone of this memo from the office manager to her staff after unusually heavy rains had flooded the firm's supply room:

As you know, the recent flood conditions in the city have affected us along with other businesses in this area.

At least 20 cm of water have accumulated in the basement, making access to the supply room difficult if not impossible. Much of the equipment and paper stored there is now unusable.

I am asking, therefore, that all of you share whatever supplies you have until conditions return to normal. Mr. Vanderkamp has offered his office as a central clearing base. Please bring him whatever you can spare and pick up what you need in return.

Your co-operation will be appreciated so that we can all get through this emergency with as little disruption as possible.

In analysing the diction of this memo, we can see how the following contribute to its favorable tone. Note, also, the contrast in tone between this memo and the preceding one.

The You-attitude. The writer uses the word *you* five times and *I* only once. She refers to herself along with the other employees, using *we* and *us* frequently to maintain the human element.

Courtesy and consideration. The writer *asks* for the co-operation of the employees rather than ordering them to turn in their supplies. An authoritative tone would probably have had the opposite effect from the one she wanted, or would have caused resentment. She uses the word *please* but not *beg*.

Explanation. Even though the employees are well aware of the reason for the request, the writer repeats it. People are more apt to comply when reasons are given.

Appreciation. She expresses *appreciation* for the expected co-operation. People like to be thanked.

154

Parts of the Memo

Since the purpose of the memo is to get a short message out fast, a standard form with headings already printed saves the writer's time. Some memo forms include the company name and department followed by space for the message.

Date. On an informal memo, one in which you are addressing a colleague by first name only, you would probably abbreviate the month (Sept. 16, 1981). Otherwise the date should be typed or written out in full.

To-From. The recipient's name and title (if he or she has one) are sufficient here. No Mr., Miss, or Mrs. is necessary. The usual practice is to use initial and last name or, in some cases, initials only.

TO: A. Brown
FROM: C. Dawson

Re: This is the line that gives the most trouble. The *subject* or *re* is followed by a summation of the subject matter of the memo. A full sentence is never necessary. Think of this line as the title of your communication. It lets the reader know right away what you are writing about.

The Message. The body of the memo should be treated much the same as the body of the letter. The message should be attractively arranged and paragraphed for easy reading. Use the modified block form, starting each line at the left-hand margin except where special sections are idented for emphasis. The salutation and complimentary closing are omitted from the memo. Signature is optional.

Longer Memos

Besides being an interoffice letter to communicate instructions, requests, and notices, the memo also can be a kind of short report. In most instances, this longer memo will be written in response to a short memo you have received or a conversation you have had: a new set of safety standards has been established by your superior, and you, as shop foreman, register your objections to these new rules because you expect they will slow down production and will not create greater safety; the head of marketing and sales has asked you, as one of the top salespeople, if you have any ideas for breaking into a new regional market because he plans to suggest this at an executive meeting the next day, so you respond with a list of possible approaches for opening this potential market.

What makes these longer memos different from short reports? Both of these examples could be reports, but they probably shouldn't be for the following related reasons:

- Time is a significant factor. There simply is not enough time to produce a well-organized and logical report. Your memo will be organized and logical, to be sure, but it can't be based on extensive research and shouldn't have the formal organization of a report. You may include some subheadings in the memo, but you won't have anything like an introduction, body, and conclusion.
- No one asked for a report. If you presented a report, with its formality and all its parts, there would be the danger of "overkill" — who is this person trying to impress? why can't this person be forthright and informal?
- A memo, because of its informality, creates less distance between writer and reader. If a report is submitted when it hasn't been asked for, you impose a stiffness on the communication that will not be to your benefit.
- A memorandum can be based on intuition and common sense; a report should rely on facts to support its conclusions. This difference, also, makes the memo more personal and informal and the report relatively impersonal and formal.

Other Considerations

If you have access to a typewriter by all means type your memo. It will be easier for the recipient to read. However, memos are sometimes written out by hand if the message is informal and intended for a close colleague. Routine report forms are usually filled in by hand if the blank spaces require only one or two words. This is faster than inserting the form in the typewriter and aligning the form with the proper spacing.

Memo forms are usually printed on less expensive paper than the company's regular letterhead stationery and, unlike letter stationery, may be in color. Memo forms printed with duplicate copies attached usually use white for the top copy which goes to the recipient of the message, and pale yellow or some other pastel color for the copy which is retained by the sender. Separate colors are an aid in identifying the memo's destination.

Exercises

1. You have been working nights as a clerk in the shipping department of a local manufacturing firm. When you were hired you were

promised a transfer to the day shift as soon as an opening occurred there. Now you have found out through the underground that several openings do in fact exist on the day shift and you suspect you have not been transferred because the night foreman doesn't want to let you go. The employment manager who hired you works days and you never see him. Write him a memo reminding him of the transfer promise and letting him know you are aware of the openings on the day shift.

2. You are the newly elected president of the student government at your college. Write a memo to all faculty introducing the new slate of officers for the upcoming year. Include a statement of your aims for the student government.

3. Draw a cartoon (without using any words) depicting a message that could be sent as a graphic memo. An example of such a message might be, "Employees are requested to use the wastebaskets and stop littering the floor of the office with wastepaper." Exchange drawings with the student next to you and interpret each other's memos.

4. You have been asked to head up the United Fund appeal for your company. Your fellow office workers have already been asked to contribute toward two wedding presents and for a gift for the retiring manager. And Christmas is coming up in a couple of months. Instead of going around to each member of the staff and arguing the merits of the United Fund, write a memo asking for donations.

5. Using the material you gathered for Exercise 1.a. at the end of Chapter Eight, write a memo to your employer summarizing your findings. Detail the facts on an enclosure.

6. What adjective would you use to describe the tone of the rewritten memo on page 153? Is the purpose clear now? What does the first paragraph do? The second paragraph? The third? Could you improve the diction?

7. You are the chairperson of a committee, either at school or at your place of business. Write a memo to the committee members, announcing that a meeting is to be held in three days. Be sure that your memo provides all the necessary information, including an agenda. If possible, use the "you-attitude."

8. You were hired six months ago as a department head for Astral Insurance. The office where you work is open plan, so that employees are generally aware of anything unusual going on. The company president, Mr. Raymond Cunningham, has a very short temper and can often be heard raising his voice to an employee. As a result, morale is low and absenteeism is high. Mr. Cunningham has noticed the absenteeism and has asked each department head

to prepare a memo suggesting solutions. Prepare the memo you would send to Mr. Cunningham.

9. Rewrite the previous memo, this time assuming you are an old friend who has been with the company since Mr. Cunningham founded it twenty-five years ago.

10. You are the credit manager for an appliance manufacturer. Lately, one of your best customers, Kitchen World, has been taking a discount for paying within fifteen days of the invoice date, even though they in fact have been paying within 25-30 days. You don't want to lose their business, but this is costing you money and leaving you open to charges of giving preferential treatment. Write a memo to Linda Burnside, Sales Manager, explaining the situation and asking for direction.

Chapter Twelve

The Short Report

A report, just as the term indicates, is a communication summarizing information for someone who will need it. You may have to send in a report on any out-of-the-ordinary occurrence in your working day: an accident, a strike in the area under your jurisdiction, a convention you attended. Or part of your job may be to gather facts and write reports that are the basis of company operations. Reports within an organization generally travel up — from a subordinate who prepares the report to a superior who makes decisions based on it.

Organization of Material

The information for a report may come from just about anywhere. From market surveys to financial reports, the statistics and data for such documents and the documents themselves can be as varied as the companies and the personnel requesting them. Nevertheless, the preliminary process for creating a report is the same in nearly every case. This process includes the basic steps you followed quite naturally in preparing your résumé — getting the material together, thinking about it, organizing it, and arranging it for emphasis.

Five Basic Steps

These are the preliminary steps for orderly report preparation:
1. *Know the purpose your report is to serve.* Be very clear in your own mind about this so that you can direct the lines of your investigation into the right channels.
2. *Gather the facts.* Gather all the facts whether you are doing research for a market survey, preparing subsidiary reports for a financial

statement, or doing library and/or lab research for a professional paper.
3. *Analyse the facts.* Think about your material. If a solution or recommendation is wanted, think it out before you start to write.
4. *Organize your material.* Decide how much of the material you are going to put into your report. Next, arrange it in a logical order. Then choose headings and subheadings.
5. *Write a rough draft first.* Then revise and rewrite.

Purpose

Purpose needs an additional word or two of explanation. Before you proceed with your investigation, determine how extensive your research is expected to be. If you aren't sure what your report is supposed to do, ask for clarification. If, for example, you are asked for a report on safety conditions in the shipping department where you work, are you expected to prepare a safety manual for the whole firm, compile lists of national statistics, or simply describe safety hazards you find as you probe the department? Are you supposed to turn in a recommendation with your report or just gather facts? These are questions for which answers are essential right at the start.

Parts of a Short Report

After you have compiled the information for your report and analysed it, you can begin arranging your material for writing. The facts and ideas on notecards and sheets of paper have to be organized into a lucid document. If report writing is a new activity for you, you will want a set of plans to follow.

What constitutes plan? In high school you mastered a simple three-part guide that is always valid whether you are writing an essay, a business report, or a novel. You will recall that these are: (1) introduction, (2) body, (3) conclusion.

The Introduction and Conclusion

The introduction may be a simple statement of the purpose of your report or it may outline a problem. It may recommend a course of action if a recommendation has been requested. In any case, the introduction should contain a thesis sentence, which states succinctly the topic and purpose of the report. If you are writing a very brief report, a sentence or two each will do for the introduction and conclusion. If your report is several pages long you will need at least a paragraph each for the opening and for the closing.

If you have trouble getting started with the actual writing, skip the opening sentence and come back to it later. An introductory sentence

160

will probably occur to you while you are are writing up the rest of the text. Or write down anything that comes into your head. Your first writing will be a rough draft anyway and you will be revising and polishing it later. One thing you don't have to do is strain for your reader's attention right at the beginning, as in a work of fiction. But just because the person who asked for your report is a captive audience, it does not mean that you can get by with indifferent writing. An adequate introduction, and all that is necessary for many short reports, is a simple

The purpose of this report is . . . .
    or
As you have requested, here is the report on . . . .

In a short report you can lead up to your recommendation so that the summation of your findings is at the end. Note, though, that in a long report this process is reversed. In any case, avoid ending your report so abruptly that the reader is left hanging at the edge of a cliff. One way to give your writing a sense of completion is to sum up briefly and then indicate a course of action based on your own opinion.

Under the circumstances, I feel that the best thing for us to do is . . . .

Block in the thinking, if not the detail, for your introduction and conclusion before you start writing your report. This way you know where you are going.

The Body of the Report

The body of the report contains the facts you have gathered and needs to be organized to present these facts clearly and concisely. This section, obviously, requires most of your attention.

Discarding Information. When you start looking over your notes you may find you don't need all the information you have so carefully gathered. Even though you have worked hard to get it and find it extremely interesting, if it isn't strictly relevant to the report you are preparing, leave it out. Discriminate between what is relevant and what isn't. Don't throw the surplus away, though. You may find you need some of it later, if not for this report then for another one or for an oral presentation. Some of this discarded information may come in handy if you have to answer any questions about your report.

Grouping of Ideas. After you have laid aside what you don't need, the next step is to group the rest of the material into workable units. Just as a well-written paragraph is a unit made up of thoughts relating

161

to a single topic, so each part of a good report is a unit of closely connected data. The first major step, then, is to separate the different kinds of information into groups of related facts. This can be done quite loosely to start with.

Suppose, for example, that you work for a firm that has a policy of paying half the tuition of employees who take night classes at the local university or college. You are enrolled in a class at college under the company plan and you are expected to turn in a report at the end of the term. Such a report should be very brief, one page or a page and a half at the most. Your grouping of material might be along these lines:

1. Details of the course — when and where the class was held — how it fits into an overall program toward a degree or diploma — the grade you received.
2. One or two highlights from the course material — the value of the course to you in your present job.
3. Your thanks to the company for making it possible for you to attend.

The Outline. A report based on the situation above probably could be written up without breaking the material into further units. But for a longer report than this, one that involves more material, you will need more bones for your skeleton outline. Suppose you have been asked to do that report on safety conditions in your department. Such a report might run to five or six pages and would mean dividing different kinds of data under headings and subheadings. There is a standard outline that all report writers use for organizing their data into coherent units before starting to write. This outline form is shown on the following page.

The number of major headings in your outline will depend on the complexity of your material. Usually, in a short report, two or three are all that are needed. The outline will help you collect your thoughts so you can write your report in a coherent manner with the detail presented logically. You will not submit the outline with the report. The outline is merely your guide, just as a recipe is a guide for making a cake — it doesn't have to be pinned on the cake afterwards. The outline, like the recipe, ensures that all the ingredients go into the product in the right order.

As you become more experienced in business writing you may find you no longer need a formal outline for a short report. You may be able to work from a mental blueprint or from a few condensed notes. Until you reach that stage in your career, however, the written outline is an indispensable preliminary so that you can begin writing in an orderly manner without wasted effort.

Organizing for Emphasis. There are two positions of emphasis in a report — the beginning and the end. In a short report, the one unit of information that stands out above the rest can occupy either of these positions. Just don't let it get lost in the middle. In a long report the usual place for the recommendation or summary is at the beginning. Organizing the material so that the most important unit is given the proper emphasis is sometimes overlooked by business writers. Yet the effectiveness of any kind of writing depends on the writer's ability to present the material so that the importance of what is said stands out.

Three days ago you requested a report on safety conditions in the Receiving Department. The results of my investigation point to the urgent need for a new *safety program* . . . .

Introduction:

I. Major heading
   A. Subheading
      1. detail
      2.
   B. Subheading
      1.detail
      2.
      3.
II. Major heading
   A. Subheading
      1. detail
      2.
      3.
   B. Subheading
      1. detail
      2.
III. Major heading
   A. Subheading
      1. detail
      2.
   B. Subheading
      1. detail
      2.

Body
of
Work

Conclusion:

163

A Final Word on Organization

Organizing material, whether for a research paper, a report, or a book-length study, always sounds more difficult than it really is. Generally speaking, if you have done the research to your satisfaction, a logical organization will present itself. In other words, if the gathering of data has been complete and has been focused on answering a specific problem or question, then that mass of data will demand to be organized in a particular way. Keep in mind while you are doing the research that you also are synthesizing and organizing. This is a natural, often unconscious part of the research process.

Further, and despite warnings to the contrary, when you research and write a report or research paper of more than a few pages, you may in fact not know what your conclusions or recommendations will be until you get to that point in the writing process. Ideally, of course, you should know where you are going before you set out, but some of the best holiday trips *and* some of the most successful and convincing studies and reports occur serendipitously. Thus, in some cases (and with experience you will know when these are) it is best to let your collected data take you where they will, rather than insisting on your taking them where you first thought they should go.

Finally, think of your report as a book with a table of contents, even if it is only a short report. Turn your previously made outline into a table of contents, as you would find in a book. Remember, though, that you won't normally include this table of contents in the finished report. The more detailed this "Contents" page is, the better organized your report will be. And be sure that each heading and subheading in the "Contents" is indicated in the text itself.

The Personal Progress Report

One short report you might have to write up on the job is a personal progress report. Some companies require all new office employees, after they have been on the job a month or two, to send in a report on what they have been doing, to justify the company's keeping them on the payroll. You won't be fired because you can't write up a good report on yourself, but you won't be promoted in a hurry either. If you write up the personal progress report asked for in Exercise 1 at the end of this chapter, such a company request won't catch you unprepared some day in the first crucial period of your career. In fact, progress reports are a routine part of many jobs.

Socrates' statement made over 2400 years ago about the unexamined life not being worth living is as pertinent today as when it was first made.

An indispensable criterion for getting the most out of life is to take stock of yourself periodically to see how you are doing and where you are headed. Two months after Paul Masterson began classes in his first college semester he sat down to examine his efforts up to that time and to prepare a personal report on his progress.

For an evaluation of himself in the early stage of his college career, Paul had plenty of information at his finger tips. He began by jotting down his mid-semester marks, noting that he was very weak in Economics but was making straight A's in Math. He didn't include the fact that his cousin Mabel was married the previous month and that he had attended the wedding. He limited his progress report to activities related to his college career. For one thing, Paul was very sports-minded. He had tried out for the hockey team in September but to his profound disappointment he hadn't made it. The coach seemed interested in Paul, however, and told him he would have potential if his stick-handling improved.

Now Paul had a conflict of interests. His part-time job limited the time available for extracurricular activities. On top of this he was finding the subjects at college more difficult than those at high school. He knew he was going to have to work hard to keep up with the rest of the class, and if he did so he wouldn't have time for additional hockey practice. But the hockey team! After a long struggle and much soul-searching, Paul decided to let his hockey hopes go for the first term and to concentrate on getting a good start in his Business Administration course. If he had actually made the hockey team earlier, his decision at this point might have been different. (What would you have done in Paul's place? What other decisions were possible?)

After he had determined his goal for the present, Paul arranged the material he planned to use under the following preliminary headings:

Accomplishments
Evaluation
Problem areas

After writing down these three categories and thinking about them, he rearranged them by putting his overall evaluation last. Next he divided his material further under subheadings:

I. Accomplishments so far
   A. Academic
   B. Sports
   C. Social
II. Problem areas
   A. Adjustment to new routine
   B. Academic problems

165

III. Evaluation
    A. Improvement needed
    B. Future plans

In his outline Paul quite naturally gave first place to the subjects he was doing well in, and this led to an important decision affecting his future. Since the purpose of a progress report of this kind is to see where you are headed, Paul at this point solidified his plans toward a career in accounting. His decision here was the most important revelation in his whole report. Again, quite naturally, he emphasized it by leading up to it and placing it in the final position. His next step was to backtrack and fill in the detail that belonged under each sub-heading. With the addition of introductory and concluding statements Paul had his blueprint for writing up his personal progress report.

Outline

Introduction: College life presents new challenges and new interests, but the time available to me presents problems.

I.   Accomplishments so far
    A. Academic progress
       1. B-average
       2. Interesting new subjects
    B. Sports
       1. Hockey
       2. Swimming
    C. Social
       1. New friends
       2. Friday night pub
II. Problem areas
    A. Adjusting to new routine
       1. Not enough time
       2. Conflict of interests
    B. Academic problems
       1. That C in economics
       2. Too many tests
       3. Personal study habits
III. Evaluation
    A. Improvement needed—reschedule time areas
    B. Future plans—to major in accounting

Conclusion: Will have to spend more time on core area subjects.

Your Progress Report

In your own personal report you can be as subjective as you wish. You can include your impressions of college life as compared to high school, or your opinion of whether your subjects are relevant or not. But your summary — if it is to have any value for you — will contain your estimation of your own efforts to date and your decision for the future.

In any walk of life and in any organization there are two kinds of people — those at the top of the ladder who make decisions and those on the lower rungs who carry them out. Unless you are going to be content with the bottom rung (and certainly some people are happier there) you will need practice in making decisions. Your personal progress report should start you in this direction. You can use your report, as Paul did, to firm up your plans for the future after you have taken stock of your efforts and accomplishments up to the present. Moreover, the information you gather for your progress report may be useful when you write — or revise — your résumé.

Exercises

1. Now that you have been in college for a while you will have some opinions of how college life differs from high school.
   a. Draw up the outline for a personal progress report based on your college career so far.
   b. Write the report based on your outline.
2. Major project (continued)
   a. Prepare an organizational outline for the body of your major research paper.
   b. Write the first draft for the body of your research paper. (The next chapter discusses the other parts of the format that precede the body of a long report.)
3. Prepare an outline for a confidential report, based on the following situation:

   You are the superintendent on the afternoon shift at a large manufacturing plant. There are about 300 men and women under you who work from 4 p.m. until midnight. The union contract is up for renewal and there have been rumblings among the men about working conditions. The company is particularly anxious to avoid a strike at this time because of a large order it has received from a new customer, a national distributor.

   At 10 o'clock one evening Mike Jacobs, the union steward, comes to your office to tell you that his people have walked off the job because paint fumes from the spray booth are spreading through the plant: a motor on an exhaust fan is overheating and the fan isn't working right.

   You know Jacobs has been implicated in other walkouts although the company has never been able to discipline him for his actions.

You recall that he was involved a month ago in a dispute with Ben Ecclestone, the foreman, over the firing of a worker who was drunk on the job.

After Jacobs leaves you call Ecclestone in and ask him for his version of the walkout. He tells you it's true that one motor has been giving trouble but the other fans are working and there are no more fumes than on any other night. He tells you that he considers working conditions perfectly safe. "The workers are spoiling for a fight," he says. "Any excuse will do."

Ecclestone has been with the company twenty-two years. As you walk over to the trouble area with him he says, "These people are a big bunch of crybabies." He reminds you that he worked in the company foundry when there were no fans there at all. "Besides," he adds, "I hear Jacobs is after the union presidency. He's out to make a name for himself."

You don't notice any paint fumes in the plant. However, the faulty motor will have to be replaced or repaired. You call Jacobs and tell him there will be a new motor installed for the next shift. He says if so the workers will be back on the job the next night. He also says, "Ecclestone is a slave driver. My men and women don't have to take that any more."

You have to send in a report to head office on the walkout. But first you have to decide how much background information you are going to include.
a. Prepare an outline.
b. Write the report.
4. Write a job description for a job you are holding or have held. Assume your employer needs the information to train a new employee who will be taking over your job when you are promoted.
5. Following the format used by *Canadian Consumer* or a similar publication, prepare a report comparing at least four brands of one of the following products:
   a. canned drinks
   b. take-out pizza
   c. fast-food-chain hamburgers
   d. shampoo
   e. pantyhose

Chapter Thirteen

The Long, Formal Report

Because of its size and complexity, a long report presents problems of organization not encountered in a short one. There is no set format for a long report since the arrangement will be based on the kind of material being submitted. The preliminary process, as covered in the chapters on field research and the short report, remains the same. It is the make-up of the completed version that will be different for a long report. A marketing report may contain results of surveys and little else. An annual report may consist almost entirely of financial statements. A consultant's report may — and usually does — begin with a summary that contains recommendations. Format, then, is flexible and adaptable to the kind of report being presented.

The Parts of a Long Report

Any one of the basic parts of a report — introduction, body, conclusion — can be expanded to include sections not necessary in a short submission. A large amount of material may necessitate breaking the introduction into subsections. You may need additional paragraphs here to explain to the reader your method of investigation, the handling of the material, or the estimated cost of following your recommendations. If so, you will need separate headings like "Procedures Followed" or "Implementation of Recommendations" or perhaps "Financial Implications" for these sections. Any or all of these will precede the body of the report.

Cover or Title Page

First in visual importance, although last to be considered when putting the report together, is the cover. Since this is the first thing the reader

169

The Regional Municipality Of Niagara
Department Of Public Works

BEECHWOOD BRIDGE
Investigation Report

Project 7182·01 July 1973

Sample Cover of a Formal Report
Courtesy of M.M. Dillon Limited
Consulting Engineers and Planners

sees, it should make a favorable impression. If the report writer uses his or her imagination a cover can be designed to incorporate some of the features of the report. A simple background drawing or photograph with title, writer's name, and date superimposed over it can be very effective. Background illustration should not overpower the words themselves, though. The title is the most important part of the cover. The rest of the information is basically the same as that on the *title page* illustrated in Chapter Eight, although the lines are usually arranged somewhat less rigidly than this for a commercial business report. The firm name and date, for example, might appear on the lower right-hand side instead of in the middle. An off-centre design makes a more contemporary appearance.

Letter of Transmittal

The *letter of transmittal* is the report writer's introduction to the report. This letter, which is inserted inside the front cover and included as part of the format, usually announces that the report is now being submitted to the person who requested it in accordance with terms previously agreed upon. It may mention some prominent feature of the report or perhaps refer to further investigation the current report necessitates, or to implementation of the recommendations. If the report is being submitted to an outside firm it is usual for the report writer to express appreciation for having been selected to do the study.

Preface and Foreword

This section explains why the report was requested and contains references to the contents or perhaps outlines the extent of the investigation. It may link the report to the company operation it is intended to aid or tie the report to further studies. If the report is intended for a superior within the company the letter of transmittal can be omitted and some of its features incorporated in the *preface*. A separate memo will then accompany the report when it is submitted. As in book publishing, a *foreword* may be written by someone other than the author of the report, but a *preface* generally is written by the author. Hence, it is preferable to title this section as the *preface*. If the report is intended for wide circulation the person who requested the report may write the *foreword*.

Table of Contents

For a very long report a formal outline is an absolute necessity and always appears in the printed version as the *table of contents* or *contents*. The table of contents reproduced here is taken from a book-length report of an investigation conducted for the city of Windsor, Ontario.

A consultant's report the size of this one (85 pages) is usually the team effort of a number of specialists, each of whom prepares a subsidiary report on one aspect of the problem. These subsidiary reports are then incorporated into a final version by the project manager or chief consultant for the study. An analysis of the table of contents for the Windsor Transportation Study reveals the classic outline form, expanded to cover this particular operation, complete with headings, subheadings, and detailed points. A large number of illustrations, diagrams, or charts may necessitate separate listings and if so these will be included as a separate list following the table of contents.

Summary or Abstract

The *summary* is a kind of précis of the report itself. In a long report the summary is included in the introductory section and highlights the main ideas covered in the body of the report. The summary in the table of contents illustrated on the following pages has become the first chapter and includes two subsections entitled "Background" and "Recommendations." Each of these subsections is further divided with pertinent detail listed in point form. The *abstract* at the beginning of a professional paper is usually a short statement of one or two paragraphs outlining the main ideas and containing conclusions based on the research that was conducted.

The Body of the Report

The ideas and information for your report proper, as organized in your outline, are now integrated as the chapters or major sections of your work. The organization for a very long report will involve preparing separate lesser outlines for each chapter. These chapter outlines, however, are guides only and are not included in the report itself. Little more needs to be said here about the main part of the report — principles and methods for preparing this section have been set out for you in previous chapters.

Conclusion

A separate *conclusion* at the end of your report is optional. If you feel you have covered your findings and have summarized them sufficiently in the *summary* that preceded the main part of your report, a conclusion may be redundant. On the other hand, one may be necessary to round off and sum up. Whether or not you need a separate section here depends on the nature of the report. If you decide not to use one, your concluding remarks can be incorporated into the last paragraph of the body of the report.

172

TABLE OF CONTENTS

Table of Contents reproduced from the Windsor Urban Transportation Study
(Report on Phase I) by permission of De Leuw, Cather & Company of Canada,
Ltd., Engineers and Planners.

Appendix

An *appendix* is the place to put supplementary material not essential to the report but which may aid the reader's understanding of it in some way. One or more appendixes may be needed especially when the report is of a complex, technical nature and the audience for the report (those who will read it and act upon it) is not broadly conversant in the methodology or content of the topic. The appendix may include more detailed description of technical aspects of the report, a careful delineation of research procedures, including questionnaires used, and additional diagrams, maps, or photographs. Putting these together at the back makes them available for easy reference if they are needed, yet saves you from stretching your text around them and thus weakening the cohesiveness of your report proper.

Glossary

A special kind of appendix, and one often found in books and reports of a technical nature, is a *glossary*. This simply is a list of technical, difficult, or especially important words and terms, with a definition for each as it is used in the text.

Bibliography

Most business reports are based on firsthand investigations or company information — which obviates the need for footnotes and bibliography. If you have quoted five or more sources, however, you should include a *bibliography*. A long list of reference materials gathered from various places can be subdivided in the bibliography under subheadings like "Books," "Periodicals," and "Interviews." The bibliography appears in a separate section following the appendix and is the last item in the formal report.

"Is This Report Necessary?"

If a business report has been specifically commissioned, somebody wants the information and will make good use of it. Reports that provide a basis for company operations or future policy are indispensable. But not all reports are necessary. Before you dash off a report on your own, ask yourself if a written report is indicated. After too many reports containing duplicate information had been arriving on the desks of its company executives, one firm decided to do something about it. Stickers called *Rethink* were issued to all management personnel to be affixed to all reports. The *Rethink* sticker asked, simply, "Is this report necessary?"

The Formal Report

For obvious reasons of length, long, formal reports similar to the Windsor Urban Transportation Study could not be included in these pages. The following reports, however, have enough of the elements of the long report to illustrate its practical application. The *Computer Room Investigation Report* is a student field-research report. The *Rideau River Flood Plain Mapping** is a consultant's report.

Exercises

1. Expand the outline for your major report to include the necessary parts of the introduction (summary, etc.) and conclusion.
2. Write your report in finished form.

*Courtesy of M.M. Dillon Limited, Consulting Engineers and Planners.

C O M P U T E R   R O O M

INVESTIGATION

REPORT

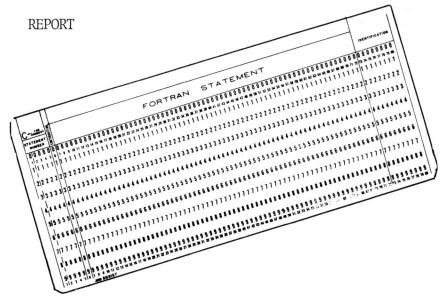

V I R G I N I A   C A R L Y L E

P E T E R   K O W A L S K I

J O H N   M A Z Z O N I

Prepared for

BUSINESS COMMUNICATION 101

CORDON COLLEGE

MARCH 10, 1980

179

March 10, 1980

Mr. Donald Adamson
School of Business
Cordon College
Central City, Canada
M9Z 9Z9

Computer Room Report

Dear Mr. Adamson:

We take pleasure in submitting our report regarding
the computer room at Cordon College.

Our findings indicate that the present facilities
are not being used to maximum advantage. Data
Processing teachers and students will both benefit
from a more efficient use of time and supplies.

With a new computer about to be installed in the
computing centre, our recommendations for
improvement should be very useful.

Thank you for giving us the opportunity for doing
this study.

Sincerely,

Virginia Carlyle

Virginia Carlyle
Project Director

C O M P U T E R   R O O M
INVESTIGATION REPORT

CONTENTS

COMPUTER ROOM INVESTIGATION REPORT

INTRODUCTION

The Data Processing students are qualified upon graduation to become Junior Programmers. A short time after employment they can take on the more advanced work of Senior Programmers. They deserve the best training facilities Cordon College can provide.

Purpose

The purpose of this report is to aid the Computing Centre to provide students with an efficient, well-operated computing room. Our investigation revealed that conditions could be improved in this area. This report outlines the problems we found and offers our recommendations for improvement.

Method

The investigation was carried out by three student researchers during the period from February 3-24, 1980, at Cordon College. A questionnaire was distributed to 50 students who were presently enrolled in a computer course. Information was also obtained from interviews with the Data Processing teachers and the manager of the Computing Centre.

EXISTING CONDITIONS

Cordon College has two computers at this time - an IBM 1130 and an IBM 360. The IBM 1130 computer has been rented over a five-year period. This period will end June 1, 1975, when ownership will pass to the college.

1

Financial Aspect

The cost of the IBM 1130 was approximately
$70 000. The IBM 360 computer has cost $55 000
a year. A new computer will be installed in May.
This one, an IBM 370, will cost $70 000 a year.
All machines are rented.

Another expense of the Computing Centre is wages.
Students are hired from 5:00 to 9:00 p.m. every
night to supervise in the computing room. They
are paid $2.25 an hour.

PROBLEMS

The IBM rentals and the wages paid student
helpers are fixed expenses and not much can be
done about them. Following our initial
discussions with teachers and students, however,
we concluded that the use of punch cards and
the allocation of time are real problem areas.
Improvements are possible here.

Waste of Materials

The main problem we are concerned about is the
waste of paper and cards and the amount of money
spent for these. It costs roughly $12 000
a year for paper and cards for student use. In
the last two years the price of paper and cards
has increased 110%. The manager of the Computing
Centre estimates that there is a 30% waste of
paper. Dozens of perfectly good cards are thrown
out each day.

Two years ago it cost $3.65 for 1000 sheets of
paper. Today it costs $8.25 for the same amount
of paper. The price is expected to increase.
It also costs approximately $3.25 for 1000 cards
and the price of these is also expected to rise -
probably to $4.00 by September.

2

The manager has already gone over his budget
this year because of the increase in prices.
These prices are actually very low because the
merchandise is bought in bulk. But something
must be done to reduce the waste.

Time Allocations

Under the present set-up, not enough time is
allotted for students to do their programs.
Class labs are held from 9:00 a.m. to 5:00 p.m.
Students can also run programs between 5:00 p.m.
and 9:00 p.m.

Year 1 students who average about six hours a
week in the computing room shouldn't find it
too hard to run their programs after 5:00 p.m.,
but Year 2 and Year 3 students who spend an
average of 26 hours or more will find it
difficult. Year 2 students have five hours a
week of scheduled labs, therefore they must
make up approximately 20 hours.

To compound the problem, the buses stop running
after 7:30 p.m. and students must provide their
own transportation home.

78% of the students found it difficult to obtain
a keypunch machine during the time allotted.
When you have to punch out cards and there
are approximately 25 students in your class
you may have to wait a long time for a machine.
Students realize this and some skip classes
rather than waste an hour waiting for a machine.

78% of the students questioned, however, did
attempt to use the class time allotted for labs.
87% found it difficult to get a program run
during times other than the periods scheduled
for their class labs. By this we can see that
there definitely is not enough lab time allotted
for the students.

3

Lack of Assistance

Another problem in the computing room is not
enough help for the student who needs it.
91% of the students surveyed said an additional
teacher's aide or a senior student would be
beneficial. Many first-year students have
trouble debugging the errors in their programs.
If they spend an hour trying to figure out
their errors then their computer time is wasted.

RECOMMENDATIONS

It is worth noting that 78% of the students
thought that paper and cards were being wasted
in the Computing Centre. Since the students
do realize that there is a waste, the next question
to ask is, are they willing to do their part to
minimize this waste?

These are our recommendations:

- If students were to use the "OPTION NOLOG" and
  the "ACTION NOMAP" cards together with careful
  proofreading of source cards, the amount of paper
  used could be cut down as much as four pages per
  student.

- Another recommendation is to insist that the
  students pay roughly $3.00 for 1000 cards.
  This has been done in other colleges and has
  proven a deterrent to waste. Students who have
  to pay for cards are more careful how they use
  them.

- Limiting the number of runs per student for each
  program according to the difficulty of the program
  is another suggestion. By doing this the student
  will take more time and be more careful when
  writing the program and when keypunching it.
  This would also produce more accurate programmers.

4

- By using 200 mm by 390 mm paper with smaller printed letters instead of the paper being used at present, the cost of paper would be reduced.

- More keypunches should be available. A room equipped solely with keypunches would be useful not only for the business students but for the keypunching classes that sometimes take up half of the room practising.

- Students should clean their keypunch machines after using them. Any unused cards lying around should be placed back in the machine.

- Students should do their keypunching during other lab periods than their own. This way extra time would be available for running their programs during their scheduled labs.

- An additional teacher's aide or a senior student should be provided to help the students debug their programs and to answer any questions they may have.

- A bus should be provided for students at 9:00 p.m. Having one bus available at this time would be helpful for the students who wish to stay after school and who cannot provide their own transportation.

CONCLUSION

From our investigation we can conclude that both teachers and students are aware of the waste in the computer room. It is up to the college to give us ideal conditions to work with and up to the students to give full co-operation in return.

If this could be achieved the cost of cards and paper could be reduced by as much as $3000 a year. Even more important, Cordon College would be graduating accurate and responsible programmers.

5

Q U E S T I O N N A I R E

Course _____   Year _____

1. Approximately how many hours a week do you
   spend in the computer room?

0 - 2	_____
3 - 4	_____
over 4	_____
if over 4, how many	_____

2. Do you use the computer room after 5:00 p.m.?

   _____

3. Do you ever find it difficult to obtain a
   keypunch?   _____

4. Have there been times when you could have
   used an additional teacher's aide to help
   you with your problem?
   Yes _____
   No _____

5. Do you use the time allocated for your class
   labs for that purpose?
   Yes _____
   No _____

6. Do you find it difficult to get a program
   run during times other than the periods
   scheduled for your class to use the computer?
   Yes _____
   No _____

7. Do you feel there is a waste of paper and
   data cards in the computer room?
   Yes _____
   No _____

8. Any additional comments would be greatly
   appreciated:

   _____

6

rideau river

flood plain mapping from Ottawa River to Kars

Rideau Valley Conservation Authority

DILLON

M. M. DILLON LIMITED

consulting engineers and planners

280 METCALFE STREET, OTTAWA 4, ONTARIO • 613-236-9869

OUR FILE: 6771-01
YOUR FILE:

Chairman and Members
Rideau Valley Conservation Authority
Box 518
Kemptville, Ontario

Rideau River Flood Plain Mapping
Ottawa River — Kars Bridge

Dear Chairman and Members:

We are pleased to submit the results of our hydrologic and hydraulic studies on the Rideau River flood plain.

The results of the study will not only provide the necessary information to prepare fill and construction regulations but will also identify locations where methods of flood prevention will be necessary.

Yours truly

M. M. DILLON LIMITED

J. H. Kearney, P. Eng.
Manager, Ottawa Branch

FIL/h

189

Table of Contents

List of Exhibits

Summary

The results of the flood plain studies indicated that considerable area of developed land can be inundated by the Rideau River during high floods. The Rideau Valley Conservation Authority, which is responsible for the flood plain management of the Rideau River, will shortly be in the position to proceed in passing regulations for the control of construction and dumping of fill based on the results of the flood plain studies.

It is hoped that this report together with the existing co-operation among the officials will accomplish the goal, which is to achieve a workable solution on the flood plain management.

Acknowledgements

In presenting this report, we wish to acknowledge the assistance and co-operation which we have received from Provincial and Municipal officials.

1   Introduction

Shortly after the formation of the Rideau Valley Conservation Authority in 1966 an overall report was carried out by the Conservation Authority's Branch on the Rideau River Watershed. This report covered the history, recreation, wildlife, forests, land, and water and its purpose was to guide the Authority in developing its conservation program for the whole watershed. Following the recommendations contained in the above report the Authority requested M.M. Dillon Limited to prepare flood plain maps of the Rideau River between Ottawa River and Kars Bridge, a distance of 24 miles.

One of the most important functions of the Authority is to play a leading role in flood plain management in order to minimize the suffering, hardships, and loss of life caused by severe floods and to achieve economical use of the flood plains with regard to benefits and related costs.

Flood plain land along the lower reaches of the Rideau River played an important role in the development of the Rideau Valley in terms of transportation and water supply. Although technological advances during the past decades diminished the advantage of flood plain development, the continued growth of flood damage potential has not been halted. The establishment of flood plain limits is the first step in the property management of flood plains. The following flood plain study will assist the Authority in taking a positive control over developments in flood prone lands and in the future planning of flood control structures.

It deals with the frequency and magnitude of design floods, the estimated flood levels, and the compilation of flood plain maps. This will enable the Conservation Authority not only to prepare fill and construction regulations but also to identify areas to be protected by future improvement works. Separate reports will be issued shortly on fill and construction regulations and on proposed improvement works along the Rideau River between Hog's Back and Ottawa River.

2 History of Flooding

Each year in the spring when the snow starts melting, the Rideau River brings down spring freshets which can create flooding over the low-lying areas. Newspaper reports on flooding in the vicinity of Ottawa go back more than 100 years. The rapid development within the flood plains and the clearing of upstream drainage areas for farming increased the frequency and severity of the floods and flood damages. More than twenty serious floods have been reported since the earliest report dated 1862; the majority were due to a combination of high flows and ice jams particularly occurring at restrictions in the river caused by bridges and piers.

The first record of successful cutting and blasting of ice dates back to April 1887. Previous attempts in 1870 and 1885 proved that cutting alone or blasting after the ice jams occurred would not result in significant reduction of flood levels. During the past 15 years the cities of Ottawa and Vanier, with the co-operation of the Department of Public Works and the Rideau Canal Authority, eliminated the damage of ice jam formations by their efficient cutting, blasting, and flashing techniques.

3 Hydrology

3.1 Drainage Area

The Rideau River watershed shown on Exhibit 1 covers an area of 1,500 square miles, out of which 73 square miles are made up by the numerous lakes in the source area. The head waters are located south of Mountain Grove in the Carnahan Lake area 115 miles from the Ottawa River at an elevation of 800 feet above mean sea level. The Rideau River is formed at the downstream end of Rideau Lake and flows first in an easterly direction then turns north-northeast and travels a total distance of 80 miles before entering the Ottawa River at an elevation of 134 feet.

Major tributaries in the drainage system are:

Jock River	221 square miles
Kemptville Creek	177 square miles
Tay River	176 square miles
Irish Creek	65 square miles

The average gradient between the head waters and the Ottawa River is 5.6 feet per mile.

The Rideau Canal follows the river from upper Rideau Lake to Hog's Back Dam. Levels within this range are regulated during the April-to-October navigation season.

Physiography for the drainage area is rather varied. In the upper part of the watershed, upstream of Rideau Lake, the land is formed by broken plains. From Rideau Lake to Ottawa the river is formed mainly in clay plain except in isolated locations where sand plains and drumlins are evident. The majority of the drainage area is comprised of farm land or natural, uncultivated areas.

3.2 Flood Calculations

Flow calculations in flood plain mapping are usually based — in absence of suitable flow records — on hydrologic analysis, i.e., on the relationship between rainfall and runoff. Fortunately, in the case of the Rideau River, actual recorded flows observed in Ottawa are available for analysis.

The first gauging station was set up at the Canadian National Railway Bridge upstream of Hurdman's Bridge in 1911 and regular observations started in 1916. However, data on flows and elevations were not published prior to 1945. In 1966 the gauging station was moved upstream to Carleton University in Ottawa.

Data for the 1916-to-1944 period were obtained and checked. Analysis of this unpublished data is shown on Exhibit 2 together with the 1946-to-1966 period flow records. The good correlation of annual peaks indicated that both published and corrected unpublished data could be used for flow analysis. All 56 flood peaks used in the analysis occurred during the spring breakup period.

The highest daily mean flow of 19,400 c.f.s. observed at the Ottawa recorder occurred twice — in 1927 and 1929. Flows above 15,000 c.f.s. occurred 14 times during the past 56 years. A study of the shape, size, and type of drainage area indicated that only a combination of excessively high snowfall and a cross-sections were used in this analysis. These were based on bathymetric soundings and ground elevations derived from recent contour maps. In the absence of such ground elevations, levels were obtained by site survey. Details of every structure crossing the river were also obtained by site survey and the effect of these structures on the flood water profile was taken into account during the analysis.

The backwater analysis was carried out using the standard step method with the aid of an IBM 360/75 Computer.

Calculated design flood levels at selected points are shown in the Appendix for reference purposes.

4.2 Ice Jams

The effect of ice jams on design water levels was investigated. Ice formation on the Rideau begins in December and by March the average observed thickness of ice is 1 foot 9 inches at the edges and 1 foot at the centre of the river. Past floods, especially before the turn of the century, were caused by ice jams. These jams are formed when the capacity of flow under ice cover is not sufficient to carry away all incoming ice. In such cases, the ice cover will thicken and onset of ice jams will occur. Ice-cutting combined with explosives proved successful and prevented ice jams occurring on the Rideau. Therefore the effect of ice jams on design water levels has not been taken into consideration in the backwater calculations.

4.3 Soil Erosion

A survey of the 48 miles of river banks from the Ottawa River to Kars Bridge revealed several locations where stream bank

sudden rise in temperature could produce such high flood peaks.

A list of high floods and a correlation between snowmelt and peak flows are shown in the Appendix.

Considering the hydrologic and economic factors, the 100-year flood has been selected as the design criterion. This design flood is expected to occur on the average of once every 100 years.

Annual peak discharges for the period 1916 to 1972 were plotted on Gumbel-type probability paper and a flood frequency analysis was carried out. Exhibit 3 shows the 56 years of flow data and the calculated line of best fit. Extrapolation of frequency data is accepted within twice the period of flow records. The resultant 100-year flood peak obtained from the extrapolation is 26,000 c.f.s. Separate synthesized flow calculations based on a 100-year rainfall resulted in a much smaller discharge than the design flow obtained from observed snowmelt peaks. Design flows estimated for various locations between the Ottawa River and Kars are shown on Exhibit 4.

4 Hydraulics

4.1 Flood Profile

The estimated design flows were used to compute water surface elevations at various points along the River. Almost 200

5 Flood Plain Mapping

Flood levels obtained from a 100-year design flood computed at all the selected cross-sections were transferred to contour maps. These contour maps were obtained from the National Capital Commission showing the Rideau from the Ottawa River to Long Island. Mapping for the remainder of the river to Kars Bridge was prepared by General Photogrammetric Limited for the Conservation Authority. Copies of these contour maps, to a scale of 1 inch equals 100 feet or 1 inch equals 200 feet, will be secured with the Authority indicating not only the flood plain limits but also the fill and construction limits.

Exhibits 5a to 5g, at a scale of 1 inch equals 800 feet, show the flood plain limits transferred from the detailed contour maps. The limits of flood plain shown in blue are calculated from the 100-year flood based on existing conditions. Future improvements, which may change the design flood or the river cross-sections, will necessitate an adjustment in the flood plain limits. The same exhibits also indicate locations where bank erosion is taking place.

erosion is taking place. Although these erosions are not presenting immediate danger to property or human life in view of the presence of "Leda" Clay in the area, close watch should be kept on some of the erosion spots.

Erosion at the toe of slope by the fast flowing river or waves created by the ever-increasing number of power boats can cause unexpected movement of a large mass in such "Leda" Clay slopes. The majority of stream bank erosions are formed in sand plains where removal of toe material will result only in a gradual removal of slope material. Local improvement works have been carried out in many locations, some with limited or no success.

In many cases future bank failure can be easily prevented by flattening the slopes or by simple erosion protection measures such as mats, riprap, gabions, etc. Until such permanent measures are taken, further erosion of stream banks will occur during high floods. It is recommended that the Authority investigate these strips of banks after each major flood and at least once every two years. Areas of possible concern where advanced erosion is taking place have been marked on Exhibits 5a to 5g.

Historical Floods 15,000 cfs or greater

Year	Maximum Daily	Instantaneous
1917	18,500	
1927	19,406	
1929	19,406	
1934	15,800	
1938	19,100	
1946	15,000	
1947	19,000	
1950	15,800	
1955	17,400	
1960	18,800	
1963	15,600	
1970	15,600	
1971	17,500	18,100
1972	18,900	20,300

Design Flood Levels

Location	Elevation
Sussex Street Bridge — East Branch	179.0
Sussex Street Bridge — West Branch	180.7
Minto Bridge — West Branch	182.0
Minto Bridge — Middle Branch	181.5
Minto Bridge — East Branch	181.3
New Porter Island Bridge	183.6
Old Porter Island Bridge	183.7
St. Patrick Street Bridge	184.6
Cummings Bridge	186.0
Old Hurdman Bridge	190.2
Smyth Road Bridge	193.0
Billings Bridge	193.7
Dunbar Bridge	194.3
University Gauge	198.8
Heron Road Bridge	204.3
Hog's Back Dam — Upstream	248.2
Black Rapids Dam — Downstream	254.0
Black Rapids Dam — Upstream	258.6
Long Island Dam — Downstream	264.0
Long Island Dam — Upstream — East Branch	280.2
Manotick Dam — West Branch	277.8
Kars Bridge	286.3

Part Six
Oral
Communication

Interpersonal Communication

Listening and Speaking

Chapter Fourteen
Interpersonal Communication

A recent survey of top executives in a large Canadian city revealed, as one would have expected, that such persons considered communication skills essential in their positions. What was surprising in the survey findings, however, was the large number of management personnel who rated the ability to speak well above the ability to write well, although both were considered important. They were referring, not to speech-making ability, but to tact and finesse when talking to customers and clients, employees, and other administrators. This is where the human element is especially important. Faults of attitude and personality that can be subtly altered or hidden in a written communication are apt to show up in face-to-face dialogue with devastating results.

Personal Interaction

Communicating in today's complex business environment involves more than just doing your job, important as that is. You have to give of yourself as well in terms of personal effort if you are going to get along with others. Personality plays a large part in the operation of the modern office. A pleasant personality can smooth a lot of splinters from the chairs of those around you, to say nothing of your own. Remember that pleasantness will gain you far more than rudeness will.

J. D. Slater, founder and chairman of Slater Walker Securities Ltd., who in five years snowballed $5000 into an empire with assets of a billion dollars, says if he were asked what personal characteristics executives of Slater Walker should have, a good sense of humor would be high on the list. He maintains it is vital for business to be fun as opposed to being a chore. Maintain your ability to laugh and to laugh at yourself occasionally.

199

Other qualifications being equal, personality is the decisive factor that governs which employee gets the promotion. You won't get it if you are the kind of person who never has anything to contribute to a conversation or who takes offense at the remarks of others or who pushes into elevators first.

Knowing who you are plays a large part in how you communicate. Ask yourself what image you want to project and set out to become that person. It won't be a simple operation. It's easier to change an ugly nose than an ugly disposition. But miracles still happen and nothing is impossible where personality is concerned. Try to get an objective viewpoint of yourself first and take it from there.

Keeping Your Temper

Managers know they can't run a modern business by swearing and shouting at employees and customers. They have to maintain a calm exterior no matter what they are feeling inside. Not that an honest expression of anger isn't justified at times, provided those times are rare. Temper has to be kept under control in the office. As one successful manager says, "People who fly off the handle seldom go up."

If you have a low emotional threshold and you think it would give you ulcers to bottle up your feelings all the time, you are probably right. In that case maybe you should consider some other line of work — keeper of a lighthouse, for example. Alone on your rock you can shout at the elements instead of at people. But most of us live and work in cities where on-the-job interaction with others is part of our lives and where stress and tension have to be coped with in other ways than by a display of anger.

Courtesy

Courtesy is a form of lubricant that takes the friction out of the tension and impersonality of our industrialized society. Good manners need not be a form of hypocrisy. Real courtesy stems from thoughtfulness, from respect for other people, and from a willingness to consider their interests and feelings as well as your own. By being courteous to others, you encourage them to treat you in the same way. As a result, both you and your co-workers find your business environment more congenial. Finally, the regular practice of courtesy results in greater productivity for the company.

How can you consider the interests of someone you know nothing about? To adapt Hamlet's advice, "Assume an interest if you have it not." The more you appear interested in another person, the more you will learn about that person; and the more you learn, the more interested you will become. Such concern soon becomes genuine.

Expressing interest in others, however, does not mean prying into the personal affairs of your colleagues. Respect for other people also means leaving them alone if they don't want to talk. Someone may be busy, or mentally composing a speech, or just in a bad mood. Tact springs from a sensitivity to the moods of others.

Think before You Speak

The success of Dale Carnegie's book, *How to Win Friends and Influence People,* which has gone into 94 printings and has sold over 3 000 000 copies to date, is based on one important observation: most of us want to be liked. If you want to be liked you have to become really aware of the other person and his or her feelings. Be friendly and approachable yourself but don't overdo it. Most people don't want an impulsive puppy jumping all over them at work.

It is not enough to stop and say to yourself, *think before you speak,* just so you won't put your foot in your mouth every time you open it. This is a negative approach, though a useful one if you are overly impulsive. On the positive scale, *think before you speak* means decide what you want to say and how you want to say it.

If you have your purpose clearly in mind beforehand, you won't be stumbling around searching blindly for the right words to get a conversation off the ground. Pause and organize your thoughts before you say anything. If your purpose is to overcome an antipathy toward you on the part of one of your colleagues, try paying the person a sincere compliment. Likewise, how are you on accepting a compliment yourself? Can you receive it gracefully or does it make you uncomfortable? If you have to come back with a wisecrack you still have a long way to go.

Style in Conversation

On the one hand oral communication is a subjective skill that starts with the inner person. It affects our chances for getting a job in the first place, our on-the-job relationships afterwards, and our chances for promotion. Looked at objectively it also is a skill that can be learned and measured.

The principles of effective communication are as applicable to the spoken word as to the written one. Speak clearly, concisely, and courteously, and be sure your message is complete and that your facts are accurate. (The Five C's.) Have something to say and keep your purpose in mind. Try to see the point of view of others before you throw them out of your office. (The you-attitude.)

201

Over and above these there is another quality to aim for in oral communication — style. Style in conversation, as in writing, is the extra that makes speech interesting and distinctive. It encompasses each individual's way of talking, gesturing, behaving, and being, which again is intensely personal because each of us is so different from the other. And since no one lives in a vacuum, style also reflects the times in which we live.

All the world's great orators have had, above all else, this double consciousness of themselves and of their time and place. Winston Churchill's magnificent war speeches are the supreme example of style in this century. His sentences breathed a pride that amounted to arrogance but they inspired a whole people in the dark days of the Second World War. In his radio broadcast after Dunkirk the simple yet powerful rhetoric of "We shall fight on the beaches, we shall fight on the landing grounds, we shall fight in the fields and in the streets, we shall fight in the hills; we shall never surrender . . ." still rings with centuries of British determination. There is a poignant footnote to this speech. Churchill is reported to have added to those in the studio after he went off the air, "Though God knows what we shall use for bullets — empty beer bottles, maybe." After the defeatist Petain said that Hitler would wring the necks of the English like chickens, no one who heard Churchill's "some chicken, some neck" speech — delivered to the Canadian Commons in Ottawa on December 30, 1941 — will ever forget it.

Substandard Expressions

Most of the time when you are speaking with your friends your language is informal and colloquial. That is as it should be. Language should be adapted to the audience. The trouble with most of the slang in use, however, is that it is stale and overused. It becomes counterfeit coin when used as a substitute for thought. Words and phrases like *right on, groovy, like man* pop up ubiquitously in everyday conversation. Coarse, common, and difficult to eradicate, slang chokes off the more colorful and original diction that should be growing in its place.

On the other hand, slang is sometimes effective when it develops out of an attempt to find a newer and more pungent means of expression. A word like *rubbernecking* used in the proper place is full of vitality. But the turnover rate of most slang terms is terrifically high. (Who now says, *twenty-three skidoo* or *oh you kid?*) However, when slang isn't discarded it eventually becomes an accepted part of the language (*okay*). In a good vocabulary slang is an appendix, effective if used humorously or as an exclamation point, but boring when it dots every sentence.

The preceding observations on the overuse of slang are doubly true of obscenity. These substandard expressions not only violate good taste, but also suggest you lack the ability to function as an educated person. If you aren't aware of your own speech imperfections, use a tape recorder to catch some of your conversations with your friends so that when you play the tapes back you can hear yourself as others hear you. (This has *real* shock value.) If your endings are slurred, if you say *git* instead of *get,* *yeah* instead of *yes,* *ain't* instead of *isn't,* if your sentences are sprinkled with *you know* and *uh . . . uh,* if you are unable to find anything except slang or four-letter words to express yourself — then your more sterling qualities will be obscured.

Your spoken language is the basis of a prospective employer's preliminary evaluation of you. The employer is conscious, as you will have to be, that you project the company image when communicating with others outside the organization as well as within it, and will expect you to speak like an educated person. Furthermore, earning power is directly related to word power. The more poverty-stricken your language, the more poverty-stricken your pay cheque.

Body Language

The study of communication through gestures, facial expressions, and similar nonverbal displays is called kinesics. Students of kinesics know that a person's body language often betrays his or her true emotional state because gestures and unconscious mannerisms communicate just as much as words do. If a friend asks how you are feeling and you answer fine, he or she will rightly suspect differently if your shoulders are slumped forward and your mouth is pulled down.

Much of our body language is used in social situations in ways that are expected of us. We obligingly look happy at parties and sad at funerals whether we actually feel that way or not. Thus, cultural conditioning plays some part in many of our kinesic expressions. In some cultures men greet each other by hugging and kissing, but in secular Canadian Anglo-French society they shake hands. Furthermore, the handshake itself is expected to be firm and not limp and flabby.

Moving the eyes, face, hands, and other body parts frames the verbal activity and accentuates its meaning for others. A skilled speaker usually uses body language for reinforcing effect. A closed fist brought down on an open palm at the right moment can be as explosive as an exclamation mark or a rifle shot. Consciously or unconsciously, when people interact they use body language to punctuate their speaking and listening behavior.

You don't need to become an expert in kinesics to increase your own understanding of nonverbal communication. Once you become aware of the basic gestures, you can make them work for you instead of against you. Gestures, however, do not appear in isolation. Body language communicates through a number of interrelating actions (gesture-clusters) just as the English language expresses meaning by using a number of interrelating words in a sentence.

Understanding how gestures work in congruence or harmony with each other is the important thing. For example, sales representatives who believe in the product will match the enthusiasm of their words with everything about them. They will stand erect and confident or will sit on the edge of the chair leaning toward the client. They will use their hands for emphasis. Their facial expressions will reinforce their posture: eyes alert, mouth smiling slightly, forehead unfurrowed. If they do *not* believe in the product, then one incongruous gesture — for example, a nervous laugh — will give them away to the astute customer. Since a laugh usually signifies amusement or well-being, a nervous laugh can mean discomfort caused by lack of confidence or loss of integrity. Unless salespersons are consummate actors, they will unconsciously exhibit one or more gestures that will give the rest of the performance the lie.

Television pitchmen and politicians who go in for fabricated or phony kinesics invariably blow the deception. The insincerity of those who use stylized imitations of emotion is usually apparent to the viewer, doubly so to the sophisticated viewer. Look for the incongruities in the gesture-clusters of a few of our top politicians and you will see how true this is. In the long run, there is no substitute for sincerity.

Positive Gestures

Hands can be used for dramatic effect in many ways. When speaking, you can emphasize action words by accompanying them with such gestures as opening the hands, sweeping the air, chopping, pointing, levelling, and so on. In fact, most of us do this automatically in informal situations. A hand brought to the chest traditionally signifies honesty and loyalty, so much so that it is an easy gesture to burlesque. Steepling — that is, joining the finger tips in imitation of a church steeple — usually indicates that the person is confident and very sure of what he or she is saying. On the other hand, steepling can indicate a smug and egotistical attitude.

Confident persons look you in the eye and maintain eye contact longer than those who are unsure of themselves or have something to hide. Confidence also results in less blinking and in squared shoulders. Again, this latter is an easy gesture to burlesque. To avoid comic

204

overtones, gestures of confidence should arise from within the individual.

If a listener's head is tilted, it often indicates interest in what is being said. A hand on the cheek can also suggest attentiveness in the listener. However, if the index finger extends along the cheek with the remaining fingers below the mouth and if the other gestures in the cluster include the body drawn back, the pattern can denote a skeptical, critical, or even cynical attitude toward the speaker. The total picture has to be taken into account to avoid misinterpretation.

Pinching the bridge of the nose, if accompanied with closed eyes, can communicate deep thought and concern about a decision to be made. If the communicant is your client or maybe your boss, this is the time for you to be silent while that person makes up his or her mind. Silence at the right time can also be a positive gesture.

Pacing is a very forceful gesture. Many people seem to feel they think better while pacing, and this gesture can indicate that the pacer is wrestling with a problem. Pacing or moving around can also indicate confidence. It can add tremendously at times to a presentation if it isn't carried to the point of distracting the audience. All motions should add to, not detract from, the speaker's words. An interesting lecturer seldom sits down to deliver the material. Notice how a good teacher moves around the room, uses a chalkboard pointer, emphasizes spoken words with hand and arm gestures, and so on. A deadpan figure is just as boring as a deadpan voice.

Negative Gestures

There are some individuals who will react with resistance or outright hostility to whatever you say. Such people cannot help betraying their attitudes in their nonverbal gestures, which will close all the doors between you no matter how good you are at selling a product or yourself. Although situations differ, the gesture-clusters that communicate doubt, suspicion, or rejection all project the same *no*. If you can read the signs correctly, you can learn with experience when to change your tactics or even when to retreat entirely.

Crossed arms or crossed legs can indicate a negative reaction, especially if accompanied by a leaning-away position of the body. Closed or clenched hands, of course, are a danger signal. Touching, rubbing, or pulling the nose can mean doubt or indecision. A sudden shift in position on the listener's part so that feet and body are turned away from you can mean the listener is restless and probably wants to break off the conversation. You may risk antagonizing the person if you persist in continuing.

A Word of Warning

Those who are inclined to take an isolated gesture as final and definitive need to be reminded that individual gestures are open to misinterpretation. Crossing the arms might indicate a shift to a more comfortable position rather than resistance to an idea. Rubbing the nose might mean simply that it is itchy. Pinching the bridge of the nose, rather than suggesting deep thought, could mean the person has a bad headache. These variations in meaning are readily understood by having an awareness of the full context of interpersonal communication — the relationship between speaker and listener(s), the content and tone of the verbal communication, the time of day, the physical environment.

Kinesics indulged in superficially can result in a misreading of body language and do more harm than good. Yet, a sharpened awareness of the true attitudes underlying others' gesture-clusters and a heightened sensitivity to the feelings and reactions of other persons can be of immeasurable value in business and social situations. Bear in mind, too, that just as we all "speak" unconsciously with gestures, so do we listen to and understand the gestures of others without consciously analysing them. Kinesics is a serious science. If you are going to understand it in depth so that it can be really useful to you, you are going to need more information than has been given here. For a start, a number of books are available. A few of these are listed in the bibliography. If you are planning a career in management or marketing, a seminar course in kinesics will be the most beneficial way to develop insight in this direction.

Exercises

1. Do a little research into the background of an achiever, a person who has "made it" in the business world. Speak for two or three minutes on the qualities of this person. Speak without notes. Use your body language advantageously.
2. Make a list of slang expressions and colloquialisms you have heard since you have been on campus.
   a. Write out a definition in formal English for each of these terms.
   b. Express the meaning of each term through an image of your own.
3. Act out, without words, an attitude or emotion for the others in the class to interpret. (This exercise is not intended to teach "contrived" kinesic behavior, but to raise your awareness of gesture-clusters.) Act out with appropriate accompanying gestures one of the following:
   a. dejection (I didn't get the job.)

b. elation (I got the job!)
c. confidence (I'm the person for the job.)
d. lack of confidence (I'm afraid I'm not good enough for this position.)
e. courting behavior (Hey, look me over! I'm interested in you!)
f. anger (You can't fire me. I quit!)
g. dominance (I'm the boss here.)
h. an emotion of your own choosing

4. Prepare, with a partner in class, a three-minute example of how not to conduct a conversation between employer and employee — the employee is being called on the carpet for excessive absenteeism. Then present the same conversation as it should be conducted.

5. Prepare a short biographical fact sheet about yourself, using point form. Exchange with a partner in class. After two minutes' preparation, "introduce" your partner to the class.

Chapter Fifteen
Listening and Speaking

Listening to the Other Person

Since approximately one-third of all business communication is now oral, listening and speaking are a big part of any employee's or employer's business day. But the art of listening is one aspect of communication that has been too long overlooked. (Most people are not good listeners — most would rather talk than listen.) It is important to be able to communicate your ideas to the other person, of course, but it is equally important to listen to what the other person is saying.

Oral communication in business is used to inform, instruct, or persuade. On the job you will probably receive oral instructions on how to do the work that is expected of you. Understanding what is being said in the first place is the grounding for good listening and if you don't grasp instructions right away, ask the instructor to repeat them. Ask questions. He or she won't think you are stupid if you don't understand the first time round, but will certainly think so if you don't understand and don't say so. (This applies equally to classroom instruction.)

Both speaker and listener share the responsibility of seeing that communication takes place. Clear your mind of mental barriers so that you can concentrate on what is being said. If other ideas are competing with the instructor's words, you won't be able to listen with full attention. Finally, if you are being given a particular set of instructions, jot them down. Even though you think you will remember, it is possible you may forget later.

In any conversation the rules of simple courtesy ought to govern behavior for listening as they do for speaking. Restrain your impulse to interrupt in the middle of another's sentence. It is just as rude to break in when someone else is talking as it is to shove ahead of someone in the cafeteria line. Wait your turn. Besides, if you are listening — really listening — to what the other person is saying, you will be as interested in that as in adding your own comments.

Never brush anyone off impatiently. (No matter how busy, the successful careerist makes a point of listening as carefully to subordinates as to superiors.) After all, there might be something useful in what the other person is saying even if the content is familiar to you. Suppose, in spite of your good intentions, you find you cannot suffer a crashing bore gladly, then use the time to your advantage. (What does this person's conversation reveal about him? Am I also guilty at times of . . . ?)

There are ways to get rid of unwanted ear-benders tactfully. A favorite technique of managers and supervisors is to have the secretary come in at the end of a set time or on signal and announce, "Mr. Bigboss, may I remind you that you have an appointment with Mr. Suchandso?" Tact means achieving your purpose without unnecessarily wounding the other person.

Listening to Criticism

In the previous chapter I suggested that you develop an image of the person you want to be and work toward it, but that you look at yourself objectively first. Most of us find it difficult to form an objective viewpoint of ourselves, particularly if it includes adverse criticism from someone else. This can be so damaging to our self-image that we react defensively against it. Then, instead of listening, we throw up mind-blocks in the form of excuses for our conduct or our work, and these blocks prevent us from profiting from what the employer or teacher is saying.

If you ask a superior, "How did I do?" on a piece of work, be prepared for the truth. As a matter of fact, you will get such criticism whether you ask for it or not, especially if you are new on the job. A supervisor's remarks are usually justified so be prepared to listen attentively. Jot down any comments, and by all means analyse them in relation to your work to see how you can improve. Constructive criticism can ease you into the routine of a new situation and help you to adjust.

Accepting criticism from your equals is another matter. Here you may have to evaluate the remarks for the motive behind them. Jealousy, the competitive instinct, psychological compensation — any of these may play a part. (If I can tear you down, I look better by comparison. If I'm only a metre and a half tall, every little centimetre helps.) Usually you can safely disregard any remarks that are made behind your back and repeated to you by someone else. Usually, but not always. Criticism from colleagues can be valuable at times, no

209

matter what the motive, if you and they face similar job problems. It will pay you to sift such remarks carefully. If you find some truth in their criticism, accept it and profit from it. Criticism can be used as a tool for self-appraisal and self-improvement.

Body Language When Listening

Just as a speaker's body language can be distracting at times, so yours can be as a listener. The following pointers are for courteous and attentive listening.

- Remain relatively quiet. It is distracting to a speaker if you are rattling papers or drumming with a pencil. As far as possible, avoid head-scratching, chin-stroking, foot-jiggling, and other nervous habits.
- Meet the speaker's gaze occasionally but don't stare into that person's eyes. A prolonged stare-down can indicate aggression.
- Show signs of comprehension by nods or by verbally expressing an occasional comment. If you don't understand, of course, ask questions at the appropriate moment.

Note-taking

Many positions in business, apart from the obvious secretarial ones, require skill in note-taking — at business meetings and conferences, during personal interviews, on the telephone, etc. The following discussion focuses on note-taking in college, but the skills you develop now will be useful later on in business.

Much of your time in college is spent listening and taking notes in the classroom. Difficulties arise when you find you can't concentrate on a subject that does not appeal to you. The resulting boredom is likely to generate restlessness and inattention. Teachers complain that students don't listen but nobody tells them *how* to listen. If you are a poor listener you can do something about it. Just as you can become interested in other persons, so you can become interested in any subject if you are willing to make the effort.

Listening with Interest

Think for a minute about what interests you as a student. Usually the subjects you know and like, or those you realize will be useful to you later on, hold your attention. If you are not interested in a subject, here are several tips that will help you to develop some liking or enthusiasm for it.

Lack of information is the most common source of lack of interest. Learn more about the subject in question and some degree of interest

210

will follow. Do some extra work for the course. Read up on the subject in the library. The more you know about it the more interested you will become.

You may resist a subject because you can't see any practical reason for it. Course developers, however, do not put subjects on a curriculum unless there is a need for them. Usually the ones you resist are those that relate to the course indirectly or that are designed to develop you as an educated person as well as a trained one. If this is the case and you cannot understand why you have to take a subject that is of no practical use to you, go back and reread the chapter on theory and practice (Chapter One).

These are the three main reasons for failure of interest — lack of information on the subject, lack of previously developed enthusiasm, and failure to see the need for it. If you can overcome these three obstacles, you will be able to take class notes more intelligently.

Listen Discriminately

Listen for the main ideas in the speaker's sentences. Then choose key words as headings for each idea and jot down supporting points under the headings. Don't try to take down complete sentences when taking class notes. Some teachers will put the subject headings of their lectures on the blackboard or on a transparency for an overhead projector, and if so the main ideas will be outlined for you. Not all discussions and lectures, however, lend themselves to this method. You may have to do most of the selecting and arranging yourself. Some anecdotes or stories used to illustrate lecture material are worth noting, many are not. Try to distinguish what will be useful and keep notes you will be able to make sense of days, weeks, or months later. If you know the subject fairly well and are interested in it, your ability to discriminate between the significant and the inconsequential will be greatly enhanced.

How to Not-listen

This is the era of information overload. So much is thrown at you daily that you can't pay a high degree of attention to everything you hear. To protect your own sanity, you have to choose not to listen occasionally. The trick is to know when and how. If, in the classroom, you have to let your mind wander sometimes, let it wander on the periphery of the lecture material. Think of something related in some way to the subject under discussion. You can, if you try. Shut out extraneous material such as yesterday's basketball game or Saturday's dance. If you keep your mind from spinning too far out of orbit, it will slide back in again with no trouble when the speaker says something important.

211

Review

Immediately after the lecture, go back over your notes and fill in any blanks while the material is still fresh in your mind. If you don't have time to do it right after class do it that same night at home. If you review your notes then, and again on the weekend, you will have no difficulty understanding your notes when you study before exams.

Listening Creatively

Finally, do keep in mind that you are a thinking human being and not a tape recorder. You are not expected to play back word for word at the flip of a switch whatever you hear in the classroom. Creative listening means selective listening so that you can use some of the material to spark ideas of your own. Leave a wide margin beside your class notes for jotting down comments as they occur to you. Keep your trigger finger on your imagination and become a creative listener.

How to Take Notes

- Date each set of notes in the upper right-hand corner.
- Take notes in pencil preferably, so that changes can easily be made.
- Leave a wide right-hand margin for added information or for questions. Bracket comments of your own to keep them separate from the speaker's words.
- If possible, listen to an idea fully before summarizing it in note form. This may take some practice on your part. Don't try to take complete sentences. You can go back and fill in later if you need to.
- Use abbreviations. This can be a code of your own, like *imp* for *important, eff* for *effective.*
- Pause periodically to scan your notes to see how the speaker is developing the topic.
- Use headings and subheadings. Practise arranging ideas this way as you go. Train yourself to catch key words and use these to hang the speaker's other ideas on.
- Review your notes immediately after the discussion while the material is still fresh in your mind.
- Use a separate notebook for each subject. Keep notes in the front, assignments and other material in the back.

The Daybook or Desk Diary

It is impossible to remember — without help — all the details of a busy working day, particularly details that are brought to our attention orally.

212

Here the daily business diary is indispensable for keeping track of appointments and work to be done, whether in the classroom or the office. A desk diary is an efficient little memory helper that no business person can do without.

The desk diary is usually notebook size, 90 mm by 140 mm approximately, with blank spaces for notes on one page and blanks for appointments on the facing page. The pages are dated so that future appointments can be noted ahead. If you use a business diary now for marking down due dates for assignments and dates for your tests, you will be forming another good habit.

The Desk Diary

Brownline Jumbo Calendar Pad and Stand

213

Telephone Use

In today's fast-moving world the average business man or woman sends more words over the telephone than through the post office. The reasons aren't hard to find. In most cases, since it takes two days to exchange letters even under the best of conditions, time is the crucial factor. Can you imagine the frustration and delay if all business had to be conducted by letter or messenger? Today we take the wonder of electronic instruments for granted, yet for an English merchant of two hundred years ago, the idea of speaking directly from London with a customer in Montreal would have been considered (a) the fraudulent scheme of a swindler, or (b) miraculous, or (c) impossible. Now we accept the telephone as just another vehicle of communication, useful some dozens of times a day for everything from making plane reservations to getting a repeat order quickly to a wholesaler.

There are many reasons besides speed for the increasing use of the telephone in business communication. Cost is a factor. The cost of a three-minute daytime call from Toronto to Vancouver, which cost $3.00 in 1963, cost only $3.15 in 1980. Conversely, a letter now costs $5.00 (or more, depending on the source you accept) from the time it is dictated to the time it is dropped in the mail chute. The same letter cost $1.00 twenty years ago. When the cost of letterhead stationery, stamps, office overhead, and the dictator's and the secretary's time are averaged in, the letter costs do not seem out of line. Circumstances, however, alter cases where long distance calls are concerned. The advantages to be gained from direct and speedy contact have to be weighed against the cost of the call. Not all long distance calls are necessary. They may or may not justify the individual expense.

Telephoning speeds decision-making. It scarcely needs stating that direct discussion of a problem is more satisfactory than distancing it in an exchange of letters. Both the receiver and the sender can voice immediate reaction and response over the telephone to simplify communication. Also, because a speaker's words are not being filed and kept on record, a telephone conversation nearly always allows for more frankness than a letter does.

When Not to Phone

On the other hand, the fact that a telephone conversation cannot be filed for future reference can be an inconvenience. Very often, if the content will have to be written down anyway, the telephone conversation becomes a time-waster instead of a time-saver. If such is the case the whole operation might better be conducted by letter in the first place. If you need a written record, or information to study in detail, then don't phone, write.

Know Your Purpose

Telephone calls can be an imposition on the receiver's time. Even your best friend doesn't appreciate being dragged to the phone at an inconvenient time for an aimless chat. Friends, bless them, make special concessions for us, but business people do not. You should have your purpose firmly in mind before you dial so that you can be as brief as possible. Ask yourself, is this call necessary? If it is and if you are making the call, then you are responsible for seeing that your message is organized and to the point. So plan ahead.

Plan your telephone message as carefully as you would the content of a letter. Until you become an experienced telephoner, jot down ahead of time the points you want to make during the call. That way you can bring them up in order without unnecessary sidetracking or stumbling around.

The Corroborating Letter

Very often, after preliminary details have been satisfactorily ironed out over the telephone, a corroborating letter will be needed as a record of an agreement reached. Such a letter should refer specifically to the details of the conversation. This:

Dear Mr. Quick:

This will confirm the agreement reached during our telephone conversation yesterday.

Your request for a change in plans for your new office layout is being implemented today in the blueprints.

The idea of partitioning the large central office into two separate offices for your assistants is a good one. The new arrangement will allow for two private offices each 2.5 m by 3.7 m with a joint reception area between.

The revised blueprints will be in the mail to you tomorrow.

Sincerely,

Not this:

Dear Mr. Quick:

This will corroborate our telephone conversation yesterday.

Sincerely,

Unsolicited Phone Calls

If you are making a call that the recipient hasn't asked for and isn't expecting, make sure that it is to his or her advantage to listen to you. An unwanted phone call is more than a nuisance to a busy career person. It costs time and time is money. And don't tie up a business telephone with social or personal calls. Save them for afterhours.

Telephone Courtesy and Common Sense

Bell Canada urges common sense and courtesy when receiving and placing calls. The entertaining and informative film, *How to Lose Your Best Customer without Really Trying*, dramatizes the following guidelines for telephone use in the modern office.

Placing a Call

- Have a personal directory for frequently dialed numbers and keep it handy on your desk.
- Plan ahead before placing an outgoing call. Have a pad and pencil ready. Have handy any notes or documents you might need in relation to the call.
- Dial your own calls. Let the switchboard operator run the switchboard. The operator's job is to direct incoming calls. She or he shouldn't have to look up numbers for you or dial your calls.
- Dial long distance direct. It's cheaper and faster than going through the long distance operator.
- Stay on the line once you have placed a call. It is extremely rude to have a secretary place a call for you, say you are on the line, and then have to ask the person who answers to wait while the secretary tries to locate you in another part of the building.

Answering a Call

- When answering a business call, don't say "Hello." It wastes time and isn't necessary. Simply identify yourself by name.

216

- If you answer an outside call direct, identify your company as well as yourself. "Roberts and Grayling. Miss Hindmarsh speaking. May I help you?" When answering an interoffice call, identify your department as well as yourself. "Stockroom. Rogers speaking."
- Speak distinctly and talk into the mouthpiece. Keep cigarettes, cigars, coffee cups, pencils, pens, etc. out of your mouth while you are on the phone.
- If you are away from your phone, leave a message with the secretary or switchboard where you can be reached.
- If you take a call for someone else, say: "Mr. Brown is not in right now. May I have him call you?" or "May I tell him who called?"
- If you must keep a caller waiting on the telephone, be sure he or she knows why. A plain "Just a second!" can antagonize a client unnecessarily. Rather, say, "Please hold on while I get the information you need."
- If you put callers on "hold," be sure not only to let them know in advance, but also remember that they are there. For most people, there is nothing more frustrating than the hopeless sense of having been left permanently on "hold." If you must leave callers on "hold" for more than a couple of minutes, stop and speak to them every few minutes to let them know they haven't been forgotten.

The image of the company is in the voice of everyone who uses an office phone.

Exercises

The section in this chapter on note-taking concentrates on the classroom activity. Note-taking, however, is a skill that is applicable to all kinds of business situations — meetings, conferences, even telephone conversations. The obvious exercise for developing the skill is to begin taking comprehensible notes in the classroom.

1. Attend a meeting of your choice. Perhaps a speaker is coming to your college. Or perhaps an election is in the offing — if so, attend a political rally. Take notes of the meeting, following the suggestions on page 212.
2. Watch the evening news on television. Take notes, arranging your material under headings and subheadings. Add creative comment of your own in the right-hand margin.
3. Plan a telephone skit of approximately two minutes for yourself and a partner. Make notes ahead of time on the points you intend to cover.

    a. Write out the dialogue for yourself as job applicant phoning to request an interview and for your partner as recipient of the call.

    b. Act out the skit with your partner for the rest of the class.

4. Evaluate the following telephone comments:

    a. Ask the switchboard operator to place the call for you.

    b. Get the number from directory assistance.

    c. Data Processing, Mr. Hare speaking.

    d. Mr. Smith isn't in yet; I don't know what's keeping him.

    e. Miss Kelly isn't in her office now and I don't know anything about credit memos.

    f. Good morning! Filch Enterprises here. Hang on a minute.

    g. Mr. Drew is out in the warehouse somewhere.

    h. I don't care if you're calling from Timbuktu. Mr. Chinstrap instructed me not to put any calls through to him.

    i. Stop! Stop! You don't want me. You want Mrs. Milroy, and I just saw her disappear down the hall.

    j. I believe you were connected with the wrong department. Hang on while I connect you with Mr. Bimblewit in Accounting.

Part Seven
Working with Others

Chairmanship

Teamwork

Chapter Sixteen
Chairmanship

Employers are always looking for leadership potential. Today, as you well know, the market is glutted with graduates who hold degrees and diplomas that testify to the owner's technical ability in accounting, marketing, architecture, or whatever. The person the employer wants is the one who has technical knowledge plus the ability to express ideas imaginatively and enthusiastically, to inspire enthusiasm in others, to assume responsibility.

One of the most conspicuous qualities of leadership is willingness to become involved. Look for ways to pave your path in the direction of leadership during the years you are in college. Join that student group or club. Offer to serve on one of its committees. Run for office. Start a club yourself. Above all, *participate now* so that you can acquire practice in group action. It will make it so much easier for you to chair that first important meeting later.

There is increasing emphasis in our country on participatory democracy. People want more say in their own affairs, particularly at the local level. In any number of organizations people are getting together to make their collective voices heard — from neighborhood citizens' groups to societies of political, cultural, athletic, business, social, humanitarian, environmental, and professional interest. But no individual can make his or her voice heard at group meetings unless some rules of conduct are observed by those present. Without rules everyone would be babbling at once and nothing would be accomplished. All groups need a leader or chairman to see that the rules are observed and that the meetings proceed as planned so the purposes of the group can be achieved. To do this effectively, the leader and also the members need a good grasp of parliamentary procedure.

Parliamentary procedure refers to the method commonly used to manage any meeting — not just a session of the House of Commons — so problems can be discussed and decisions reached in a fair and orderly manner. The system actually originated in the Roman Senate, but the principles have come down to us from the English Parliament, hence its name. There, parliamentary procedure grew out of the customary way of conducting the country's affairs. The English, who seem to have more respect for custom and precedent than we do if only because they have been where they are longer, never wrote the rules down. It remained for an American, Henry Martin Robert, to adapt the rules for use in ordinary societies and to print them, in 1876, in reference form.

Robert's Rules of Order is still the preferred manual for most group meetings, although in Canada *Bourinot's Rules of Order*, which is used by the federal government, is our final authority. No set of rules is sacrosanct, however. At best, rules are guidelines. Any group, to meet its own particular needs, can change the rules in its written constitution or bylaws. (If you think rules aren't necessary, picture what would happen at the main intersections in your city during rush hour if there were no traffic lights or traffic laws.)

Group meetings are usually held to take action on common problems. We read newspaper accounts daily of concerned delegates petitioning city hall — which you *can* fight — or the House of Commons for legislative change. A neighborhood citizens' organization demands a halt to construction of a freeway. Another wants a community swimming pool built. Another wants industrial pollution curbed. Special interests want restrictions on other interests. Politicians certainly seem to listen more readily to lobbies than to individual voters. Groups have more clout. In the business world this is as true for professional associations as it is in the industrial world for labor unions or at the college level for student government.

Everywhere there is a need for leaders to channel the concerns of such groups into strong and effective rivers of action. But, for two important reasons, it is necessary for all members of the group to understand the basic principles of group action along with the leader. First, each member will then be in a position to contribute more effectively to the group's activities. Second, each participant can be on guard to see that the group's privileges and purposes are not abused by unethical or selfish members.

Principles of Parliamentary Procedure

The democratic system of parliamentary procedure evolved out of a respect for fair play and common sense. The three main principles are: (1) that the will of the majority prevail; (2) that the minority has a right to be heard; (3) that the group conduct its business in an orderly way by considering one thing at a time. These principles are based on good manners, freedom of speech, and equality and justice for all. A meeting that observes these principles is democracy in action.

Business and Democracy

Now, before we move on to the details of a parliamentary meeting, a few words of warning are in order on the limitations of participatory democracy and on the subject of leadership and participation. First, an effective leader or chairman: (1) has a clear sense beforehand of what should be the outcome of the meeting or the decision-making process; (2) is open to the possibility of having a change of mind if new and convincing facts and ideas are presented; and (3) is able, by methods of logical persuasion and strength of personality, to convince a majority that his or her studied opinion is the one to follow. In politics, such an ideal leader would be called a statesman, a leader who truly leads the people. During the Second World War, Winston Churchill was such a leader. Yet, if you think about it, you will soon realize that such qualities are rare, especially today with the dubious emphasis in society on people "doing their own thing."

Those in leadership positions in business did not get there by popular vote. Thus, the second qualifying factor for an understanding of participatory democracy is that even if a majority of subordinates suggests one course of action, this doesn't mean that a superior can't sway or overrule the majority opinion. Most people in business are responsible to others who are above them in the company hierarchy. Those who make decisions, at any level, gather facts and ideas from subordinates who *submit* these data in reports, memorandums, and informal and formal meetings. But the final decision is the boss's. The business world is far from "democratic," and to pretend otherwise is either a subtle form of hypocrisy or simple ignorance.

Leadership, or authority, carries responsibility with it, most especially a responsibility to *listen* to others and to *consider* what they have to say. If we assume, as we have done here, that business is not conducted as a pure democracy, then we must look at the implications of such an assumption. Those who are under the authority of leaders, as all of us are, must take the responsibility of submitting our ideas to those leaders. They may not accept our ideas; they may not act upon them; but they usually will *respect* us for having proposed them. In business today, to be sure, there still are people who "succeed" in a superficial way by being "yes men," those who gain and maintain the boss's favor by supporting every move or word the boss makes or says. And there are companies where being "a good company man" means putting one's job ahead of family, working long hours to impress people, and silently accepting company policy even when it conflicts sharply with one's personal opinions and morality.

Many more businesses, however, do not foster such attitudes and behavior. It remains the responsibility of the sheep to help the shepherd

223

find the best patch of grass in the field of business. The shepherd's task, in this ongoing search, is to direct and guide the sheep to see that they, too, prosper and don't lead the company into pitfalls.

As many of you with business experience will know, pretty much everyone in business is a sheep to some and a shepherd to others. This offers you a dual perspective that is important to keep in mind at all times. In the final analysis, then, the distinction between leaders and followers is significant, but always shifting according to the situation. Both positions require responsibility.

Format for a Formal Meeting

It isn't always necessary to invoke the protocol of "rules of order" to conduct a meeting. The smaller your group, the more informal your meetings can be. Once you have tied down and mastered the rules to your own satisfaction, you can loosen them to suit the situation. A committee of four or five members, for example, can gather around a table and discuss a problem without any formality whatever. In most cases the less rigidity the better. But if a general membership is meeting to discuss a topic that requires the consent of the majority of the members — sending delegates to a national convention, for example — then a more formal procedure is in order.

The list of items, the business to be brought up at a meeting, is called the *agenda*. The *order of business* refers to the sequence of events from the time the meeting begins until it adjourns. The order of business for a regular meeting has a standard format in seven steps. These are:

1. *Call to Order.* The meeting is opened by the chairman or president who says, "The meeting will now come to order."
2. *Reading the Minutes.* The minutes (record of events) of the previous meeting are read by the secretary who then asks if there are any corrections or additions. If there aren't, the minutes are approved as read and become a permanent record of the group's transactions.
3. *Treasurer's Report.* The treasurer's report is read next, but is not adopted as read unless it has been audited.
4. *Correspondence.* The chairman asks the secretary to read or report on any correspondence received or sent since the last meeting.
5. *Unfinished Business.* Unfinished business of the last meeting or business arising out of the minutes is taken up next. If there is a printed agenda, unfinished business heads the list of items to be considered at the meeting.
6. *New Business.* New business is usually presented in order of importance and will be so listed on the agenda.

224

7. *Adjournment.* After reading any announcements, including the time and place of the next meeting, the chairman declares the meeting adjourned.

Responsibilities of the Chairman

Too many people are content to leave the thinking and planning to a leader who will produce all the answers for them. That is how dictatorships get started. In a democratic group, producing answers isn't the job of the chairman alone. Like a good panel-show moderator, the chair draws in all the participants and solicits their opinions. He or she doesn't monopolize the conversation and doesn't force people into decisions he or she favors. The chair remains as fair and impartial as possible.

At some point in your career you likely will be called upon to chair a meeting or even to run for elected office in an association. Familiarity with the responsibilities of chairmanship and a knowledge of parliamentary law will go a long way toward overcoming any initial nervousness when you reach that milestone. These are the duties of the chairman of a formal meeting:

- To acquire a working knowledge of parliamentary law and procedure and an understanding of the bylaws of the organization.
- To draw up the agenda for each meeting ahead of time and to distribute it to the members within a reasonable time.
- To appear at the front of the room a few minutes before the meeting is scheduled to begin.
- To announce and cover all the items on the agenda, using tact and courtesy to keep the members from straying off topic and getting involved in irrelevant discussions.
- To maintain order and decide all points of order, including accepting only one main motion at a time and seeing that each motion is properly made and then discussed and voted on in the proper sequence.
- To stay out of the discussion and to talk as little as possible.
- To appoint committees when authorized by a motion.
- To abstain from voting unless his or her vote is needed to break a tie.
- To be scrupulously impartial and courteous to all members, even the most troublesome, and to encourage courtesy in return.

Put the members at ease by displaying a friendly and courteous attitude. There are times when you might have to control an angry or impetuous member, and at such times a sense of humor is a wonderful asset if you don't have to strain for effect. Never display anger yourself, and avoid showing off just because you know the rules. Remember that your job is to keep things running smoothly and to assist the members to cover the business at hand.

Minutes

The secretary, who should be seated near the chairman, takes down the minutes of the meeting. If the chairman is absent, the secretary can open the meeting and preside until a temporary chairman is chosen, but the secretary's main duty is to record the minutes of the meeting and to attend to the correspondence. The minutes presented at a regular meeting include:

- The date, place, and time of the last meeting.
- Whether it was a special or a regular meeting.
- Whether the minutes of the last meeting were approved as read or were corrected.
- All main motions and the names of the members who made the motions. The name of the seconder does not have to be recorded although it sometimes is.
- Reports of committees (summarized).
- The time the meeting adjourned.
- Signature and approval of the chairman or president.
- Signature of the secretary.

The secretary takes down the minutes in rough form during the meeting and later summarizes them and copies them in ink in the official record book. The format on the opposite page is standard for the minutes of a regular meeting.

Motions

Motions, or resolutions, record the opinion of the group and commit the organization to action after the majority approve the motion. All the business is introduced by motions, and the primary rule is that only one motion can be considered at a time. The chairman has to remember that a motion is already before the group if, during the discussion, someone gets carried away and attempts to make another main motion. Let's follow one chairman as he guides his group through the process of adopting a motion.

Handling a Motion

- *Obtaining the Floor*. Mr. A obtains the floor by rising or, less formally, by raising his hand. He says, "Mr. Chairman" or "Madam Chair-

MINUTES OF THE MONTHLY MEETING

of the Sales and Marketing Department

February 2, 1981

The regular monthly meeting of the Sales and Marketing Department was held in the office of Mr. Lander, Sales and Marketing
Director, who presided at the meeting. Mr. Lander opened the
meeting at 2:00 and the following were present:

Lee MacPhail	Ann Seghri
Joan Steinbrenner	Ed Tremayne
George Lander	

OLD BUSINESS

The secretary read the minutes of the previous meeting. They
were approved as read.

Mr. Tremayne reported that the coupon ads that had been run
in the city newspapers have proved notably successful. His
follow-up report noted that 1500 persons requested the
illustrated brochure and 280 persons wanted a salesman to
call.

NEW BUSINESS

Mr. Lander reported that the department has been directed to
increase advertising expenditures for the coming quarter.
An additional $2800 has been allocated for this purpose.
Discussion following this announcement centred on three
possibilities:

1. Increasing direct mailing to householders
2. Insertion of an ad in Sales Ad Magazine
3. Increasing space in city newspapers

Mrs. Seghri reported that the flyers for direct mailing to
householders were being run off now and that another 5000
could be printed at minimal cost. Postage would cost approximately $500 more. Mr. MacPhail moved that the additional
flyers be ordered. The motion was carried. Mr. Tremayne was
delegated to contact Sales Ad Magazine regarding their advertising rates.

The meeting adjourned at 3:30 on motion of Miss Steinbrenner.

Minutes approved by

George Lander, Director

Minutes prepared by

Sarah Smith, Secretary

227

man" and is recognized by the chair who answers, "Mr. A."

- *Making a Motion.* Mr. A says, "I move that . . ." and states or reads his resolution.
- *Seconding the Motion.* The chair asks, "Do we have a seconder?" Another member raises a hand and says, "I second the motion."
- *Restating the Motion.* The chair says, "It has been moved and seconded that . . . . Is there any discussion?"
- *Discussion.* The motion, or question, is now before the members for discussion and debate. The person who makes the motion speaks first giving reasons for the proposal. After this person finishes speaking, the chair gives the floor to anyone who wants to oppose the motion.
- *Restating the Motion Again.* After all the pros and cons have been heard, the chairman again repeats the motion. So many things — amendments, for example — can happen to a motion in its progress through the discussion period that it is important for the chair to read the motion as it currently stands, or to have the secretary read it back so that all the members will know exactly what they are voting on.
- *The Vote.* Voting usually takes place by a show of hands. The chairman says, "All in favor raise their right hands." The count is taken, and then the chair says, "All those opposed." Again the count is taken. Finally he announces the results: "The motion is carried (or defeated)."

Main Motions

A main motion is one which concerns the business of the organization and if passed binds the group to do something. Once such a motion has been made and seconded, no other main motion can be entertained (received). Although main motions are low in priority they are high in importance since they are the ones that decide the group's activities.

An example of a main motion: "Mr. Chairman, I move that we raise the annual dues of our association from $10.00 to $20.00."

Privileged Motions

Privileged motions have nothing at all to do with the subject under discussion but concern points of such urgency that they can stop proceedings at any time. The chairman must deal with them right away. They are highest in order of priority and are not subject to debate. These include:

1. *Adjournment.* A motion to adjourn has a higher priority than any other motion (except to set time to adjourn) simply because there

is no point in keeping a meeting going if a majority want to leave. A motion to adjourn can be made only when a member is able to obtain the floor. It must be seconded. Any business interrupted by adjournment is placed first on the agenda for the next meeting.

2. *Recess.* A motion for a recess, like a motion to adjourn, is high on the list of priorities and for the same reason. It makes sense to stop proceedings for a short time if a majority of the members want to.

3. *Point of Privilege.* This usually relates to the physical safety, comfort, or dignity of the members, or to the rights of the assembly which are being deliberately abused. If the matter is urgent, it can interrupt a speaker. Any member who resorts to insulting another member, for example, should be silenced under a point of privilege. This motion does not have to be seconded.

4. *Orders of the Day.* A call for the orders of the day is a motion designed to get the discussion back on track if the speakers have wandered away from the topic. If certain questions are of such importance that they are to be discussed at a certain time, they become the orders of the day.

Incidental Motions

Incidental motions are those that are connected in some way to the motion under discussion, although they do not refer specifically to it as secondary motions do. Like other special motions, they are allowed to interrupt the proceedings and must be taken care of before discussion can continue. They have no order of priority among themselves, but they take precedence over all except privileged motions. Such incidental motions as point of order and point of information do not have to be seconded.

1. *Point of Order.* Any member who notices a breach of rules can insist that the rule be enforced. It is the responsibility of the chairman to know the rules and to enforce them. All members have the right to insist that this be done.

2. *Appeal from the Decision of the Chair.* Occasionally, members may disagree with the ruling of the chairman and appeal his or her decision. If the appeal is seconded, the chairman asks the secretary to call for a vote and to indicate the result. The chairman should accept the decision if the vote goes against him or her and should change the ruling.

3. *Point of Information.* If, while one member has the floor, another member wants clarification of some remark, he or she may interrupt during an appropriate pause. The member requesting information never addresses another member directly, but always addresses the chair first. He or she is out of order otherwise. The

chair will then request a response or recognize the willingness to respond from the other member.

4. *Withdrawal of a Motion.* If a motion is a waste of time or detrimental to the interests of the group, it may be withdrawn any time before the vote. A withdrawal motion does not require a seconder if the original mover makes the motion. A simple majority vote decides the matter. (In the Commons, a motion can be withdrawn only by unanimous consent of the House.) If a motion is withdrawn, the secretary should strike out all reference to it from the minutes.

Subsidiary or Secondary Motions

A subsidiary motion is applied to a main motion to delay or dispose of it in some way and is made while the main motion is being discussed. Subsidiary motions are the most frequently used of all motions and thus their order of priority is important. When made and seconded, a subsidiary motion has to be voted on before the vote can be taken on the main motion. Some of the subsidiary motions, in order of precedence, are:

1. *Table a Motion.* To table a motion means to lay it aside temporarily so that something more urgent can be attended to. This motion is not used in the Canadian Commons where other motions have the same effect but it is useful in community organizations. It is not debatable.

2. *The Previous Question.* To call for the previous question means to close debate and vote on the motion. This is used when the discussion drags on too long. It is not debatable and requires a two-thirds vote. If it is defeated, the discussion continues.

3. *Postpone to a Definite Time.* This motion is used to postpone a question to a later meeting. The term, like the motion to table, is not used in the Canadian Commons but other organizations find it useful.

4. *Commit, or Refer to a Committee.* When more study on a subject is needed, it may be referred to a special commitee. When the investigation is completed, the committee brings back to the membership meeting a report or recommendation. The motion is debatable.

5. *Amend.* A motion can be changed by an amendment. This requires a new motion which proposes to alter the wording of the main motion by adding or deleting words, phrases, or sentences. A motion to amend must be seconded, discussed if necessary, and voted on before the main motion is again considered. It is possible to amend an amendment by the same process. Then the amendment to the amendment must be voted on first, then the amendment as revised, and finally the amended motion.

230

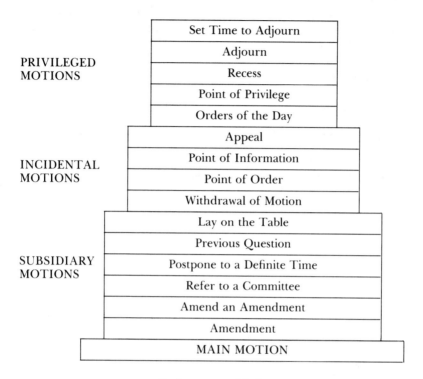

PRIVILEGED
MOTIONS

Set Time to Adjourn
Adjourn
Recess
Point of Privilege
Orders of the Day

INCIDENTAL
MOTIONS

Appeal
Point of Information
Point of Order
Withdrawal of Motion

SUBSIDIARY
MOTIONS

Lay on the Table
Previous Question
Postpone to a Definite Time
Refer to a Committee
Amend an Amendment
Amendment

MAIN MOTION

Parliamentary Motions
Most Often Used in Ordinary Societies

Conclusion

The individual's right to propose and discuss change, to press for legislative action, to speak out against leaders, to remove them from office if they are not doing the job as he or she considers it should be done, to run for office — all these, aligned with a free press, are the fundamental differences between a democracy and a dictatorship. Those who live in an authoritarian state have no legal means for protest and none of the privileges of free discussion that we take so for granted.

Parliamentary procedure is the muscular framework for exercising these privileges, but like any set of muscles if they aren't exercised they will atrophy. A handbook of parliamentary "rules of order" is a manual every would-be leader has to become familiar with. Take your copy with you to the meetings you attend. Then if you are called on to chair a meeting, you will be ready.

Exercises

1. Attend a meeting that is run along the lines of parliamentary procedure and take the minutes as if you were the secretary. Some suggestions for a meeting you might attend:
   a. Student government.
   b. Regular council meeting of your city council.
   c. Formal meeting of a club or organization to which you belong.
2. Watch at least one hour of a television talk show. In approximately 200 words, evaluate the host/hostess as a discussion leader, considering such skills as keeping the discussion on course, encouraging contributions from all participants, controlling dominating speakers, creating a releaxed atmosphere, and managing time.

Chapter Seventeen

Teamwork

Getting jobs done today means group effort. Middle management personnel, especially, are in contact daily not only with groups of people under them but with groups of people over them. Every employee is part of a team somewhere along the line. In your career either as employee or employer you will be participating as a group member and you will be doing so in many ways. Your individual efforts can contribute to the success or failure of the company projects on which you work.

Speaking to Others

Group effort means interaction, particularly through oral communication. Some aspects of this important method of communication are covered in Interpersonal Communication (Chapter Fourteen), but speaking *to* others is a little different from conversing with another person, especially if it involves preparing remarks ahead of time. It isn't likely after you start working that you will be called on to deliver a formal speech — you are much more likely to have to report orally to your superiors on some aspect of your job, to instruct others in some way, or to contribute to the discussions at department meetings.

Overcoming Nervousness

Some fortunate people seem born with the gift of gab. They love to talk, and facing an audience is a delight for them. But others, for whom speaking to a group of any size is an acutely painful and nerve-wracking experience, are just the opposite. If you are among the latter you may derive some comfort from knowing that a good many others — from teachers to performing artists — share or have shared your affliction.

233

Practice and experience usually take care of the problem of stage fright, but a little nervousness is a good thing, really. It starts the adrenalin flowing and this keeps you on your toes mentally and physically. So preliminary nervousness isn't anything to worry about and usually disappears after five or ten minutes. But if excessive nervousness is a real problem with you when speaking in front of others, here are some suggestions for keeping things under control.

- Know your subject thoroughly. Nothing will give you confidence like having done your homework ahead of time and being well-prepared.
- Don't wear your best clothes if they are going to make you feel self-conscious. Dress casually in clothes that are familiar, neat, and clean. Then forget about them and concentrate on your talk.
- Find a comfortable posture and take a few deep breaths. This will help to relax your whole body. If you are sitting down, lean toward your audience. This is a psychological device for bringing you and the audience closer together.
- Look at your audience. Eye contact is important. Experienced speakers are able to rotate their gaze to keep the interest of the whole group. Until you master this, you can pick out one person in the audience, particularly someone you know, and speak directly to that person, at least to start with.
- Keep your head up and speak loudly enough for everyone in the room to hear. If you are afraid your voice will betray your nervousness, practise at home with a tape recorder until you can control your pace and pitch. Practise speaking slowly and enunciating clearly.
- Finally, once you start speaking let your enthusiasm for your subject show. Interest and enthusiasm are contagious. The key is a desire to share with others what you have learned.

Speaking to Instruct Others

A common job-application question is, *Have you ever trained anyone to do a job?* If you are asked to take a trainee or a group of trainees under your wing, advance preparation on your part is a must. It isn't enough just to let them watch you on the job. You have to explain and demonstrate as you go. Decide beforehand what you are going to say and organize your instruction into a step-by-step procedure. Stick to the situation at hand and don't introduce irrelevant instruction — for example, if you are demonstrating the use of the photocopier don't start talking out of the blue about the dictaphone. Choose a suitable place for instructing and see that you have all the materials and equipment ready ahead of time.

234

The first step in the actual instructing of others, whether you are giving orders to a subordinate or training new employees to do a particular job, is to ensure that you have their attention. Switch them on first. You can do this by asking them a question about the job at hand to see that they are listening and that you are both talking about the same thing. If you are explaining how to operate a new piece of office equipment, you might ask your trainees if they have ever used a similar piece of equipment before. After you have their attention, show them what you want done, how it is to be done, when and where it is to be done, and why.

You are more apt to get through to others if you explain the reasons why a particular operation has to be done or done in a certain way. And giving instructions in short segments so that the others don't have to remember too much at one time is preferable to a long monologue. Finally, involve the others in what you are doing and saying. Ask them to play back what you have just said or have them run through the operation themselves.

Committee Work

Someone once remarked that if Moses had depended on a committee to lead the Israelites out of the wilderness they would still be there. Unfortunately, this attitude is prevalent. A large number of career persons consider all committee meetings a big waste of time — and I have attended some that are just that. Nevertheless, a committee that meets to discuss problems and reach solutions is one of the most democratic processes we have, and no one person has all the answers or even the best answer.

The problem with committees — and sometimes they do create more problems than they solve — is that they can take up a lot of a person's time that perhaps should be used more fruitfully at some other task. And, a not entirely unfair criticism is that committees often are established to do the work that no one wants to do alone — although a single person *could* accomplish the task more quickly and just as well. In this instance, a wise leader might better simply ask one person to do it. Committees also can be *used* to delay decision-making or to make a preordained, autocratic decision appear to have been made democratically. These are points for you to remember both when you are a leader and when you are being led, which means all the time.

Serving on a Committee

A committee is a group of persons who have been asked to help out with an activity (planning the annual company dinner-dance) or to

235

solve a problem (reducing operational costs in a particular department). Once you have the good firm feel of responsibility, you probably will be asked to serve on a committee or even to chair one.

Participation in a committee discussion is usually informal, spontaneous, and conversational. As a committee member you will make a contribution to the group if you have ideas and can express them clearly. Conflicting opinions are desirable for discussing all aspects of a problem. (Who needs a person who says "yes" to everything?) So contribute to the conversation but don't monopolize it. You should listen to what the other members have to say so your comments fit in naturally and help build toward a course of action. Decisions are always made by vote, even at informal meetings, to ensure that the opinion of the majority prevails.

The Committee Chairman

The role of the committee chairman is slightly different from that of the chairman of a formal meeting. For one thing, the committee chairman is not only expected to lead off an informal discussion but may take part in it throughout. Or, depending on the size and the inclination of the group, the chair may stay out of the discussion. He or she does not force opinions or decisions on the group and draws all members into the discussion. Here are some additional ways good committee chairpersons fulfil the leadership responsibility.

- They introduce the subject or problem and are familiar enough with it to interpret the questions of the group.
- They set the tone for the meeting — either brisk and business-like or relaxed and casual. Not all committee meetings are conducted in a comfortable atmosphere. The situation — a meeting to find ways to reduce business losses, for example — may call for a more serious attitude.
- Effective leaders see that the members have enough information to work with. They may bring in films, charts, or reports they have prepared ahead of time. They are responsible for seeing that the committee members get any additional information needed.
- They do not do all the work themselves. If additional research is necessary, they ask the various members to accept such tasks.
- They guide the discussions and keep them on track. It is the chair's responsibility to see that the group makes progress and does not waste time. But adequate discussion has to be allowed.
- They summarize (1) at the end of a long discussion before the group moves on to another point and (2) again at the end of the meeting to sum up the group's decisions and accomplishments.

236

Problem-solving Committees

Although all committees work under a chairman, not all of them need to follow the established rules of parliamentary procedure. A small group can use a more relaxed form of meeting. It may employ some rules of order or may dispense with them altogether. To stimulate creative thinking and new approaches to business problems, small groups can use any of a number of techniques that would be impractical for a large general meeting. Three of these methods are explained below.

Freeflowing Discussion. At an informal discussion-meeting, it is not necessary for the members to be recognized by the chair before speaking. They can discuss the problem with each other, exchanging and encouraging ideas so that the conversation flows naturally. If the group is small and if the seating arrangement is relaxed, the members probably will be uninhibited about speaking out. The danger at an informal gathering is that one or two persons will do all the talking. An alert chairman prevents this from happening by drawing everyone into the conversation.

Brainstorming. This is a method of thinking out loud by the group. Whatever comes to mind, anything and everything even remotely suggested by the problem, is "tossed into the pot." One idea triggers off others in a rapid-fire exchange. None of the ideas is discussed or commented on at a brainstorming session. The chair or secretary takes them all down, no matter how ridiculous they may seem, and saves them for analysis and discussion at a subsequent meeting. A brainstorming session can last as long as the chair feels it is productive.

The Fishbowl Method. This is similar to brainstorming in that ideas are tossed into a pot. In the fishbowl method, however, the ideas are written out by their originators, though not necessarily signed, and put into a container. The leader "fishes" them out randomly one at a time and open discussion follows each. Thus, the appraisal process takes place during the same meeting. This method is perhaps less time-consuming than brainstorming. It may or may not be as productive of ideas.

Conventions

Conventions are becoming more and more popular as a means of bringing specialists and career people together. Some day you may attend a professional convention or conference on behalf of the company you work for. Since the featured speakers at conventions are usually experts in their field, any information you gain will be the most up-to-date possible. If your expenses are being paid in full or in part by your company you will be expected to report the gist of the meetings orally if not in writing when you return. This way the information may be shared with your colleagues. Some day you may be asked to introduce the speakers at a conference session or to take part in a panel discussion.

The Conference Report

If you represent your company at a conference or convention, you will be expected to submit a short report when you return, summarizing some of what you heard and saw. Such a report should not be an exhaustive account of every minute you spent. It should be a concise report, preferably not more than two or three pages in length. In it you summarize briefly the highlights of the conference. Then on separate enclosures you detail any outstanding information that will be valuable for others. You might also attach some of the literature you received.

The Panel Discussion

The panel discussion is one of the most popular methods of presentation at conventions. Provided one panel member doesn't monopolize the entire program — and it's up to the moderator to see that this doesn't happen — the panel discussion usually proves the most interesting method of illuminating all sides of a question. It is particularly stimulating when conflicting points of view are presented by the speakers. The following explanation sums up the panel method.

To insure an unbiased presentation of all sides of a question, a panel of experts, especially selected to represent various shades of opinion, is often asked to discuss a subject before the group. The moderator or chairman guides the discussion along the lines that will be of most use to the members of the listening group. He is the only member of the panel who should make a speech. His opening talk presents the topic for discussion.

The members of the panel are usually people who have made a special study of the topic. They do *not* present their points of view in the form of speeches. The discussion should follow naturally and not become a symposium of prepared addresses. A "cut-and-dried" panel is so obviously artificial that much of the interest is lost.

The discussion is carried on for a set period of time and then the meeting is given over to questions and follow-up discussion by the whole group. Each question from the listeners should be answered briefly and clearly by the panel members within whose field that particular question falls.*

*Notes for Community Leaders No. 6, "Effective Meetings," Youth and Recreation Branch, Ministry of Community and Social Services, Ontario.

Knowledge is confidence. For a panel member, there is no substitute for knowing your subject. You can be sure someone in the audience, if not one of the other panel members, will challenge you if you make an erroneous statement. So do whatever research is necessary first and prepare a few notes beforehand. Jot down on notecards the points you intend to cover. Be sure of your facts — then talk about them. Don't read anything. If you know your topic thoroughly — up and down, forwards and backwards, inside and outside — you will be able to contribute spontaneously to the discussion once it gets under way. Don't worry about forgetting what you want to say — you can't forget what you know, only what you have memorized.

Exercises

This chapter, with its concluding exercises, might have been entitled "Getting It All Together." Almost everything you have been learning and practising up to now will be brought into play for doing the two final exercises. Both as a panel member when your group makes its presentation and as a delegate in the audience taking notes for a written report, you will be getting practical experience in oral and written communication. Each member of your group will be doing research on some aspect of your topic. You may have asked a guest speaker to join you for your presentation, in which case you will be writing letters or making phone calls beforehand. You will need the skills of oral communication for contributing to the discussion. You will have to be familiar with the basics of parliamentary procedure. And finally, as a member of the audience when each of the other groups makes it presentation, you will be taking notes and then writing a report.

Your class should divide into seminar groups to discuss a topic and prepare a panel presentation for the rest of the class.

1. As a group, present your panel discussion.
2. As a member of the audience, take notes and prepare a concise report of the other presentations.

A Brief Handbook for Writers

Proofreading
Difficult and Confusing Words

A Brief Handbook for Writers*
Proofreading

Sentence Errors

People usually define the sentence by saying it expresses a complete thought. However, don't "Wow!", "Beautiful, man!" and "Dumb!" express complete thoughts? In one way, of course, such expressions are complete in themselves; indeed they are often used in creative writing where their context gives them appropriate significance. Nonetheless, for the more formal situations which call for the clear, precise, and complete explanation of an idea to a reader, such expressions are not normally adequate. Good expository writing calls for the use of complete sentences, for the structure of sentences demands a clear definition of the ideas being presented to the reader: they require that something (a *subject*) be carefully defined as *being* whatever it is, or as *doing* whatever it is doing. A complete sentence, that is, demands a subject and a predicate.

Thus, if you read "The growling dog" you find yourself waiting for more information: Did the growling dog bite the writer? Did it turn tail and run? The fragment lacks an action (i.e., a verb or predicate) that would give you a complete idea of what actually happened. If, on the other hand, you read

The growling dog stood across the body of his fallen master.

you have a complete idea of the situation; you have read a sentence.

Since most people use complete sentences when they find themselves talking in formal situations such as job interviews or visits from the

*Adapted and abridged from Ray Matthews and Gary Webb, *Who's Going To Read This Anyway?* (Toronto: Holt, Rinehart and Winston of Canada, 1980). Used by permission.

minister, it is usually easy to write using complete sentences. Occasionally, however, you will find that in the heat of the battle to get words down on paper, you use incomplete sentences or run several sentences together into one: you must reread carefully everything that you write to make certain that in your haste you have not actually obscured your meaning by presenting the reader with incomplete ideas, or with ideas that have been run together with others.

The Sentence Fragment

I came home late one night to find garbage strewn all over my front lawn. An awful mess.

Read the second "sentence" of the above statement again, without rereading the first sentence. Obviously this does not really tell the reader anything by itself, for it depends on the first sentence for its meaning. Such partial sentences are called *sentence fragments*. Sentence fragments are usually created in only three situations:

1. When you isolate *words in apposition* to the last words in the previous sentence.

Children love plants such as venus flytraps, pitcher plants, eggplants, or sensitivity plants. Any plant that is odd or unique.

The writer of this fragment tried to stress the concept that children love unique plants, but instead created a sentence fragment. A dash should have been used, as its purpose is to give dramatic impact.

2. When you isolate a *subordinate clause* (used to expand upon the idea of the previous or following sentence).

He could always find an excuse to go out after dinner. Especially when he did not want to help with the dishes.

Such words as "when," "if," "since," "as," "because" alter the meanings of the sections of a sentence that they introduce by making them "subordinate," or secondary, in meaning to the main idea of a sentence:

I was late (main idea) because I took time for a cup of coffee (secondary or subordinate idea that simply adds further information to the main idea).

But a subordinate idea always needs a main idea to expand upon. By itself, the subordinate clause "Because I took time for a cup of coffee" is meaningless.

3. When you isolate verbal phrases containing a verb ending in "ing." Consider, for a moment, the following:

244

having been there already
being an example of ingratitude
doing what should have been done
after having arrived in Hong Kong

Obviously none of these statements makes any sense; "ing" verbs depend upon other words for their meaning: used alone, as they are in these examples, they are meaningless. Yet how often in our rough drafts do we write such things as the following:

We must never use verbs ending in "ing" as independent verbs. The reason being that they depend on other words for their meaning.

(If you didn't catch the problem with the second "sentence" the first time you read the example, reread that second "sentence" through again without looking at the first sentence).

As you have seen in examining the examples given above, you subconsciously know already how to recognize a sentence fragment when you view it in isolation. The way to recognize them in your own rough drafts, then, is to isolate them from the rest of the essay.

Put the paper or article away for a day or two; rereading a paper some time after you originally wrote it makes you more objective. This tends to place you in the situation of a reader coming upon a work for the first time and allows you to recognize fragments more easily. Reread your paper one sentence at a time. Reread your work aloud, making certain that you read what you have actually written (keep in mind that all too often we "see" with our minds; that is, we know what we meant to write and this knowledge causes us to think that we see things like complete sentences when indeed we have written only sentence fragments).

Since the sentence fragment is not independent because it usually depends upon the sentence that precedes or follows it for its meaning, there are two methods for correcting sentence fragments:

1. Make the fragment independent by adding a subject or a verb. For example, change

From that time on he was a perfect citizen. Doing what should have been done from the beginning.

to

From that time on he was a perfect citizen. He did what should have been done from the beginning.

2. Incorporate the fragment into the preceding or following sentence. Change

245

From that time on he was a perfect citizen. Doing what should have been done from the beginning.

to

From that time on he was a perfect citizen, doing what should have been done from the beginning.

The Comma Splice

The *comma splice* occurs when a writer uses a comma to replace the period at the end of a sentence. In almost every instance, the comma has been used to replace a period between two sentences that are very closely related in their meanings. The second sentence may illustrate the point made in the first one; it may add additional information about the point made in the first sentence; or it may give the effect of a cause that was outlined in the preceding sentence. Example:

We are robots, our ideas and opinions are often not our own.

The writer of this comma splice was trying to create a certain effect in the reader's mind, but unfortunately fell into a trap. The purpose was to drive home to the reader just how people are like robots. Subconsciously the writer realized that a period would bring the reader to a full stop and that such a full stop would destroy the dramatic impact of the second point. Therefore, a comma was used rather than a semicolon, which would have been correct and would have avoided the full stop of the period.

The easiest way to spot comma splices is to listen to yourself carefully as you read your written work over *aloud*. Make certain that you read exactly what is written on the page. Most people, when they try to explain something with precision to someone else, think in sentences; thus you will find that when you encounter a comma splice and read it aloud as it is punctuated, with only the short pause symbolized by the comma, the passage will not sound right; your mind recognizes the confusion that the use of the comma can create. You will see the point being made if you read the following "sentences" aloud:

I knew that I had made a mistake, when she slapped my face, it was all too obvious.

Whenever I came to call, no one seemed to be at home, maybe they were giving me a hint.

Many recent films have tried to imitate *Star Wars*, not one has succeeded.

In many cases the identification of comma splices is made easier because they often occur just before *adverbial connectives*:

246

I had no warning about the test, *therefore*, I was not prepared.

A person who owns a small piece of land can save money, for *instance*, one might grow vegetables.

Some other adverbial connectives are: so, yet, thus, hence, however, moreover, consequently, henceforth, furthermore, nevertheless, otherwise, therefore, on the other hand, namely, for instance, that is, for example. However, do not confuse adverbial connectives with *co-ordinate conjunctions* (and, or, but, for, nor), which take commas.

I was late for work; *however*, I wasn't put on report. I was late for work, *but* I was not put on report.

You can correct the comma splice by using any one of the following three methods:

1. Use a semicolon between the two sentences. It is designed specifically to draw the reader's attention to the close connection of the ideas that precede and follow it, and thus gives the impact to the second idea that you mistakenly sought when using the comma. For example, change

My English class was cancelled today, my instructor was sick.

to

My English class was cancelled today; my instructor was sick.

2. Subordinate one of the ideas (i.e., one of the sentences) to the other by introducing a subordinate conjunction. Change

My English class was cancelled today, my instructor was sick.

to

My English class was cancelled today because my instructor was sick.

Be careful to subordinate the appropriate idea: "Because my English class was cancelled today, my instructor was sick" completely changes your meaning by changing the emphasis given by the subordination.

3. Join the two sentences with a co-ordinating conjunction (and, but, for, or, nor). Change

My English class was cancelled today, my instructor was sick.

to

My English class was cancelled today, for my instructor was sick.

Pay careful attention to make certain the meaning you are striving for stays the same when you add a co-ordinating conjunction: "My English class was cancelled today, and my instructor was sick" has

247

completely different meaning from the one you had in the original comma splice.

The Run-on Sentence

The *run-on sentence* occurs when a writer uses no punctuation at all at the end of a sentence.

My English class was cancelled today my instructor was sick.

Actually, the run-on sentence is exactly the same error as the comma splice, except that here even the comma has been left out. The writer is trying to achieve the same effect as the writer of the comma splice (i.e., the writer is trying to point out the connection between the ideas of two sentences by speeding the reader through to the second idea). You can use exactly the same methods outlined in the section on the comma splice to identify and correct the run-on sentence.

Agreement

Subject and Verb Agreement (Number)

The subject and the verb of any sentence must always have the same number (i.e., singular or plural). Most of the time we have no difficulty with *subject/verb agreement* because our use of the language has so accustomed us to using correct agreement that errors immediately strike us as not sounding right. None of us would have difficulty in recognizing the problem in such sentences as "He go to the store" or "They goes to the store."

Occasionally in more complex sentences or in constructions that we do not use frequently, we become confused or forget just what word is the subject of the verb, or what the number of the subject really is. The following section outlines the most common instances in which writers make errors in subject/verb agreement and suggests how they can be corrected and avoided.

Common Problems of Subject/Verb Agreement in Number

SITUATION	EXAMPLE OF ERROR	CORRECT FORM
(i) A group of words comes between the subject and the verb, one of which is a noun	One of the eggs are rotten.	*One* of the eggs *is* rotten.
	Life with all its trials	*Life* with all its trials

248

SITUATION	EXAMPLE OF ERROR	CORRECT FORM
of a different number than the subject.	and tribulations are hard to bear.	and tribulations *is* sometimes hard to bear.
(ii) When the word "there" begins a sentence. In such cases the number of the verb (e.g., "is" or "are") is determined by the number of the noun that *follows* the verb (the real subject).	There is many cases of unnecessary surgery. There was times when I almost gave up. There is a man and his wife at the door.	There *are* many *cases* of unnecessary surgery. There *were times* when I almost gave up. There *are* a *man* and his *wife* at the door.
(iii) When a *collective noun* is the subject of the sentence. Collective nouns represent groups of people or things: e.g., group, herd, crowd, jury, audience, class.	The class are late for the examination.	The *class is* late for the examination.
If the group is acting as a unified whole, a *singular* verb is used.	The jury agree on the verdict.	The *jury agrees* on the verdict.
If the members of the group that comprises the collective noun are not acting as a unified whole, use a *plural* verb.	The crowd disagrees on what to do.	The *crowd disagree* on what to do.

Actually you can avoid the entire problem of awkward sounding plural verbs in these circumstances by rewording the subject of the sentence.
REMEMBER:
(i) When the members of the group agree, use the singular verb.
(ii) When the members of the group are not unified, *change the subject* to a noun that represents the members of the group:

The herd are going off in all directions.

249

to

The *cows* are going off in all directions.

or

The *members* of the herd are going off in all directions.

SITUATION	EXAMPLE OF ERROR	CORRECT FORM
(iv) When the usual order of the sentence is reversed, so that the subject follows the verb, make certain that you have the same number for the subject and the verb.	In the doorway was standing two gigantic policemen. What was I to do?	In the doorway were standing two gigantic policemen. What was I to do?
(v) Indefinite pronouns such as the following are *always singular* and therefore always have *singular* verbs: one, each, everybody, no one, nobody, someone, somebody, either, neither, anyone, everyone.		*Neither* of the men *is* able to do the job. *Nobody is* interested. *Each has* its proper place. *One* of the men who were imprisoned *is* my uncle.
(vi) Two separate subjects of the same verb, joined by "and," form a *plural* subject; they require a plural verb.		*My brother and I are* going to travel this summer. *Halifax and Quebec City have* citadels.
(vii) Two subjects of the same verb, joined by "both . . . and" constructions, always form a plural subject; they require a plural verb.		Both my father and I are going.

250

SITUATION	EXAMPLE OF ERROR	CORRECT FORM
(viii) Two subjects of the same verb, joined by "either . . . or," "neither . . . nor," "not only . . . but also" may take either a singular or a plural verb: if the subject *closer* to the verb is singular, use a singular verb.		Neither mother nor *Aunt Helen is* able to go. Neither the children nor *Aunt Helen is* able to go. (Note that even though "children" is plural, "Aunt Helen," which is singular, is closer to the verb; therefore, the verb is singular.)
If the subject closer to the verb is plural, use a plural verb.		Either the instructor or the answers in the book are wrong. (Note that even though "the instructor" is singular, "answers," which is a plural subject, is closer to the verb; therefore, the verb is plural.)

REMEMBER:

When in doubt, or when you get caught up in an awkward, confusing situation, take the easy way out. Reword the sentence so that "either" comes before one subject *and* its verb and "or" comes before the second subject *and* another verb; "Either *the textbooks are wrong* or *the instructor is.*"

SITUATION	EXAMPLE OF ERROR	CORRECT FORM
(ix) Who, Which, That (relative pronouns). When these words introduce a subordinate clause *and* act as the subject of the verb in that clause they always refer to a specific word used earlier in the sentence and take their number from that word.		The *stories* that *are* told about him are all lies. The *story* that *is* being told about him is a lie. The *girl* who *is* telling the story is a liar. The *girls* who *are* telling the story are liars.

Agreement: Pronouns and Antecedents

A pronoun always agrees in number with the noun to which it refers.

The *men* said *they* were tired.

Most of the time you will have no difficulty with pronoun/antecedent agreement, but four situations might cause you confusion:

SITUATION	EXAMPLE OF ERROR	CORRECT FORM
(i) Collective nouns (crowd, jury, pack, group, etc.) are considered singular if all the members of the collection are acting as a unified whole.	After the *jury* deliberated for six weeks, *they* reached a verdict.	After the *jury* deliberated for six weeks, *it* reached a verdict.
(ii) Collective nouns are considered *plural* if the members of the collection are *not* acting as a unified whole.	The *jury* still disagreed on whether *it* should ask for advice.	The *jury* still disagreed on whether *they* should ask for advice.
(iii) Indefinite pronouns (one, each, everyone, either, neither, etc.) are *always* singular.	*Everyone* did as *they* were told.	*Everyone* did as *he* was told.
(iv) Make certain that you know which word the pronoun refers to.	Neither of the boys knew what they wanted to do (the word which the pronoun refers to is not "boys" but "neither").	Neither of the boys knew what he wanted to do.

Agreement: Possessive Pronouns (my, your, his, her, its, our, their)

Just as a pronoun takes its number from the noun that it replaces, so too does the possessive pronoun. Usually a writer has little difficulty in recognizing the appropriate number of the pronoun to use; we do it almost every time we speak:

Where is Hilda's hat? *It's* with *her* coat.
Here come the kids. Do they have *their* coats on?

A problem normally occurs only in the same four situations that we encountered when discussing pronoun agreement:

SITUATION	EXAMPLE OF ERROR	CORRECT FORM
(i) Collective nouns (crowd, group, jury, etc.) are considered singular if all the members of the collection are acting in a unified way.	The *flock* was sleeping quietly in *their* fold as the wolf crept closer.	The *flock* was sleeping quietly in *its* fold as the wolf crept closer.
(ii) Collective nouns are considered *plural* when the numbers of the collection are *not* acting in a unified manner.	The *flock* ran off in all directions as the wolf attacked *its* fold.	The *flock* ran off in all directions as the wolf attacked *their* fold.
(iii) Indefinite pronouns (one, someone, somebody, everybody, each, either, etc.) are *always* singular.	*Each* of the men did *their* homework.	*Each* of the men did *his* homework.
Feminist objection to the impersonal "his" has meant that some writers and some publications now purposely use indefinite pronouns incorrectly. But such usage still is wrong. Don't fall into this trap yourself.	Everyone has their work order now.	*Everyone* has *his* work order now. or, preferably: *All* have *their* work orders now.

SITUATION	EXAMPLE OF ERROR	CORRECT FORM
(iv) Make certain that in a complex sentence you know exactly to which word the pronoun refers.		Miss Evans is one of those *instructors* who never forgets *their* students' names.

Pronoun Reference

Pronouns are used to substitute for, or take the place of, nouns. Using them frees us from the boring and unwieldy repetition of nouns. Without pronouns we would have to write the following, for example:

Tom is a doctor. Tom lives in London, Ontario. Many patients think Tom is the best doctor that these patients have ever had.

Since we can use pronouns to substitute for specific nouns, however, we can avoid the rigidity and childishness that using them brings:

Tom is a doctor *who* lives in London, Ontario. Many patients think *he* is the best doctor *they* have ever had.

When using pronouns, be careful to observe the following two rules.
1. There must be a specific noun to which that pronoun refers.
2. There must be only one noun to which the pronoun could possibly refer.
Look at the confusion that the lack of a specific noun to refer to causes in the following sentences:

My uncle, an old college friend, and Doctor Peter Smith came for a visit yesterday. *He* is from Montreal.

This sentence causes confusion by not clearly defining which person the "He" refers to. In this case, the second sentence would have to be changed to "*Dr. Smith* is from Montreal."

They don't know what they're doing in Ottawa.

Who does "they" refer to? the Cabinet? the civil service? Members of Parliament? the Ottawa tourists? The sentence would have to be changed to replace the first "they" with a specific noun; e.g., "*Our Members of Parliament* don't know what they are doing in Ottawa."

Runaway inflation, increasing unemployment, and a mounting trade deficit are three major problems our country faces. *This* often causes people to turn to dictators.

The failure to have one specific noun to which "this" refers causes the reader confusion. To convey a clear meaning the second sentence would have to be changed to read: *"These economic difficulties* often cause people to turn to dictators."

Modifiers

Modifiers — words or groups of words that "modify" or alter the meanings of other words — attach themselves to the closest appropriate word in a sentence. Thus, unless you are very careful in placing modifiers, they may change the meaning of the wrong word and cause your reader to misunderstand your meaning, become confused, or end up laughing at what you intended to be a serious point. Note how the change in the positioning of the following modifiers changes the meaning of the sentences:

He handed the book to the customer with the leather cover. [*This would be a rather strange looking customer.*]

He handed the book with the leather cover to the customer.

She took a loaf of bread from the refrigerator that Aunt Bessie had made. [*Aunt Bessie, we must suppose, had a job in a factory that made refrigerators.*]

She took a loaf of bread that Aunt Bessie had made from the refrigerator. [*Here Aunt Bessie has changed jobs to become a cook.*]

I only asked for one ticket. [*Everyone else, apparently, purchased two or more tickets.*]

I asked for only one ticket. [*The writer was going Dutch treat.*]

He lived in the house built by his great-grandfather for ten years. [*Either Great-grandfather apparently didn't want to take up permanent residence, or else he was a very slow worker.*]

He lived for ten years in the house built by his great-grandfather.

Walking down the street, a skyscraper came into view. [*An advance in bionics has apparently been made.*]

Walking down the street, I saw a skyscraper come into view.

Such problems arise from the fact that *we* know precisely what *we* mean when we write the sentence, but forget that all others will not know what we mean unless we put our modifiers in exactly the right place. We know that Aunt Bessie never worked in a factory, so it doesn't occur to us that someone else could think that she did. We're just trying to get down on the paper that Aunt Bessie makes her own bread: doesn't everybody know that she does? The answer, of course, is no, not unless *you tell them*. Make your modifiers say what you mean by placing them with the word that you want them to modify.

If modifiers are a problem in your writing, the easiest way to spot *misplaced modifiers* is either to read your own work aloud (preferably a day or so after you wrote it) or to have someone else read it aloud for you while you read it to yourself. By putting yourself in the role of a stranger coming to the work for the first time, you will recognize the confusion or the change of meaning that results from misplaced modifiers.

Verb Tense Consistency

Whenever you write, you must make certain that you always present the reader with one consistent point in time from which to view your material. In the following example the writer mistakenly presents two points of time (one present, one past):

In *The Edible Woman*, Marion *intends* to marry Peter until she *discovers* he *is* trying to dominate her. When she *realized* what he *was* doing, she *refused* to marry him.

In the first sentence, the writer views the book as existing in the present tense; therefore, the action taking place in the book is presented as occurring in the present tense. In the second sentence, the action of the book is presented as if it happened in the past. The writer fails to maintain a consistent point of time in the present, and should have determined in advance which point of time (i.e., verb tense) would be used throughout the essay.

Not all cases of changing the tense of your verb are as obvious as the above example.

How many times have you had to hit the brakes because someone else *decides* to pull out onto the road?

The incident has become so vivid in the writer's mind that midway through the sentence the immediacy of the situation has caused a shift in tenses. Nevertheless, although the switch in time was a natural occurrence for the author, who knew exactly what the situation was, it still strikes the reader as awkward and disturbing, and distracts from the content of the argument. If the author had written

How many times have you had to hit the brakes because someone else *decided* to pull out onto the road?

the reader would have been taken through a complete and unified experience.

256

Difficult and Confusing Words

A number of words are often mistakenly interchanged or confused by people when they speak and write. Sometimes the mistake can bring a ridiculous meaning to the sentence that completely destroys the seriousness of the message. "They found his body in the middle of the dessert" brings up an image in the reader's mind of a 6'4" detective found dead in a giant bowl of jello, a good scene from a Woody Allen movie, perhaps, but definitely not the tragic *desert* scene the writer meant to depict.

The following section is intended to give you a quick reference to check the most commonly confused words whenever you have the slightest doubt over whether you have used the right word or not. It is a good idea to read this entire section over a few times anyway. All too often people assume they know the correct word or the correct form of a word when in fact they have been making an error for years.

ACCEPT—EXCEPT

ACCEPT means to receive something or to agree with something.
> I *accepted* the certificate from the Dean.
> I *accept* that concept.

EXCEPT means other than or but.
> Everyone *except* Joan had to rewrite the test.

ACCESS—EXCESS

ACCESS means coming toward or a way to approach something or permission to approach something.
> I had *access* to the library.
> The only *access* to the mansion was through a guarded gate.

EXCESS means an extreme, too much.
> His head felt like a race course for the Austrian cavalry because he had drunk to *excess* the night before.

AFFECT—EFFECT

AFFECT means to cause change or to influence something.

Smoking *affects* your breathing.

EFFECT, as a *verb*, means to result in, or to produce a result.

The Prime Minister was unable to *effect* his legislation.

EFFECT, as a *noun*, means the result of something.

Troubled breathing is the *effect* of excessive smoking.

Note: "Effect" is most commonly used as a noun. Except in a few obsolete or technical cases "affect" is not used as a noun.

ALREADY— ALL READY

ALREADY means previously.

We were *already* there.

ALL READY means that everyone or everything is prepared to do something.

We were *all ready* to go.

AMONG—BETWEEN

AMONG means to be in the midst of more than two things, or to divide something for more than two people.

The five of you will have to decide *among* yourselves.

BETWEEN means to be located or to happen so as to separate two things, or to divide something for two people.

I was caught *between* the devil and the deep blue sea.

I divided the last of the wine *between* my girlfriend and her brother.

AMOUNT—NUMBER

AMOUNT means the quantity of something.

The *amount* of snow that fell last night was incredible.

NUMBER means a collection of persons or things.

A *number* of people came to our house on Christmas Eve.

Note: Errors usually occur in the use of these words when a writer confuses a collection (i.e., a group of people or things) with a quantity, and puts down, for example, "The amount of people who favor tax reform is changing." The correct wording recognizes that the people involved are individuals gathered into a collection, not a lump of undifferentiated flesh: "The number of people . . . ."

ARE—OUR

ARE is a form of the *verb* "to be."

We *are* going to the store.

OUR is the possessive form of the *pronoun* "we."

Our house burned down.

Note: The confusion of these two words results from the pronunciation of "our" in some Canadian dialects. If you are in any doubt about whether you have made the error when you reread your paper, see whether you can reword the phrase to read ". . . belonging to us"; if you can, use "our."

A WHILE—A LOT

No one confuses these expressions, but they certainly are overused.

258

Both are colloquial phrases and usually are not appropriate in business writing. Avoid them if at all possible, but if you must use them, at least note that they are both spelled as two words.

CAN—MAY
CAN means to be able.
> A cheetah *can* run at 80 miles per hour.

MAY means to have permission.
> *May* I attend the board meeting?

CHOICE—CHOOSE—CHOSE
CHOICE is a *noun* which means selection or choosing, or option.
> What *choice* did I have?

CHOOSE is a *verb* which means to select. The "oo" is pronounced the same as the "oo" in "loop."
> *Choose* the loop, not the roller coaster.

CHOSE is the past tense of the *verb* to choose. The "o" in "chose" is pronounced the same way as the "o" in "elope."
> They *chose* to elope.

COARSE—COURSE
COARSE means rough.
> This sweater is made of *coarse* wool.

COURSE means a plan of action or direction.
> Of *course* this *course* is the *course* to a brilliant future.

DESERT—DESSERT
DESERT, as a *noun*, means a place where there is little rainfall.
> Cacti grow in the *desert*.

DESERT, as a *verb*, means to abandon.
> He *deserted* his family.

DESSERT means those delicious, fattening goodies at the end of a meal.
> No more *dessert* for me, thanks. I'm obese already.

DEVICE—DEVISE
DEVICE, as a *noun*, means a tool, a scheme, an invention, etc. The "ice" is pronounced the same as the frozen substance, ice.
> That *device* will never fly, Orville.

DEVISE is a *verb*, meaning to plan or invent. The "ise" is pronounced the same as the "ies" in "lies."
> You had better *devise* some good lies to account for the pies.

EMIGRATE—IMMIGRATE
EMIGRATE means to leave a country.
> He *emigrated* from Canada to avoid paying his taxes.

IMMIGRATE means to come to a country.
> He *immigrated* to Canada to find a better life.

EMINENT—IMMINENT—EMANATE
EMINENT means important, distinguished.
> She is an *eminent* lawyer.

259

IMMINENT means about to happen.
> From the darkness of the clouds we knew a cloudburst was *imminent*.

EMANATE means to originate from, to come from.
> Daylight *emanates* from the sun.

FEWER—LESS

FEWER is used to refer to a collection of things that can be counted.
> *Fewer* people watch the late movie than watch the National.

LESS is used to refer to the amount of a material or thing.
> *Less* time was lost when a stoplight replaced the stop sign.

I—ME

I is the subjective form of the first person pronoun.
> When *I* forgot the punchline, *I* became the joke.

ME is the objective form of the first person pronoun.
> When he hit *me* with the pie, the joke was on *me*.

ITS—IT'S

ITS is the possessive form of the pronoun "it." Remember, no personal possessive pronouns (my, your, his, her, our, their) use an apostrophe; therefore, "its" is no exception.
> *Its* tail drooped between *its* legs.

IT'S is the contracted form of "it is."
> *It's* about time for supper, isn't it?

KNOW—NO

KNOW means to be aware of.
> I *know* when I am right.

NO means not in any way or not any.
> We have *no* merchandise made by Pretty Boy.

LATER—LATTER

LATER means subsequently. The "a" in "later" is pronounced the same way as the "a" in "play."
> Stephanie can come out to play *later*.

LATTER means the last mentioned thing out of two things mentioned. The "a" in "latter" is pronounced the same way as the "a" in "ladder."
> John and Bert helped us elope. The *latter* brought the ladder.

LAY—LIE

LAY, in the present tense, means to put something somewhere.
> *Lay* the book on the table.

LIE means to assume a position as opposed to being placed in a position.
> *Lie* down, please; it's time to go to sleep.

The problem: the past tense of the verb "to lie" is "lay."
> John *lay* in bed thinking, "Shall I just *lie* here and hope that I *laid* the book on the table?"

Remember: You *lie* down each night.
> You *lay* something down on a table.
> You *lay* in bed last night.
> You *laid* your coat down yesterday.

260

LESS—LEAST

LESS, the comparative form of little, means not so large, etc. "Less" is often used with adjectives and adverbs to create a negative comparative.

> likely . . . . less likely
> beautiful . . . . less beautiful
> sure . . . . less sure

LEAST, the superlative form of little, means smallest in size, quantity, etc. Least is often used with adjectives and adverbs to create a kind of negative superlative.

> certain . . . . least certain
> long . . . . least long

Do not make the mistake of thinking that adding an "-er" or "-est" suffix to the end of a word accompanied by less or least adds emphasis: it simply reduces your phrase to nonsense. Never write such things as "least likeliest" or "less fiercer."

LETS—LET'S

LETS means allows.

> She always *lets* him go early.

LET'S is the contracted form of "let us."

> *Let's* go to the show.

LIKE—AS—AS IF

LIKE, when used to compare one thing to another, is always a *prepositon*. The group of words that it introduces never contains an independent verb.

> I wish I were *like* him.
> He was out *like* a light.

AS, when used to compare one thing to another, is always a *conjunction*, i.e., it joins two clauses (groups of words that each contain a subject and a verb).

> He is the same age *as* I am.

Remember: the verb used after "as" is often left out or understood: if you are in doubt as to whether you should use "like" or "as" see if you can use a form of the verb of the sentence after the word that will follow the "like" or "as"; if you can, use "as."

> I am the same age *as* — Joan (is). Therefore, "I am the same age *as* Joan" is correct.

AS IF — You will often find that when your first impulse was to use "like" as a conjunction, the words you really wanted were "as if."

> He lay there *as if* he were dead.

LOOSE—LOSE—LOSS

LOOSE, as an *adjective*, means not tight, and as a *verb*, means to untie. The "s" is pronounced in the same way as the "s" in "moose."

> Who let the moose *loose*?
> Is the skin of a moose *loose*?

261

LOSE means to mislay. The "s" is pronounced in the same way as the "z" in "booze."

> Did you *lose* the booze in the ooze?

LOSS (rhymes with "toss") means something lost.

> The *loss* of the toss cost my boss a dime.

The confusion between these words simply results from not knowing which spelling goes with which sound: remember one and you have them all.

MORE—MOST, -ER, -EST

MORE is the comparative form of much; it means greater in quantity or quality.

> I have had *more* to drink than I should.
>
> *More* haste makes *more* waste.

"More" is often used together with an adjective or adverb to create a comparative form for that word.

> likely . . . . more likely
>
> certain . . . . more certain

MOST is the superlative form of much; it means greatest in quantity or quality.

> I love you *most* of all.
>
> She had the *most* money of all of us.

"Most" is often used together with an adjective or an adverb to create a superlative form for that word.

> certain . . . . most certain
>
> quickly . . . . most quickly

ER is a suffix added to the end of many adjectives and adverbs to create the comparative forms of those words.

> great . . . . greater
>
> large . . . . larger
>
> late . . . . later

EST is a suffix added to the end of many adjectives and adverbs to create the superlative forms of those words.

> sure . . . . surest
>
> full . . . . fullest
>
> late . . . . latest

People are often confused over which of these alternatives to use when they want to create comparatives and superlatives, but there is a relatively simple guideline to use that regularly works: If the word that you want to make into a comparative or superlative form has three or more syllables, use "more" or "most."

> su-per-cil-i-ous . . . . most supercilious
>
> ri-dic-u-lous . . . . most ridiculous

(Any dictionary will give you the number of syllables in a word by breaking the word into its compound syllables as we have done here.)

Never use both -er or -est and "more" or "most" with the same word: "most fiercest," "more faster," etc.

PASSED—PAST

PASSED is the past tense of the *verb* "to pass"; it means went by.

> We *passed* the bus.

PAST means that something happened earlier.

> That's all in the *past* now.

PERSECUTE—PROSECUTE

PERSECUTE means to oppress, to harass, to cause someone trouble.

> Hitler *persecuted* the Jews.

PROSECUTE means to put on trial, to try to prove charges against someone in court.

> Trespassers will be *prosecuted*.
> Of course, you could always try to *persecute* trespassers, but you would probably be *prosecuted* for doing so.

PERSONAL—PERSONNEL

PERSONAL means private.

> These are my *personal* belongings.

PERSONNEL means the staff that works for a firm, college, etc.

> The *personnel* in this store are unfriendly.
> Watch out for *personnel* directors who advertise for *personal* positions.

PRACTISE—PRACTICE

PRACTISE is the *verb*, and means to do, to do repeatedly in order to learn a skill, etc.

> He must have *practised* in order to do that badly.

PRACTICE is the *noun*, and means a custom, a repetition of a skill in order to learn it well, etc.

> *Practice* makes perfect.
> Make it a *practice* not to *practise* your drums after midnight.

PRINCIPAL—PRINCIPLE

PRINCIPAL, as an *adjective*, means the most important.

> The *principal* cause of the flood was a broken dam.

PRINCIPAL, as a *noun*, means the person in charge of a school.

> The *principal* is your pal.

PRINCIPLE is used only as a *noun*; it means fundamental truth or rule of conduct.

> The main *principle* behind our action is to get the *principal* fired.

STATIONARY—STATIONERY

STATIONARY means standing still.

> The bus remained *stationary*.

STATIONERY means paper for writing.

> If you remain *stationary* too long in front of a *stationery* store, you might be arrested for loitering.

THEIR—THERE—THEY'RE

THEIR is the possessive form of "they."

They forgot *their* heir when they left *their* money to charity.

THERE is an *adverb*, used in such constructions as "here and there," "over there," and "there are . . . "

THEY'RE is the contracted form of "they are."

TO—TOO

TO is used as a *preposition*, e.g., "to the store," "to town," etc.

TOO is an *adverb*. It means likewise or also, and more than enough.

> I, *too*, had *too* much *to* eat.

WERE—WE'RE—WHERE

WERE is the plural form of the past tense of the *verb* "to be."

> We *were* later than we thought.

WE'RE is the contracted form of "we are."

> *We're* in hot water now.

WHERE is used to ask about the location of someone or something.

> *Where* on earth are you dragging me now, Rover?

Make certain that you know where to use "were" and where to use "we're" (know which spelling goes with which sound).

WEATHER—WETHER—WHETHER

WEATHER means the rain, snow, sleet, etc.

WETHER is a castrated ram.

WHETHER is used in such constructions as "Whether you're ready or not, I'm going."

> A *weather* man knows *whether* it will rain or shine.
>
> *Whether* the *weather* be sunny or cloudy, I hope you don't meet an angry *wether* on your hike.

WHO—WHOM

WHO is the subjective form of the pronoun.

> *Who* is coming to the party?

WHOM is the objective form of the pronoun.

> *Whom* do you prefer?

WHO'S—WHOSE

WHO'S is the contracted form of "who is."

> *Who's* going to the meeting night?

WHOSE is the possessive form of the pronoun "who."

> *Whose* hat is this?

WORSE—WORST

WORSE is the comparative form of "bad."

> His condition is *worse* than it was yesterday.

WORST is the superlative form of "bad."

> Of all of those lazy bums, he is the *worst*.

YOUR—YOU'RE

YOUR is the possessive form of "you."

> Here's your hat; what's *your* hurry?

YOU'RE is the contracted form of "you are."

> *You're* here because this meeting will determine *your* future.

264

Bibliography

Part One: Background for Writing

Blumenthal, Joseph C. *English 3200; a Programmed Course in Grammar and Usage*, rev. ed. New York: Harcourt, Brace, Jovanovich, 1972.

Canadian Government Style Manual. Ottawa: Queen's Printer, 1962.

Compact Dictionary of Canadian English. Toronto: Holt Rinehart and Winston, 1976.

A Concise Dictionary of Canadianisms. Toronto: Gage, 1973.

Dictionary of Business Terms. Toronto: Coles, 1973.

The Dictionary of Canadian English. Toronto: Gage, 1967.

The Dictionary of Canadianisms on Historical Principles. Toronto: Gage, 1967.

Ehrlich, Ida. *Instant Vocabulary.* New York: Pocket Books, 1972.

Fowler, H. W. *A Dictionary of Modern English Usage*, 2nd. ed. Revised by Sir Ernest Gowers. London: Oxford University Press, 1965.

Funk, Wilfred, and Norman Lewis. *30 Days to a More Powerful Vocabulary.* New York: Pocket Books, 1976.

Lambuth, David. *The Golden Book of Writing.* New York: Penguin, 1976.

Leslie, Louis A. *20,000 Words*, 7th Canadian ed. Scarborough: McGraw Hill-Ryerson, 1977.

Matthews, Ray, and Gary Webb. *Who's Going To Read This Anyway?* Toronto: Holt, Rinehart and Winston, 1980.

Newman, Edwin. *A Civil Tongue.* New York: Warner Books, 1977.

Newman, Edwin. *Plain Speaking.* New York: Warner Books, 1975.

Orkin, Mark M. *Canajan, Eh?* Toronto: Lester and Orpen, 1974.

Orkin, Mark M. *Speaking Canadian English.* Toronto: General Publishing, 1970.

Strunk, W. S., Jr., and E. B. White. *The Elements of Style*, 2nd. ed. New York: Macmillan, 1972.

Treble, H. A., and G. H. Vallins. *An ABC of English Usage*. London: Oxford University Press, 1965.

Tufte, Virginia, and Garrett Stewart. *Grammar as Style*. Toronto: Holt, Rinehart and Winston, 1971.

Zinsser, William. *On Writing Well: An Informal Guide to Writing Nonfiction*. New York: Harper and Row, 1976.

Part Two: Letter Writing

Avett, Elizabeth M. *Today's Business Letter Writing*. Englewood Cliffs, New Jersey: Prentice-Hall, 1977.

Gartside, L. *Modern Business Correspondence*, 2nd. ed. New York: International Publications Service, 1967.

Mager, N. H. and S. K. *The Complete Letter Writer*, rev. ed. Richmond Hill, Ontario: Simon and Schuster of Canada, 1968.

Martin, George W. *Let's Communicate: A Self-Help Program on Writing Letters and Memos*. Reading, Massachusetts: Addison-Wesley, 1970.

Reid, James M., and Robert M. Wendlinger. *Effective Letters: A Program for Self-Instruction*, 3rd. ed. New York: McGraw-Hill, 1978.

Shurter, Robert L. *Effective Letters In Business*. 2nd ed. Toronto: McGraw-Hill, 1954.

Vogel, Erwin. *How to Write Collection Letters that Click and Collect (Without Really Crying)*. Brooklyn, New York: Copy-Write, 1970.

Part Three: The Job Application Package

Bolles, Richard Nelson. *What Color Is Your Parachute? A Practical Manual for Job Hunters and Career Changers*. Berkeley, California: Ten Speed Press, 1980.

Developing Your Career. Toronto: University and College Placement Association, 1979.

Donaho, Melvin W., and John L. Meyer. *How To Get The Job You Want*. Garden City, N. J.: Prentice-Hall, 1976.

Figler, Howard. *The Complete Job Search Handbook*. New York: Holt, Rinehart and Winston, 1979.

How To Prepare for an Interview. Ottawa: Manpower and Immigration, 1971.

Kao, Raymond. *Small Business Management: A Strategic Emphasis*. Toronto: Holt, Rinehart and Winston, 1981.

Payne, Richard A. *How to Get a Better Job Quicker*. New York : Taplinger, 1972.

Zeigler, Ray. *Creative Job Search Technique Is . . .* Ottawa: Manpower and Immigration, n.d.

Part Four: Research Methods

Backstrom, Charles H., and Gerald D. Hursh. *Survey Research*. Evanston, Illinois: Northwestern University Press, 1963.

Hauser, Travis L., and Lee Learner Gray, *Writing the Research and Term Paper*. New York: Dell, 1964.

Ives, Edward D. *The Tape-Recorded Interview*. Knoxville: University of Tennessee Press, 1980.

Parker, William Riley, comp. *The MLA Style Sheet*, rev. ed. New York: Modern Languages Association, 1970.

Turabian, Kate L. *Student's Guide for Writing College Papers*, rev. ed. Chicago: University of Chicago Press, 1972.

Part Five: Report Writing

Brown, Leland. *Effective Business Report Writing*, 3rd ed. Englewood Cliffs, New Jersey: Prentice-Hall, 1973.

Carr-Ruffino, N. *Writing Short Business Reports*. New York: McGraw-Hill, 1979.

Lesikar, Raymond V. *How to Write a Report Your Boss Will Read and Remember*. Homewood, Illinois: Dow Jones-Irwin, 1974.

Lewis, Phillip V., and William H. Baker. *Business Report Writing*. Columbus, Ohio: Grid Publishing, 1978.

Pearsall, Thomas E., and D. H. Cunningham. *How to Write for the World of Work*. New York: Holt, Rinehart and Winston, 1978.

Shurter, Robert L., J. Peter Williamson, and Wayne G. Broehl, Jr. *Business Research and Report Writing*. Toronto: McGraw-Hill, 1965.

Part Six: Oral Communication

Birdwhistle, R. L. *Kinesics and Context*. Philadelphia: University of Pennsylvania Press, 1970.

Fast, Julian. *Body Language*. New York: M. Evans and Co., 1970.

Frye, Northrop. *The Well-Tempered Critic*. Bloomington: Indiana University Press, 1963.

How to Lose Your Best Customer Without Really Trying, 16mm color film, 30 minutes. Bell System, 1971.

Morris, Desmond. *The Human Zoo*. Toronto: Clarke, Irwin & Co., 1969.

Nierenberg, Gerard I., and Henry H. Calero. *How to Read a Person Like a Book*. New York: Pocket Books, 1971.

Scheflin, Albert E., and Alice Scheflin. *Body Language and the Social Order*. Garden City, N. J.: Prentice-Hall, 1972.

Sondel, Bess. *To Win With Words*. New York: Hawthorne Books, 1968.

Part Seven: Working with Others

Bourinot's Rules of Order. Revised by J. G. Dubroy. Toronto: McClelland and Stewart, 1963.

Meetings, Bloody Meetings, 16 mm color film. Video Arts Ltd., 1976.

Notes for Community Leaders. Toronto: Ministry of Community and Social Services.

Robert's Rules of Order, rev. ed. New York: William Morrow, 1971.

Vixman, Rachel, ed. *Robert's Rules of Order.* New York: Pyramid Books, 1967.

Index

232, 239
Experience, *see* Job experience
Extracurricular activities, 72, 77, 165

Facts, 156, 239; gathering of, 133-4, 159-60; importance of, 89; and knowledge, 117-18
Field research, 118, 132-8
Figures, 148
File number, 47-8
Filing, 7, 123-5, 152, 214
Financial Post, 7, 84, 100
Financial Times of Canada, 7
Fishbowl method of discussion, 237
Five C's, 3-4, 13, 97, 135, 151; defined, 3-4; in letter writing, 56, 58; in oral communication, 201
Fixed-alternative questions, 134
Follow-up letter, 110-12
Footnotes, *see* Notes; Social science annotation
Foreword, 171
Form letters, 56
Fowler, H.W., 35
"Free association of provinces," 12
Freeflowing discussion, 237
Fringe benefits, 108
Full block letter style, 48, 50

Gestures, 203-6
Globe and Mail (Toronto), 8, 48, 84
Glossary, 177
Government grants, 99
Graphic presentation, 141-50, 169-71, 172
Graphs, 145-8
Gretzky, Wayne, 4

Hamlet, 200
Handwriting, 42, 46, 156
Hanging-indentation letter style, 49, 54
Headings, 144, 156, 162, 165, 172, 212, 217
Health, 73, 108
Help-wanted ads, 98; *see also* Advertisements
Help-wanted notices, 98
Hemingway, Ernest, 14
Hitler, Adolph, 202
Honors and societies, 73, 77

How to Lose Your Best Customer without Really Trying, 216
How to Win Friends and Influence People, 201
Humor, 199, 226
Hyphens, 22, 124
Hypotheses, 136, 137

Ibid., 126
Illustrations, *see* Graphic presentations
Image, personal, 200, 209; *see also* Personal appearance
Incidental motions, 229
Indexes, 118, 120
Indexing, 124-5
Inflected forms, 24
Information: discarding, 161; filing, 7; lack of, 210, 211; methods of recording, 136; proliferation and dissemination of, 117-18; sharing of, 238; sources of, 118-21, 134-5; *see also* Data; Facts; Organization; Reports; Research
Inquiry letters, 58-9
Inside address, 43
Instructing others, 234-5
Interlibrary loan service, 119
Interoffice communication, *see* Memos
Interpersonal communication, 199-207; *see also* Oral communication
Interview questions, 103-5, 110, 234; examples of, 106-8
Interview situations, 104-5, 210
Interviewing, 121, 133, 134, 138; *see also* Questionnaires
Introduction, 172
Investigation, *see* Creative investigation; Research; Scientific investigation

Job application package, 69-113
Job experience, 74-5, 88-9, 107
Job interview, 69, 72, 77, 78, 93, 94, 95-8, 101-12; anticipating interview situations, 104-5; interview questions, 106-8, 234; personality testing, 105
Job market, 76, 83, 221
Job objective, 69, 70, 73, 77; *see also* Career goal